T0354993

A BIBLE JOURNEY (AND BEYOND)

E L N O R A   D E A N

WESTBOW
PRESS®
A DIVISION OF THOMAS NELSON
& ZONDERVAN

WestBow Press books may be ordered through booksellers or by contacting:

WestBow Press
A Division of Thomas Nelson & Zondervan
1663 Liberty Drive
Bloomington, IN 47403
www.westbowpress.com
844-714-3454

Scripture taken from the King James Version of the Bible

ISBN: 978-1-6642-1201-5 (sc)
ISBN: 978-1-6642-1200-8 (e)

Print information available on the last page.

WestBow Press rev. date: 01/30/2021

About the Author and the Book

Elnora Dean was radically converted to Christianity at the age of fifty-eight. She proceeded to make up for 'lost' time by assuming a life of prayer, Bible study, and sharing her faith with others. She had an unquenchable thirst for God's word, and in her later years spent hours writing about the Bible. This book is a partially complete, roughly edited collection of her writings, compiled after she passed away in 2013.

CHAPTER I

But, beloved, be not ignorant of this one thing, That one day
   is with the Lord as a thousand years,
   and a thousand years as one day.
II PETER 3:8

God's time is not man's time. He is not limited to the laws he has imposed upon this insignificant little planet. We have no way of knowing how long his days were in the beginning of our world as he divided the waters from the firmament (heaven); as he molded this formless lump of matter into dry land and seas and planted the first grass, herbs and fruit that would be meat for life that was to come. But God saw that it was all to his liking; that it was good. Thus ended God's third day: A planet lush with every green thing.

   Mine hand also hath laid the foundations of the earth,
   and my right
   hand hath spanned the heavens;
   When I call unto them, they stand up together.
ISAIAH 48:13

In the vast darkness of the Cosmos are innumerable stars and planets, both younger and older than ours; heavenly bodies we know little about. When God gave his attention to our planet, he set it in orbit around the sun, establishing earth's path within an exact boundary suitable for mankind. Earth is the only planet in our solar system capable of sustaining human life. Surface temperatures on Venus are 900° F; it is surrounded by sulfuric acid and has an atmosphere so dense a human body would be crushed. Mars is extremely cold, a frozen planet with an atmosphere only 1% as dense as earth's and with an absence of oxygen and liquid water so essential to human existence.

God, in his infinite wisdom, foresaw the environment ideally suited for life as we know it.

> According as he hath chosen us in him before the
> foundation of the world.
>
> EPHESIANS 1:4

Thus, the sun was set in the firmament for warmth, for life and light. The sun and the moon serve as a measurement of man's time - day and night – months - years. The stars beautifully decorate the night sky. Everything seemed to be tailored to support life on earth. But what life? And why?

THE SERPENT

And the Lord said unto Satan, from whence cometh thou?
And Satan answered the Lord, and said,
From going to and fro in the earth, and from walking
Up and down in it.   JOB 2:2

From the beginning Lucifer, son of the morning, greatest of God's

angels, through rebellion against God Himself, had been cast out of heaven.

The great dragon was cast out,
That old serpent, called the Devil, and Satan,
which deceiveth the whole world,
He was cast out into the earth,
and his angels were cast out with him.
                                        REV 12:9

Because he had desired to be exalted above God, because his proud

spirit was evil continually, he continued to seek revenge against the

Almighty Creator. He had been persuasive enough to turn one third of

the angels against

God and they too were banished from God's presence. So, with his

army of fallen angels, Satan was still seeking whom he might destroy.

Now the serpent was more subtil
than any beast of the field
which the Lord had made.
And he said unto the woman,
Yea, hath God said,
Ye shall not eat of every tree of the garden?
                                        GENESIS 3:1

Eve answered that they could eat of all but the one which God had told them not to touch o-r eat lest they die. Satan, luring Eve with the same delusions that had been his own downfall, assured her that when she ate the forbidden fruit she would also be as a god, knowing good from evil. Her spirit, which had known only love and good, had ruled her life up until this point; now the flesh grew stronger as it lusted for a taste of that fruit; the human eye saw it as desirable, and the promise of the serpent, that they would be as gods was irresistible.

> Love not the world,
> neither the things that are in the world.
> If any man love the world,
> the love of the father is not in him.
> For all that is in the world,
> the lust of the flesh, the lust of the eyes,
> and the pride of life, is not of the Father,
> but is of the world.
>
> I JOHN 2:15,16

She took the fruit and did eat and gave also unto her husband and he did eat. Human flesh had sinned, becoming infected with the knowledge of good and evil. The flesh had had a taste of ruling and was not easily going to relinquish that power once again to the spirit. Indeed, they would surely die.

> And the world passeth away, and the lust thereof:
> but he that doeth the will of God abideth forever.
>
> I JOHN 2:17

When the Lord came again to the garden and found they had disobeyed the only commandment he had given them, the man justified his action by saying "The woman You gave me, she did it. I just ate what she gave me."

In essence, "God, it is all your fault." A rebellious spirit was now in control.

For the first time, they had been reluctant to f ace God because they now knew they were naked and sinful. The pattern was set at this time as God sacrificed the lives of innocent animals to supply skins to cover their sinful bodies. From then until now, the only redemption from sin would be by the shedding of blood.

The Lord had no recourse but to send Adam and Eve from the Garden of Eden lest they eat of the tree of life and live forever. No longer was God's blessing upon them as before. Now the ground was cursed with thorns and thistles and only by sweat and toil would it yield a harvest. To woman he gave pain with childbirth and she was destined to be submissive to her husband. A curse was placed upon the serpent. But God is merciful.

Although man's flesh would die and return to dust, He left them a promise, a hope to carry down through the ages. To the serpent the Lord said:

> I will put enmity between thee and the woman
> and between thy seed and her seed;
> It shall bruise thy head,
> and thou shalt bruise his heel.

GEN 3:15

Elsewhere in the Bible, "seed" is a reference to a man's offspring or posterity. This is a strange statement as it alludes to the woman. History reveals that science and religion were derived and handed down from Chaldea (from the inhabitants of the Assyrian plains) to the ancient Egyptians and Greeks. These religions, and mythology, have one thing in common. The Babylonians supremely worshipped a Goddess Mother and a Son who was represented in pictures and images as an infant in his mother's arms. From Babylon, this worship spread throughout the world. It is believed the Babylonian mother was Semiramus, also called Rhea. Her child is referred to in Ezekiel as Tammuz; throughout literature as Bacchus, or Ninus "The Son". Isis and Osiris are the mother and child of the Egyptians; in India, even today, they are known as Isi and Iswara; in Asia as Cybele and Deoius, in pagan Rorne as Fortuna and Jupiter, in Greece as Ceres, the Great Mother with a babe in her arms, or as Irene with Plutus. Even in Asia, China has Shing Moo the Holy Mother. These all have one thing in common: an immaculate conception.

> Therefore the Lord Himself shall give you a sign;
> Behold, a virgin shall conceive, and bear a son,
> and shall call his name Immanuel.
> (God with us.)
>
> ISAIAH 7:14

> For as by one man's disobedience
> many were made sinners,
> so by the obedience of one shall
> many be made righteous.
>
> ROMANS 5:19

Adam and Eve recognized God's promise of a redeemer. This promise lived in the hearts of each succeeding generation and from this promise of a savior, through a virgin birth, sprang an eternal hope.

**For I know that My Redeemer liveth,
and that He shall stand
in the latter day upon the earth.**

JOB 19:25

CHAPTER II

OUTSIDE THE GARDEN

Adam and Eve bore two sons: Cain, a tiller of the ground; and Abel, a keeper of sheep. In time, they each brought an offering to the Lord. Cain brought of the fruit of the ground and was angry when God was not pleased with an offering from the very ground he had so recently cursed. Abel, more perceptive of God's plan for their salvation, offered the best of his flock - a sacrificial lamb. Cain could not stand God's pleasure in Abel, so he killed him. Neither repenting nor seeking God's forgiveness, Cain, with his wife, went out from the presence of the Lord and dwelt in the land of Nod, east of Eden and they were fruitful. Cain's great grandchildren were said to dwell in tents, had cattle, were musicians, and were craftsmen in brass and iron. From all accounts they made great strides toward civilization as we know it in only three generations (possibly 1,000 years) or a time frame better understood as 3000 B.C. Recent excavations in Ban Chiang, Thailand, southeast Asia show evidence of a culture during that period that raised cattle, pigs and chickens and there was also evidence of bronze and iron metalwork.

An exhibition called "Ban Chiang: Discovery of a Lost Bronze Age" was displayed at the American Museum of Natural History in New York in November, 1984. Archeologists were not expecting to find metal objects during this period. It has caused scientists to rethink traditional theories about the development of civilization in Southeast Asia. Every day scientists are making new amazing discoveries. Yet it was recorded in the Bible all the time.

When Adam was one hundred thirty years old he begat a son in his own likeness, after his image and called his name Seth. Eve said "God hath appointed me another seed instead of Abel. Seth's son was Enos and in that time men began to call upon the name of the Lord. Enoch was the seventh generation in this bloodline and

> Enoch lived 65 years and begat Methuselah.
> All the years of Enoch were 365.
> Enoch walked with God:
> And he was not; for God took him.
>
> GEN 5:21, 24

This might be considered a great mystery because the Bible says all the other descendants of Adam died. But not Enoch - - for God took him. In many ways, the Old Testament is a pattern of things to come; things not understood at the time, but becoming clearer as they are revealed to us today. Paul wrote as follows to the church he founded in Corinth:

> Behold, I show you a mystery,
> We shall not all sleep, but we shall all be changed,
> In a moment, in the twinkling of an eye,
> At the last trump: for the trumpet shall sound,
> and the dead shall be raised incorruptible.
> And we shall be changed. For this corruptible
> must put on incorruption, and this mortal
> must put on immortality.
>
> I CORINTHIANS 15:51-53

Methuselah's grandson was Noah. When Noah was five hundred years old he begat Shem, Ham and Japeth. By this time men had multiplied upon the earth ·and become exceedingly wicked. The Lord said:

> My spirit shall not always strive with man,
> for that he also is flesh:
> Yet his days shall be a hundred and twenty years.
>
> GEN 6:3

God saw that man's heart was continually evil and he was grieved that he had ever made man. Only Noah, who found grace in the eyes of the Lord, prevented God from destroying all mankind and every beast and fowl of the earth.

**Noah was a just man and perfect in his generations,
And Noah walked with God.   GEN 6:9**

Nevertheless, because the earth was filled with violence and corruption, God spoke to Noah "Make thee an ark, pitch it within and without; it shall be three hundred cubits long (450 feet), fifty cubits wide (75 feet) and thirty cubits high (45 feet). It shall be three stories, it shall have one door. I will bring a flood of waters upon the earth and everything that has breath shall die." Only Noah, and his family had a promise of safety. God would spare two of every living thing - male and female. Noah was to make provision to feed every fowl, cattle, creeping things, two of every sort of creature that God would draw into the ark.

> **Thus did Noah, according to all that God commanded him,**
> **so did he.** **GEN 6:22**

So great a faith in God has never been surpassed. For one hundred years Noah and his sons labored to build and stock the ark in preparation for a flood when the world had never even experienced rain!

> **For the Lord God had not caused it to rain,**
> **but there went up a mist from the earth,**
> **and watered the whole face of the ground.**
> **GEN 2:5, 6**

Noah's faith did not sway the rest of the world. II Peter calls Noah a "preacher of righteousness". Unbelief held all mankind in its grasp. They could not believe in something they had never seen. Even Methuselah, grandfather to Noah, would not listen. He lived to be nine hundred and sixty-nine years old, and no one knows how long he might have lived, for he died the year of the flood!

Noah was six hundred years old when the flood of waters was let loose upon the earth. Noah, his sons, his wife, his son's wives went into the ark because of the pending flood. There went in unto Noah, two of every beast and fowl and after seven days **the Lord shut them in.** **GEN 7:16**

Noah could not open the door, only God could do that. Now, mankind must have come in great travail, with unleashed panic, crying out to Noah and to God. Noah had preached, Noah had warned, now he could do nothing. God had given man a space of one hundred years to repent, but they had not heeded. God was adamant. The earth would be cleansed. The windows of heaven were opened and rain poured down upon the earth. The fountains of the deep were broken up. The earth itself was in travail; great underground geysers burst forth, spewing their boiling water and steam into the flood, and formidable outpourings of lava gushed forth from fissures and volcanoes.

The flood was forty days upon the earth, and the waters increased and lifted the ark above the earth and it rode above the destruction which was occurring all around it. All flesh died that moved and breathed upon the earth. Even the highest mountain top was under water - there was no escape. Only Noah and those with him in the ark were saved. The ark rode upon the waters continuously for over seven months, at which time the waters had receded sufficiently to allow it to rest upon the mountains of Ararat. At the end of one year, Noah beheld that the face of the ground was dry but God did not open the door for almost two more months when the earth was dry. Noah had no concept of flooding, never having experienced rain or its effects, upon the ground. Seeing the "face" or surface of the ground was dry he would have ventured out of the ark into a quagmire .which would surely have swallowed him. Until the earth was given time to dry out, it could not have supported the weight of either animals or people. God, in his wisdom, knew just the right time to open the door.

Noah's first actions were pleasing to the Lord, for he built an altar and offered burnt offerings to the Lord. The Lord observed and blessed Noah and his sons, saying:

> Be fruitful and multiply and replenish the earth.
> Every moving thing that liveth shall be meat for you;
> Even as the green herb have I given you all things.
> But flesh with the life thereof, which is the blood thereof,
> Shall ye not eat.   GEN 9: 1, 3, 4

No longer would mankind and animals live peacefully together. In the beginning God said:

> Behold, I have given you every herb bearing seed,
> which is upon the face of all the earth,
> and every tree in the which is the fruit of a tree yielding seed,
> To you it shall be for meat.
> and to every beast of the earth, and every fowl of the air, and
> to everything that creepeth upon the earth
> wherein there is life,
> I have given every green herb for meat.
>   GEN 1:29, 30

Before the flood both men and beasts were most likely vegetarians. An even, constant mist enabled an abundance of vegetation to grow, supplying a reliable source of food for all. Now the climate had changed. Great seas and oceans had been formed; no doubt the earth's crust and surface rocks had cooled during the period of flooding. Now cloud formations and rain would become a common occurrence, as would periods of drought - no longer would plant life be a sufficient food source. Thus, God's permission was given to eat meat (as long as the blood was drained from it first). Man and beast would now prey upon each other. Existence on earth would become increasingly harsh and dangerous.

> Our fathers have sinned, and are not;
> and w·e have borne their iniquities.
> LAMENTATIONS 5:7

Noah became a grower of grapes and was found in a drunken state by his youngest son, who uncovered and disgraced him. Noah awoke and knew what his son had done; therefore a curse was placed upon Ham's son Canaan, while blessings were given Shem , and Japeth who would share in Shem's blessing. These blessings were not only temporal, but pertained to spiritual and eternal blessings.

Through the three sons of Noah was the whole earth overspread. But not of their own free will. Ham begat Cush, whose son was Nimrod who "began to be a mighty one in the earth." His kingdo m began with the cities of Babel, Erech, Accad and 'Calneh in the land of Shinar (Babylonia) and of Ninevah, Rehoboth and Calah in the land of Asshur (Assyria).

> He was a mighty hunter before the Lord,
> Wherefore it is said,
> Even as Nimrod the mighty hunter before the Lord.
> GEN 10:9

His is· the first mention of a kingdom and it implies he obtained power and rule over many cities, chief of which was Babel (Hebrew for Babylon); know n as "the gate of God."

> And they said, Go to,
> Let us build us a city and a tower,
> Whose top may reach unto heaven;
> And let us make us a name,
> Lest we be scattered abroad
> Upon the face of the whole earth.
>
> GEN 11:4

In direct defiance of God!

All of the area bounded by the Tigris and Euphrates rivers was aptly called Mesopotamia (the land between the rivers) and was a fertile oasis in a barren, sun-seared desert and harsh wilderness. In the midst of this land, Nimrod and his followers built the mighty city and tower of Babel.

Excavtions in the 20th Century have revealed the existence and identity of Babel, Erech and Ur. Also the pattern and design of their towers or ziggurats have been discovered. One of the best preserved is at Ur, on the southern end of the Mesopotamia. Only the first level remains today, but there is rubble and evidence of a second and third level. On top of this once rested a temple to Ur's special deity, Sin, god of the moon.

The great mound of Nimrud out of Nenevah was excavated by Layard and, about one hundred years later, on a much greater scale by Max Mallowan, which indicated the strong influence of Nimrod in Assyria. But none could compare to the ziggurat at Babel which had eight levels and a temple to the god of the sun.

For its time period, Babel was the greatest of all cities. A walled, fortified city whose people worshipped the sun god personified by Nimrod._ Inscribed clay tablets by the tens of thousands have been unearthed, making these first cities tangibly real. Records indicate that a city-state form of government was exercised and that an astonishingly high culture level existed.

From this civilization stems the most pervasive form of religion ever devised. Here began a pagan form of idolatry that would be adopted in some manner in every nation of our world. The ancient Chaldean Mysteries stem from this beginning, as does the identification of Semiramus as the wife of Nimrod and mother of the son Ninus, also known as Tam muz. She too had an important part in forming the mysteries and was worshipped by many names: as Rhea the great mot her of the gods; as Venus and as Ishtar, to na me a f ew. During the later reign of Nebuchadnezzer, Babylon had a famous gate called Ishtar which led to the palace, indicating a continued influence by her.

Nimrod has been acknowledged as the originator of fortifications (walled cities) and as the one who first carried on war against his neighbor. No doubt this is how he became king over many cities. He was acclaimed as the father of the gods and in this role was deified. He is a classic example of Anti-Christ.

Who opposeth and exalteth himself
Above all that is called God,
Or that is worshipped;
So that he as God sitteth in the temple of God
Showing himself that he is God.

II **THESSALONIANS 2:4**

The tower of Babel was in direct opposition to a true worship of God and was built in defiance of all that was holy. Men built the tower to reach heaven without God's help and through the guidance of Nimrod and Semiramus a priesthood was established to spread a false worship that was a distortion of God's original promise of the Saviour to come. A triune worship was established which prevails to this day. This religion was reinf orced by magic and astronomy introduced at this same time by Nimrod, Semiramus and their priesthood.

Is it any wonder that when the Lord came down to see the city and tower which the children of men builded, he said:

Behold, the people is one,
And they have all one language;
And this they begin to do;
Now nothing will be restrained from them,
Which they have imagined to do.
Let us go down, and there confound their language,
That they may not understand one another's speech.
So the Lord scattered them abroad
From thence upon the face of all the earth,
And they left off to build the city.

GENESIS 11:6, 7 & 8

Not being able to com municate with each other had eff ectively created the separation that God desired. Their unity of purpose was shattered but Babylon's influence went with the people as they travelled their separate ways.

Babylon was not destroyed at this time. The building program was restrained although Babylon was apparently still the center of pagan worship.

> Wherefore, behold, the, days come, said the Lord,
> That I will do judgement upon her graven images:
> And through all her land the wounded shall groan.
> Though Babylon should mount up to heaven,
> And though she should fortify the height of her strength,
> Yet from me shall spoilers come unto her, saith the Lord.
>   JER 51:52, 53

From the families of the sons of Noah all nations of our world were formed. Since there was no longer a bond to hold them together, each family went their separate way. The greatest migration the world has ever experienced was begun as families, or groups, who could still speak a com mon tongue separated themselves from the chaos that resulted when the only language known to man was lost. Communication was severed but traditions, culture and religion were an integral part of them" and only gradually changed as distances, time, climatic variations, terrain, raw materials and inherited characteristics all had a bearing on forming present nationalities.

Japeth had seven sons who travelled northwest to inhabit the region of Asia Minor (Turkey); a land largely a high plateau surrounded by rough textured mountains, the highest of which is Mt Ararat. This land is bordered by the Black Sea to the northwest, south by the Mediterranean Sea and on the east by the Caspian Sea. From this starting point, succeeding generations continued to travel - surrounding the Black Sea and travelling north. Gomer and his family settled north of the Black Sea, then sout.hward and west ward to the extremities of Europe. Magog travelled nort heast around the Caspian Sea; into the northern most parts of Asia and his descendants inhabited much of Russia. Tubal, another son, gave his name to Tobolsk in the northeastern portion of the Soviet Union. Javan was the ancestor of the "coastland people"; of the Ionians, Macedonians of Greece and of Syria. Madai, who settled south of the Caspian Sea was the founder of the Medes. Meshech, or Moschi, settled in Asia Minor. aEd his descenpants gradually migrated toward the Black Sea.

He was probably the founder of Moscow. Ashkenaz settled near Mt Ararat; his people are known as Ar menians. Riphath and his people, identified as Celts, crossed a mountain range we know as Carpathians and into present-day Europe. Kittim and Dodanim were early sea people; inhabiting the northern coasts of the Mediterranean Sea. Thus were the Gentile tribes of Japheth scattered.

Ham's descendants settled in Africa and Arabia. Cush and his sons and grandsons inhabited Ethiopia and Abyssinia; others migrated to lower Egypt and southwest Arabia. Phut travelled further to Libya, west of Egypt. Canaan settled east of the Mediterranean and north of the Philistines to Sidon. Later they expanded to both sideS' of the Jordan River into Phoenicia, Lebanon and Syria. Sheba settled in the northern part of Ethiopia. Havilah located in Arabia, as did Sabtah, and Raamah abode on the Persian Gulf. Ludim migrated to Lydia. Sidon, son of Canaan, founded the city of Sidon which is still in existence today. Heth was the ancestor of the Hittites. From Canaan originated the Jebusites, A morites, Girgosites and other "ites" too numerous to mention.

Shem was the father of the Semites and of the Assyrians, Ar menians and Persians. Elam's family settled in the area we know as Iran. Some Elamites inter-married with Sumarians; they inhabited an area south of Assyria and east of Iran. Ur o'f · the Chaldeans, and the original home of Abraham was here. Arphaxad, ancestor of Abraham and of Jesus Christ, lived east of the Tigris River, near Elam and Asshur. Aram founded Syria and Mesopotamia, between the Taurus Mountains and Damascus. Uz inhabited a region south of Edom and west of the Arabian desert which runs into Chaldea. Eber, which means "other side" settled east of the Euphrates River and possibly also east of the Tigris river. Joktan was the ancestor of thirteen Arabian tribes and a link between Hebrew and Arab stock.

These are the families of the sons of Noah,
After their generations, in their nations:
And by these were the nations divided in the earth
After the flood.

GENESIS 10:32

It seems more than coincidence that Arphaxad's great grandson

was Peleg of whom it is written:

The name of one was Peleg;
For in his days was the earth divided.

GENESIS 10:25

Is it only coincidence that Peleg and Nimrod lived at the same

time? And that

The Lord scattered them abroad from thence
Upon the face of all the earth.

GEN 11:8

And to stretch coincidence even further, modern technology and

science have determined that at one time only one land mass existed. In

1912, German geologist Alfred Wegener, and his associates, proclaimed

that the continents known to us today were once a unified land mass that

separated into segments which drifted to their present positions. The

world, and British physicist Sir Harold Jeffreys in particular, was not

ready to accept such a radical theory. Step by step, scientific discoveries

proved Wegener's concept to be correct. In 1950, a magnetometer

was perfected by Professor P.M.S. Blockett of the University of

Manchester. When rocks solidify, tiny grains of iron are magnetized into alignment with Earth's magnetic field, like compass needles. But Professor Blockett's instrument detected that the rocks of the British Isles pointed some 30 degrees away from the present magnetic poles. Either the poles had moved more than anyone suspected, or else the entire British Isles themselves had somehow rotated clockwise! In the late 1950's, a massive f ederal program to map the world's ocean floors was begun. The sea floor revealed mountains, deep trenches and valleys. Beginning in 1960, seismologists began pinpointing positions of every earthquake on a map. Soon these positions formed patterns along narrow lines. These turned out to be the now known fault lines and, most startling, to be along mid-ocean ridges and deep-sea trenches. Working independently, Robert Dietz, a United States Government geologist , and Harry Hess, a Princeton geologist, outlined theories that overcame the opposition to Wegener's theory. They agreed that there is evidence suggesting that entire blocks of continental rock, or tectonic plates, have moved as a whole relative to each other. A map will show, for example, that Africa and South America would fit together very well and even better if they were joined at the edges of their continental shelves. For instance, India would fit nicely bet ween South Africa and Antarctica.

Recently geophysicists concluded that the driving force comes from plumes, great columns from deep in the earth. To date, they have located 120 presently active plumes, as well as remnants of past plumes, which first bulge, then split across the top in three directions. A newly active example is the "Afar Triangle", a region that intrigues geologists, at the juncture of the Red Sea, the Gulf of Aden and the African Rift Valley, each of which may be a crack from the same central plume. If several plumes should line up closely enough, their cracks might become the rift where continental splitting and sea floor spreading occurs.

Who is to say a split of this nature did not occur during Peleg's lifetime? As the tribes of Japeth, the Gentiles, moved in a northwesterly direction; those of Ham in a south and southwest direction, and the sons of Shem encircled the lands of Babylon, a plume split could have caused a widening of the Mediter- ranean Sea; a second split spread to create the Black Sea; and the third to widen or create the Red Sea. Simultaneously, this would cause upheavals such as the Caucasus Mountains and the mountainous terrain of Asia Minor. (A present potential for further splitting is evidenced by the numerous pinpointing of earthquake sites in this area.)

This would greatly discourage the regrouping of Noah's descendants since the mountains would be a natural barrier and there is no evidence of sea-faring before this time. It could also explain the startling evidence of recent excavations that point to a much more advanced European culture than had been previously supposed.

A classic example of this is the Minoan civilization on Crete which lasted until 1450 B.C., at which time it may have been partially destroyed by a volcanic eruption or by conquest by Mycenaeans from mainland

Greece. During its existence, the Minoans pioneered seafaring, possibly because of their desire for bronze, and the raw material was not available on their island. Excavations by John Evans in the 1950's uncovered the deepest layer of artifacts ever found in Europe and the houses were made of mud bricks hardened in fire, possibly similar to those used in building the tower of Babel.

> **And they said one to another,**
> **Go** to, **let us make brick,**
> **And burn them thoroughly.**
>
>

GEN 11:4
>

Since this was the only layer to employ mud bricks, it was assumed this culture had been brought by the first settlers from a Middle Eastern civilization. And like so many things Minoan, the religious cult of the bull, a symbol of strength and f ertility, probably came from the East. It is interesting to note that Nimrod is also referred to in history as the Horned or Mighty one.

CHAPTER III

ABRAHAM, FATHER OF MANY NATIONS

Hebrew is a derivative of Eber, who begat Peleg. Peleg begat Reu, Reu begat Sereg, Sereg begat Nahor, Nahor begat Terah and Terah begat Abram, Nahor and Haran, and Haran begat Lot. Haran died before his father in the land of his nativity, in Ur of the Chaldees.

Ur is recognized as one of the oldest cities of ancient Sumer, located at the mouth of the Euphrates River, near its junction with the Tigris River. Its deep, rich soil fostered farming and trading, hence a high measure of civili- zation. The focal point of Ur, a walled city, was its stepped tower, or ziggurat built to worship the moon god Sin. Here priests ruled the city and its surroundings. Ur was an old city when Abram was born around 2000 B.C.

The excavation of thousands of cuneif orm tablets reveals a sophisticated written language, a knowledge and practice of mathematics and skilled craftsmen whose equal could only be found in Egypt. The graves of the "Royal Cemetary" produced treasures of exquisite beauty and expert craftsmanship, among them a lyre decorated with a golden bull's head. The most famous grave is that of Queen Shub-ad, buried with her royal attendants and carriage, as well as silver and gold vessels and jewelry.

The average house within the walled city was one or two stories of baked or unbaked mud brick with several rooms around an open court. These houses were so well suited to this sun-seared delta country that similar homes are still being built and occupied in Iraq today.

Abram's family appears to have been semi-nomadic and although familiar with city dwelling, they may have remained outside the walls of Ur. The Bible tells us that:

> **Terah took Abram his son, and Lot the son of Haran,**
> **And Sarai his daughter-in-law, his son Abram's wife;**
> **And they went forth with them from Ur of the**
> **Chaldees,**
> **To go into the land of Canaan; and they came unto**
> **Haran,**
> **And they dwelt there.**
>
> **GEN 11:31**

They would have travelled beside the Euphrates River for almost six hundred miles, travelling afoot or by donkey, with family, servants, flocks of goats and sheep and the simple needs of the nomad. As they travelled through Central Mesopotamia, they would pass Babylon, which was still the capital of all the land. They would have witnessed a well-tended network of irrigation canals. Babylon was a city-state whose borders included Ur and whose religion would have greatly influenced Abram and would continue to have impact on the lives of the Hebrews for many years. Recent Babylonian excavations have unearthed cuneiform tablets referencing the flood, as have those in other Mesopotamian digs.

As Terah and his family continued northward, four hundred miles from Ur, they would have come to Hit, interesting for its natural tar pits from which may have come the bitumen, or slime, used to bind the clay bricks used to build their towers (as is still evident in the remains at Ur).

Still further north, they would have encountered Mari, a royal city of Northern Mesopotamia and a prosperous commercial center at that time. In its ruins, near Abu Kamal, Syria, have been found tablets referencing Semitic nomads, including the Hablru (Hebrew). Other tablets record that the Benjaminites (a Hebrew name) signed a treaty with the king · of Haran in a temple of Sin, the moon god. Remains of a ziggurat, and temples of Ishtar, Dagan, Shamash, and other dieties have been unearthed at this site known as Tell el-Hariri. Of special interest is the enormous palace of Zmrilim, the last king of Mari, covering more than six acres and with more than three hundred rooms and courtyards. Details of a large mural painting discovered in one of the courtyards is similar to the description of Eden, depicting a serpent, a woman and a fruit tree. Mari clay tablets of ten mention the city of Nahor and Haran. Other indications of a relationship to Abram is the tribal name of Banujamina, similar to Benjamin and records of tribal and religious practices common to Old Testament accounts of Hebrew customs, such as killing of a young animal to establish a covenant, and the expression "the god of my f ather."

From Mari, Terah and Abram journeyed to Haran, which is still in existence and located near the southern border of Turkey. Today, domed clay houses still exist, very little changed from approximately 4,000 years ago. Haran was not a Semitic town, but one founded by Hurrians, a little known people from the northern hills. It was an important Northern Mesopotamian commercial city, a junction for the trade routes between Ninevah and Carchemish.

The plains surrounding Haran were called Padan Aram by Abraham and his kinfolk. To date no tablets have been found in Haran that coincide with the period that Abram dwelt there, but an Egyptian record by an official who dwelt in exile in this area relates that "It was a good land. Figs were in it, and grapes. It had more wine than water. Plentiful was its honey, abundant its olives. Every fruit was on its trees. Barley was there and wheat. There was no limit to any cattle...".

Even after Abram's departure from Haran, he did not lose all contact with his family, for from its neighboring city of Nahor came Isaac's wife and from Padan Aram would come Jacob's wives.

Cuneiform tablets found at Nuzu, a small Hurrian city, shed light on customs of the Hebrew Patriarchs recorded in Genesis: deathbed blessings, the use of concubines to insure children, the use of family teraphim (images). The city of Nahor is mentioned in some of the tablets as a settlement south of Haran. From this area, the northwestern portion of Mesopotamia, Hebrews brought the story of Eden, the creation epic, the flood and the Tower of Babel story. It is unique and appears to have no parallels between Canaanite and Egyptian literature, but existence of these ancient recordings lends credence to the Old Testament.

Abram appears to be connected with the Aramaeans of Haran. Several ancestors of Abraham have the same names as towns located near Haran: Peleg, Serug, Terah and Nahor.

> Now the Lord had said unto Abram,
> Get thee out of thy country
> And from thy kindred
> And from thy father's house
> Unto a land that I will show thee.
>
> And I will make thee a great nation,
> And I will bless thee,
> And make thy name great,
> And thou shalt be a blessing.
>
> GENESIS 12:1 &: 2

And so from a heritage of idol worship, from the god Sin, golden bulls, Ishtar, Dagan, Nimrod, Shamash; burial of the dead with all the material trappings of this world, preparing them to enter the next world; Abram heeded the call of the great Creator, the one and only true God.

> And departed as the Lord had spoken unto him,
> And Lot went with him;
>   And Abram was seventy and five years old
> When he departed out of Haran.
> And Abram took Sarai his wife,

And Lot his brother's son,
And all their substance that they had gathered,
And the souls that they had gotten in Haran;
And they went forth to go into the land of Canaan;
And into the land of Canaan they came.

GENESIS 12:5

"And the souls they had gotten in Haran" indicates others may have also believed in this mighty God who had called Abram and that they too left their homes and families to follow in the quest for a one true God.

Abram's first contact with the Canaanites was at Shechem (known today as Nabulus). Relations with the ruling Hivites, closely related to the Hurrians of Haran; were amiable. It was here that the Lord appeared to Abram and promised Canaan land to his posterity and here also Abram built an altar to the Lord. For the rest of his life Abram would follow God, growing in faith with each new experience.

From Shechem, Abram journeyed to a mountain east of Bethel and west of Ai. There he pitched his tent and built an altar to the Lord.

Bethel (today a modern village called Baytin) is mentioned more often in the Bible than any city except Jerusalem. It was a well-built city and neighbor to Ai (The Ruin) of which excavations in 1933-35 uncovered an Early Bronze Age city with evidence of Egyptian contact. Destruction had already hit this city and only ruins, hence its name, and only a small village existed in Abraham's day.

Nevertheless, Abram pitched his tents in the open, not seeking a man-made city.

> **For he looked for a city**
> **Which hath foundations**
> **Whose builder and maker is God.**
> **HEBREWS 11:10**

Once again Abram moved, going still toward the south and because there was a famine in the land, he continued on into the land of Egypt, probably to the land of .Goshen, a place his descendants would later inhabit.

At this time Abram had not yet acquired complete faith in the Lord and so as they drew near to Egypt he became afraid the Egyptians would kill him because they would desire Sarai, his beautiful wife.

> **Say, I pray thee, thou art my sister.**
> **That it may be well with me for thy sake;**
> **And my soul shall live because of thee.**
> **GENESIS 12:13**

Abram's fears were f ulfilled. Because of Sarai's great beauty, she was taken into Pharaoh's house and gifts of ·sheep, oxen, servants and camels were presented to Abram as payment for her. Only the Lord's intervention rescued Sarai and when the Pharaoh understood she was Abram's wife, he indignantly called Abram, inquiring why Abram had not told hi m that Sarai was his wife and the Pharaoh sent them away out of Egypt.

In this, Abram's actions were in no way honorable. Because he trusted no one, not even God, to protect him, he had told a half-truth which did not benefit anyone.

And yet indeed she is my sister;
She is the daughter of my father,
But not the daughter of my mother;
And she became my wife.

GEN 20:12

We do not understand many of the customs of that era; maybe this was "common practice," but Abram had put God's plan for them and for all future generations in jeopardy. Still the Lord had not forsaken them and His purpose would be fulfilled.

Abram and Lot returned to Bethel and to the spot where their tents had been before; where Abram had placed an altar to the Lord. Because they had grown rich in flocks and herds, the land could not support them both. Abram gave Lot first choice of the land.

And Lot beheld all the plain of Jordan
that it was well-watered everywhere.

GEN 13:11

Abram dwelt in the hills of Judea, in the land of Canaan, but Lot dwelled in the cities of the plain, and pitched his tent toward Sodom, a most wicked city.

After this separation, the Lord spoke again to Abram: Look north, south, east and west. All that you see I will give to you and to your seed forever.

Then Abram removed his tent
And came and dwelt in the plain of Mamre.
Which is in Hebron, and built there
An altar unto the Lord.

GEN 13:18

Here can still be found pleasant tree-shaded camp sites used by Bedouins where they pitch their tents under ancient oaks or terebinths.

It was while he lived near Hebron that Abra m was drawn into warf are through his concern for Lot. Kings from the Babylonian empire: from Shinar, from Ellasar, from Elam (today a province in Iran) and their ally, King Tidal, made war against the kings of Sodom and Gomorrah, Admah, Zeboiim and Zoar. This was a mighty struggle in the Vale of Siddim (now submerged somewhere under the Dead Sea). The kings from the Babylonian empire were victorious; they plundered the cities and, taking captives, started home.

When Abram heard of Lot's capture, he armed three hundred eighteen trained servants of his own household; pursued and overcame them by night near Damascus. When he returned with Lot and the other captives and all the goods which had been taken, the king of Sodom came out to meet him.

Of much more import at this meeting was the presence of Melchizedek, king of Salem, who was the priest of the most high God.

And he blessed him (Abram) and said,
Blessed be Abram of the most high God,
Possessor of heaven and earth:
And blessed be the most high God,

. Which hath delivered thine enemies
Into thine hand.

GEN 14:19,20

And Abram gave tithes of all that had been recovered to Melchizadek.

Who was this king?

First: King of righteousness,
And after that also King of Salem,
Which is King of Peace.
Without father, without mother, without descent.

Having neither beginning of days, nor end of life;
But made like unto the Son of God;
Abideth a priest continually.

HEBREWS: 7:2,3

Was it only happenstance that Uru Salem (Jerusalem), a little walled town, was only fourteen miles west of the Dead Sea. Jerusalem: God's holy city; in God's holy land.

Now Sarai, Abram's wife, bare him no children;
And she had a hand maid, an Egyptian,
Whose name was Hagar.
And Sarai said unto Abram,
I pray thee, go in unto my maid;
It may be that I may obtain children by her.
And Abram hearkened to the voice of Sarai.

GENESIS 16:1, 2

When Abram was eighty-six years old, Hagar bare him a child who was named Ishmael. Then Hagar despised Sarai and Sarai repented that she had given her hand maid to Abram. They had followed the old Mesopotamian custom, which brought nothing but strife and bitterness. It also showed a lack of faith in God, who had promised Abram he would become a great nation. But they had acted without God instead of waiting on him.

Nevertheless, when Abram was ninety years old, the Lord appeared to Abram and said:

I am the Almighty God;
Walk before me and be thou perfect.
I will make my covenant between me and thee,
And will multiply thee exceedingly.
My covenant is with thee,
And thou shalt be a father of many nations
Thy name shall be called Abraham;
For a father of many nations have I made thee.
GENESIS 17:1- 5

The Lord went on to promise an everlasting covenant between Himself and Abraham, one that would extend to Abram's seed af ter hi m; all the land of Canaan for an everlasting possession; and that He, the Lord, would be their God.

Only one thing was required of Abraham and all his generations to come. Every man child must be circumcised when they become eight days old. To this day, the act of circumcision is still honored by the Israelites. Furthermore, it has been discovered that this is sound medically since prothombin, a proenzyme in the blood which brings about coagulation, is deficient at birth but is at its highest level on the eighth day of life.

God did not intend this just to be a physical act to fulfill his covenant, but its spiritual promise is much more lasting and beneficial. It was a symbolic act that served to bind this covenant made between Abraham and God.

> **The Lord thy God will circumcise thine heart,**
> **And the heart of thy seed,**
> **To love the Lord thy God with all thine heart,**
> **And with all thy soul,**
> **That thou may live.**
> **DEUTERONOMY 30:6**

One day as Abraham sat in the door of his tent, he saw three men approaching and he ran to meet them; bowed himself to the ground and said:

> **My Lord, if now I have found favor in thy sight**
> **Pass not away, I pray thee from thy servant.**
> **GENESIS 18:3**

Abraham realized these were not ordinary men. Because of previous encounters, he knew God and knew he was in His presence. The Lord graciously accepted a simple meal and then announced to Abraham that Sarai would have a son. Sarai was past the age of child bearing and, in the tent near by, laughed to herself. The Lord knew her disbelief and repri- manded them.

> **Is anything too hard for the Lord?**

At the time appointed, I will return unto thee,
According to the time of life
And Sarah shall have a son.

GENESIS 18:14

Even after following the Lord for so long, they still didn't know Him well enough to believe that nothing is impossible for Him and that laws of man and nature do not apply to the God who originated it all.

As the men (angels) rose to go toward Sodom, the Lord confided in Abraham that because of the extreme sinfulness within Sodom and Gomorrah, these cities would be destroyed. Knowing Lot and his f amily now lived within Sodom, he dared intercede with God for their sakes, requesting their lives be saved if only fifty righteous souls could be found; God agreed. Abraham, knowing the sinfulness abounding in these cities, was still afraid for Lot's sake and continuing to seek mercy for them, asked if the city could be saved if it contained forty, thirty, twenty and finally ten righteous people. The Lord would concede no more than that and departed.

The two angels, appearing as men, met Lot at the gate of Sodom. Lot, still with a vestige of righteousness, insisted they spend the night in his home. That night the men of Sodom surrounded Lot's house, demanding the strangers come out to them that "they may know them." Lot, understanding their evil intentions and the importance of the welfare of these strangers, offered instead his own two virgin daughters to the men to do with as they pleased. Still the men of

Sodom desired the strangers and only the supernatural power of the angels could prevent their forced entry into the house. Sodom, from which is derived the term sodomy, signifies unnatural fleshly lusts, homosexuality, and all manner of unnatural carnalities. The men of Sodom were exceedingly wicked and sinners before the Lord exceedingly.

Being advised of the pending destruction of Sodom, Lot tried to warn his sons and daughters, but they mocked him. What a pity, for they would have been God's requisite number of ten. When morning came, the angels took Lot, his wife and remaining two daughters out of Sodom and to Zoar for their safety.

> Then the Lord rained upon Sodom and upon Gomorrah Brimstone and fire from heaven.
>
> GEN 19:24

All was destroyed in a day; including Lot's wif e who lingered, who looked back and was overwhelmed in the rain of destruction. This catastrophe is known from archeology. An area prone to earthquakes and accompanied by a natural supply of explosive materials, slime pits, petroleum and gases, it supplied all the materials God needed to work with. Today the remnants of these cities are buried under the Dead Sea. Nothing could save them from God's judgement.

Verily I say unto you, It shall be more tolerable

For the land of Sodom and Gomorrah in the day of judgement,
Than for that city.   (who will not heed).

Matt 10:15

Today God still sends signs to warn us. A current parallel might well be San Francisco.   A wicked city, rife with sodomy, controlled by homosexuals and sex deviants, located in an earthquake prone area, ready again for destruc-tion and fire and a possible watery grave in the Pacific Ocean.

And turning the cities of Sodom and Gomorrah into ashes
Condemned them with an overthrow.
Making them an example
Unto those that after should live ungodly.

II Peter 2:6

The influence of Sodom lived on in Lot's daughters through the incestuously conceived sons they bore, Moab and Ben-ammi (Ammon), from which the tribes of like names originated and whose territory lies in what is now Jordan. Their history was intertwined with that of the Hebrews throughout the Old Testament. Because of their common heritage, their language and general background was similar to the Hebrews, but their religion degenerated into heathen worship of Chemash, Asteroth, and crude fertility gods and godesses.

Twenty-five years after Abraham heeded God's call for separation, at ninety-one years of age, Sarah conceived and bore him a son whom they named Isaac (One Laughs). Abraha m was one hundred years old. Isaac was the son God had ordained, the son of promise.

> For it is written, that Abraham had two sons,
> The one by a bondmaid, the other by a freewoman.
> But he who was of the bondwoman
> Was born after the flesh;
> But he of the freewoman was by promise.
>   GALATIANS 4:22, 23

When Isaac was two or three years old, they held a great feast to celebrate his weaning. Ishmael mocked and ridiculed Isaac until Sarah could stand it no longer and ordered the expulsion of the Egyptian, Hagar, and her son. Abraham was grieved but God confir med Sarah's decision, reiterating that in Isaac would his seed be called; but that Ishmael would also be blessed by twelve sons or Arab nations. This was only the beginning of the strif e and enmity that exists today between Israel and those Arab nations. Hebrews believe in one Lord, Jehovah, the Almighty God, the God of Abraham, Isaac and Jacob and that those three are the Patriarchs of the Hebrew race. Moslems look to Ishmael as the chief son of Abraha m and as an ancestor of Mohammed. Abraham is indeed "Father of many nations."

Abraham dwelt in Beer-Sheba many days while Isaac was growing. It was there that Abraham digged a well. Beer-sheba had deep religious significance to him and later to Isaac. It was probably the most permanent home he ever knew.

When Isaac was a young man, God again spoke to Abraha m.

> Take now thy son, thine only son Isaac,
> Whom thou lovest
> And get thee into the land of Moriah;
> And offer him there for a burnt offering
> Upon one of the mountains
> Which I w ill tell thee of.

GENESIS 22:2

This time there was no hesitation on Abraham's part. He rose up early in the morning and departed on a three day journey to Mt Moriah. (Tradition places this mountain in Jerusalem, on the site of Solomon's Temple; presently the site of the Moslem Dome of the Rock.) Abraham prepared well to follow God's instructions. T.aking Isaac, two young servants, firewood, as well as the fire and a knife, he was ready to obey God - even to sacrificing the son through whom God had promised would come many nations. He demonstrated his faith in God's ability to save Isaac, or to raise hi m again from the dead, when he told his servants to wait with the donkeys until he and Isaac returned. As they were climbing the mountain, Isaac asked where the sacrifice was.

> **And Abraham said, My son,**
> **God will provide himself a lamb for a burnt offering;**
> **So they went both of them together.**

GEN 22:8

By faith, neither of them questioned this terrible request from God, and at the last moment the hand of Abraham was stayed.

God did supply another sacrifice - a ram caught in a nearby bush. Only then, the Lord spoke a second time. Because you did as I asked, because you obeyed, because you trusted me, I will bless you and multiply thy seed as the stars of heaven and as the sand upon the seashore.

There is a distinct parallel between this attempted sacrifice and the real one that occurred at Jerusalem 2,000 years later, at which time Jesus Christ was the sacrificial lamb who died for our sins and was raised from the dead.

Abraham, no different from people today, had to learn to listen to and trust in God. He learned this lesson well. Because of his faithfulness, God raised up a nation of people who would be his chosen people - the people of the covenant.

CHAPTER IV

THE COVENANT PEOPLE

God seemed in no hurry to bring into being this new nation. When Isaac was forty years of age, Abraham sent his trusted servant back to Padan Aram for a wife for Isaac from among his own people. Abraham knew that to be in the will of God Isaac should not marry a Canaanite. This commission was a heavy charge to put upon a servant, but Abraham assured him God would supply an angel to go before him. Their trust was fully justified as Rebekah, granddaughter of Nahor, brother of Abraham, came to the well with her pitcher while the servant waited on a sign from the Lord. Rebekah fulfilled that sign when she not only offered water to Abraham's servant, but watered ten camels! He then went to her home and asked permission to take Rebekah back to be the wife of Isaac. Her father and brother answered: ....

Behold, Rebekah is before thee,
Take her and go,
And let her be thy master's son's wife
As the Lord hath spoken.
And it came to pass, that,
When Abraham's servant heard these words,
He worshipped the Lord,
Bowing himself to the earth.
GENESIS 24:51, 52

And Isaac made Rebekah his wife and he loved her. When Isaac was sixty years old, Rebekah conceived. She was troubled by the struggle within her and inquired of the Lord. And the Lord said unto her.

> Two nations are in thy womb
> And two manner of people
> Shall be separated from thy bowels;
> And the one people shall be stronger
> Than the other people;
> And the elder shall serve the younger.
>
> GENESIS 25:23

As prophesied, twins were born. The first was born red and hairy and they named him Esau. Jacob followed holding to Esau's heel.

Sarah had died when Isaac was thirty-six. When Isaac was seventy-five, Abraham too passed on and was buried in the cave of Machpelah, which is before Mamre; the same cave in which Sarah had been buried. And Abraham gave all that he had to Isaac, who dwelt by the well La-hoi-roi. During this sojourn, Esau and Jacob grew. Esau was a cunning hunter and loved by Isaac for his venison. Jacob was a homebody and loved by Rebekah. Already trouble was brewing in this household. Esau, the first born, was by rights entitled to a double portion of their father's wealth and of the spiritual blessings, which he despised. Jacob desired the birthright above all else. From earliest times, the first born was expected to be dedicated to Yahweh (God). Therefore, Esau's conduct in selling his birthright to Jacob for a bowl of stew, when he returned from hunting empty-handed and hungry, showed his utter disregard for the Lord.

During this time, Isaac prospered as he dug again the wells of his father, Abraham; wells that had been filled in by Philistines because they were envious of his great wealth; wells that were so essential to sustain large flocks and herds and many servants. Abimelech, king of the Philistines, observed that Isaac was blessed of God as, one by one, Isaac and his servants dug wells with plentiful water supplies at Esek and at Sithan, which he gave over to the Philistines, and at Rehoboth and Beersheba, which he kept. Then Abimelech came to make a covenant of peace with Isaac.

The Lord appeared to Isaac, assuring him of blessing and fruitfulness, for Abraham's sake. But all was not well wit h Isaac's family. When Esau was forty years old, he took two wives of Hittite descent, which grieved his parents.

Even so, as Isaac grew old and blind, he prepared to pass the birthright and blessing on to Esau before his death. But first, he sent Esau for venison one more time. Rebekah heard of these plans and hastened to prepare Jacob to take Esau's place by deceiving his father. Nothing of this was honorable or pleasing to God. In the first place, Isaac knew the Lord had told Rebekah "the elder shall serve the younger." Secondly, Esau had previously despised the birthright; and third, Rebekah and Jacob used deceit and trickery in obtaining it instead of waiting on the Lord. When Esau realized Jacob had received the birthright and blessing, he wept and hated Jacob. Rebekah knew Esau purposed in his heart to kill Jacob and arranged to send Jacob to her brother Laban at Haran. At her suggestion, Isaac instructed Jacob:

Go to Padan Aram and take thee a wife from thence Of the daughters of Laban, thy mother's brother.

GENESIS 28:2

Laban had two daughters, the name of the elder was Leah, and the name of the younger was Rachel. Rachel was beautiful and Jacob loved her so much he agreed to work for Laban seven years to be permitted to marry her. But on the wedding night, Laban slipped Leah into Jacob's tent instead of Rachel. The following morning Jacob discovered he had been tricked. Laban insisted his elder daughter, Leah, must be married before the younger, but that if Jacob would abide by the marriage arrangement for one week, he might also have Rachel for his wife. With this arrangement, Jacob was obligated to another seven years labor. Jacob did so and loved Rachel more than Leah. Leah had sons: Reuben, Simeon, Levi and Judah; and Rachel had none. Rachel envied her sister and because she was unable to bare children, gave her hand maiden, Bilhah to Jacob in her stead. Bilhah gave birth to Dan and Naphtali. Leah retaliated by sending her maid, Zilpah, to Jacob. She had two sons, Gad and Asher. Then Leah again conceived and brought forth a fifth son, Issachar; and a sixth son, Zebulun. She also bare a daughter, named Dinah.

Finally, God blessed Rachel and she had a son whom they named Joseph. The fourteen years of service to Laban was at an end and Jacob desired to leave but Laban entreated him to stay, knowing the Lord had blessed him and the herds had been greatly increased during Jacob's tenure. Now, it was agreed Jacob would serve for a share of the herds. His would be all the speckled and spotted sheep and goats. Jacob sought to influence the breeding by putting ringed and spotted poplar rods before the animals as they bred. In reality, he bred the stronger animals with his marked ones and the weaker animals with Laban's plain ones. His flocks multiplied as Laban's dwindled. Unknowingly, through divine guidance, he was practicing selective breeding, a science that is understood and widely practiced today. Resentment at Jacob's success grew in Laban until the day came when Jacob knew he must leave.

> And the Lord said unto Jacob, Return
> unto the land of thy fathers,
> And to thy kindred, and I will be with thee.
> GENESIS 31:3

Jacob's stay at Padan Aram had been full of deceit, bitterness, strife and jealousy between his wives, and his leaving was by stealth, yet he departed a rich man with great herds and flocks and a large family.

> And Jacob sent messengers before him to Esau, his
> brother Unto
> the land of Seir, the country of Edom.
> GENESIS 32:3

The messengers returned to say "Esau is coming to meet you with four hundred men." Jacob was much afraid and divided all he possessed into two companies, so that if Esau captured one of them, the other might escape. He separated a large portion of the goats, sheep, camels, bulls and donkeys and sent them forth as a present to Esau, hoping to pacify him. Sending his two wives and eleven sons on, he remained alone to wrestle a "man" until the break of day. For the first time in his life, he was truly prevailing on the Lord and would not quit until he received a blessing from God and deliverance from Esau's vengence. As morning came, the "man" said:

> Thy name shall be no more called Jacob, but Israel:
> For as a prince hast thou power with God and with men,
> And hast prevailed.
> And Jacob called the name of the place Peniel.
> For I have seen God face to face
> And my life is preserved.
> GENESIS 32:28, 30

As Esau approached, Jacob bowed seven times to him, and Esau ran to meet him, and embraced him, and f ell on his neck, and kissed him and they wept. God had interceded.

As Esau returned to Seir, the valley between the Dead Sea and the Red Sea (Gulf of Aqaba), Jacob turned westward and stopped near the Jordan River where he bought land from Shechem's father and erected tents in a place called Succoth (shelters).

This was Jacob's first encounter with Canaanites; in this case, Hivites. Dinah went out to see the daughters of the land and Shechem loved her, lay with her and then asked to marry her. Dinah's brothers sought revenge for her defilement by deceit and trickery. Pursuading the men of Shechem to agree to circumcision so they might marry with the Hebrew daughters, Simeon and Levi slew all the males on the third day when they were in acute pain and too sore to defend themselves. Jacob knew they were all in danger after this act, but God said:

> Jacob arise, go up to Bethel and dwell there;
> And make there an altar to God,
> That appeared unto thee when thou fleddest
> From the face of Esau, your brother.
>
> GENESIS 35:1

Jacob ordered all his people to put aside all of their strange gods and idols and the Lord's protection was with them as they journeyed. And God confirmed that Jacob's name was Israel. The closest translation appears to be "he who has power with God and wit h men, and has prevailed."

> And God appeared unto Jacob again,
> When he came out of Padanaram and blessed him.
> Be fruitful and multiply.
> The land which I gave Abraham, Isaac, to thee I give it.
> And God went up from him
> In the place where he talked with him.
>
> GENESIS 35:9 - 13

As they journeyed beyond Bethel, near Bethlehem, Rachel died giving birth to a second son, Benjamin (Jacob's twelfth son). From these sons originated the twelve tribes of Israel. For the most part, unruly, deceitful sons who followed the early examples of Jacob and Laban. After Jacob's surrender to God and his conversion to Israel, his transformation appears to have favorably influenced Rachel's sons, Joseph and Benjamin. Although still Hebrews, the sons of Bilhah and of Zilpah had added new blood. Their origins are obscure, but recently the exodus of Ethiopian "Jews" of the Tribe of Dan sheds some light on Bilhah's ancestory.

> Now Israel loved Joseph more than all his children,
> Because he was the son of his old age.
> And he made him a coat of many colors.
> GENESIS 37:3

This was no ordinary coat, but one designating authority. His brothers saw this as a sign Jacob planned to pass them by and make Joseph his heir. Joseph had contributed to their resentment when he told them of his dreams in which they would some day bow down to him. They both envied and hated him. Jacob sent Joseph to Shechem to check on his brothers who were tending the sheep. They had gone on to Dothan, w here he found them. When they saw Joseph approaching, they plotted to kill hi m. First, they stripped him of his coat of many colors and cast him into a pit. Just at this time, a caravan of Ishmaelite, or Midianite merchants, traveling the trade route from Gilead to Egypt, passed through Dothan bearing spices and aromatic gums (myrrh, used for perfumes; and balm, used for cosmetics, embalming and for healing). Both the Ishmaelites and Midianites were descendants of Abraham. The ter m "Ishmaelites" was applied not only to a people, but to a mode of life followed by itinerant caravan traders and cameleers. The Hebrews considered them to be an inferior people. It was to such a caravan that the brothers sold Joseph for twenty pieces of silver.

> And Judah said unto his brethren,
> What profit is it if we slay our brother,
> And conceal his blood?
> Come, let us sell him to the Ishmaelites,
> And let not our hand be upon him.
> For he is our brother and our flesh.
>
> GENESIS 37:26, 27

They dipped Joseph1s coat into goat's blood and brought it to their f ather saying they had found it. Jacob knew it was his son's coat and mourned for Joseph for many days.

Joseph was taken to Egypt and sold to Potiphar, an officer of Pharoah's and captain of the guard.

A t this time, Egypt, as well as Palestine and Syria, was ruled by t he Hyksos (Rulers of foreign lands), who were a mixed and predominantly Semitic and Canaanite people. This powerful kingdom reigned during the 15th - 17th Dynasties in Egypt. They were horsemen who brought to Egypt chariot and cavalry warfare, but who were sympathetic to the Hebrews and others who came to the delta for food during times of hardship. Egypt, during this period, is well known by historians for its famous storehouses (store-cities) and for its extensive trade. Caravan cargoes were steadily pouring riches into Egypt from every direction so that the courts at Memphis, Thebes and Akhetaten enjoyed a standard of living not of ten exceeded in ancient times.

> **And the Lord was with Joseph**
> **And he (Potiphar) was a prosperous man,**
> **And he was in the house of his master the Egyptian**
> **And the Lord made all that he did**
> **To prosper in his hand.**
> **GENESIS 39:1 - 3**

Potiphar learned to trust Joseph and made him overseer of all his house-hold and it prospered until Potiphar's wife desired Joseph. All her wiles and entreating could not persuade Joseph to betray his master, so she venge- fully accused him of attacking her. Potiphar believed his wife and had Joseph imprisoned. Even there Joseph acted honorably and gained favor with the prison keeper who put him in charge of all the prisoners. The Lord was with him in everything that he did. During this time, the Pharoah's butler and baker were put into prison and each had dreams which Joseph interpreted. Shortly thereafter the butler was reinstated, but the baker was hanged as Joseph had interpreted.

Two years later the Pharaoh was troubled by a dream; he slept, and dreamed a second time. In the morning he remained troubled so he sent for all the magicians and all the wise men of Egypt, men well versed in interpretations, but none could decipher these dreams. It was then the butler remembered Joseph and the Pharoah sent for him.

As they brought him hastily out of the dungeon;
And he shaved himself, and changed his raimant,
And came in unto Pharoah.

GENESIS 41:14

(This was consistent with Egyptian custom which dictated that everyone who appeared at court must be clean shaven and dressed in clean linen.)

The Pharoah related his dreams to Joseph: Seven fat, well-fed cattle came out of the river and fed in the meadow and seven lean, hungry cattle came after them and devoured the fat ones, but still remained as ill-favored as in the beginning. His second dream was of seven full ears of corn on on one stalk and seven thin, withered ears sprung up and devoured the good ears. Joseph replied that God would supply the answer and it was the same for both dreams. What God was about to do had been shown the Pharoah. There would be seven years of abundant crops, followed by seven years of grievous famine. Joseph went on to suggest that Pharoah appoint a wise, trustworthy man over all the land of Egypt to gather and store food in the good years.

Let them keep food in the cities.

GENESIS 41:35

Pharoah was so impressed with his wisdom and godliness that Joseph was the one appointed as ruler over all the land of Egypt and given power, second only to Pharoah himself .

> And the Pharoah took off his ring from his hand,
> And put it upon Joseph's hand,
> And arrayed him in vestures of fine linen,
> And put a gold chain about his neck.
>
> GENESIS 41:42

The signet ring with its cartouche (identification of royal authority), the gold neck-chain with its scarab, and the white linen clothing are thoroughly Egyptian. Since this Hyksos Pharoah was of Semitic descent and a ruler of foreign peoples, he may conceivably have felt a bond between himself and Joseph, also a Semite, and regarded him with a trust he did not hold for the Egyptians he ruled. History records the Hyksos were well-known for their store cities. Could Joseph's suggestion have been the inspiration and example from which they originated?

Joseph was thirty years old and for seven years he went throughout the land gathering and storing an abundance of food in every city. During this time he married Asenath, daughter of an Egyptian priest of On, and two sons were born to them: Manasseh and Ephraim. At the end of the seven years, as ordained by God, there was famine in the land; not only in Egypt, everywhere.

> And all countries came into Egypt
> To Joseph for to buy corn:

Because that the famine was so sore
In all lands.

GENESIS 41:57

It had been the custom for many years for hungry nomads of Canaan and Sinai to turn to Egypt whenever there were local famines. The Hyksos appeared to be lenient and history records several times "displaced persons" were allowed to remain in the delta area when food was scarce.

Joseph's ten brothers went to Egypt to buy corn. They bowed themselves down to Joseph, not recognizing him, for surely he looked and dressed as an Egyptian. But Joseph knew his brothers. They returned to their father unaware of his identity and when the food was gone, the famine still gripped the land and they had no recourse but to go again into Egypt. When Joseph saw that this time his younger brother, Benjamin, was with them, he had to depart quickly to hide his tears. Later, when he could stand it no longer, he made himself known to them.

And he said, I am Joseph your brother
Whom ye sold into Egypt.
Now therefore be not grieved,
Nor angry with yourselves,
That ye sold me hither;
For God did send me before you
To preserve life.

For these two years hath the famine
Been in the land;

And yet there are five years,
In which there shall neither be earing nor harvest.

GENESIS 45:5, 6

Joseph understood God had foreseen and prepared the way to spare his people during this terrible period of famine but even he did not realize the full depth of God's plan. Only the Lord's omniscience had prevented Joseph's death many years before. If his brothers had remained at Shechem wit h the sheep, they would have been forced to kill hi m , for the trade route to Egypt did not pass through Shechem. Only at Dothan could he be sold to a passing caravan and his life spared.

He hastened to send his brothers back for their families, and their f ather, that they might all dwell in Egypt for the next five years. This pleased the Pharaoh and he offered to give them the best of the land; so they settled in the land of Goshen. Jacob and his sons totalled seventy people. This count did not include wives, daughters and servants.

And Joseph placed his father and his brethren,
And gave them a possession in the land of Egypt,
In the best of the land,
In the land of Ramesses
As Pharaoh had commanded.

GENESIS 47:11

(Ramesses is a name derived from the Egyptian sun god Ra, and from which later pharaohs would derive their name.)

Jacob lived seventeen years in Egypt. Before his death he included Ephraim and Manasseh in the inheritance and set Ephraim, the younger, - before Manasseh. As for his own sons, he prophesied also, and for Judah:

> **The sceptor shall not depart from Judah**
> **Nor a law-giver from between his feet**
> **Until Shiloh come. And unto him**
> **Shall the gathering of the people be.**
> **GENESIS 49:10**

Jacob's last command to his sons was to return his body to the land of Canaan, to the cave in Mamre where Abraham, Sarah, Isaac, Rebekah and Leah were buried. His body was embalmed by Egyptian physicians and his people, and the Egyptians, mourned for forty days at which time a great colony of men, chariots and horsemen went to bury Jacob in Canaan in the land of his fathers. Still Joseph and his father's sons dwelt in Egypt.

Joseph had been fruitful to God and was the instrument God had used to preserve the lives of the Hebrews (his covenant people). God Almighty, omniscient; the only one who knows the end from the beginning, had prepared the way for the Hebrew sojourn in Egypt; preparing Egypt by placing Hyksos rulers related to and receptive to them (God is not limited -- many times he uses ungodly people and nations for his purposes) by placing Joseph's brothers in the path of the Ishmaelite merchants who brought him into Egypt and all of the circumstances which led to his appointment as a trusted ruler and the assignment of the best and most f ertile lands to his people.

Joseph died at one hundred and ten years; they embalmed him and he was put in a coffin in Egypt. Before his death he told his brothers:

> God will surely visit you.
> And bring you out of this land
> Unto the lands which he swore
> To Abraham, Isaac and Jacob
> And ye shall carry my bones from hence.
>
> GENESIS 50:25

Without the land of Goshen to feed and shelter the Israelites during - the years of famine, they would most likely have starved or been forced to divide into small groups to seek sustenance. Only their continued stay at Goshen enabled them to remain together and multiply so that they might eventually become a nation. There might never have been a king David -- or Jesus Christ, without whom there would have been no hope or salvation for the world. And none of this would have been possible if Joseph's brothers had stayed at Shechem, as planned, instead of going on to Dothan!

CHAPTER V

EXODUS

For over three hundred years the children of Israel made their home in the land of Goshen.

And the children of Israel were fruitful
And increased abundantly and multiplied,
And waxed exceedingly mighty;
And the land was filled with them.
Now there rose up a new king over Egypt
Which knew not Joseph.
EXODUS 1:7,8

They saw successive Pharaohs come into power and their authority pass on to others. The Hyksos Dynasties ended in 1550 B.C. with the 18th Dynasty of Amenhotep I, an Egyptian. A ruler less friendly to foreigners than his predecessors. Later (1379 - 1362 B.C.), a most interesting and well documented Pharaoh was young king Amenophis IV who changed his name to Akhenaten after the god he worshipped. He was married to Queen Nefertiti, renowned for her beauty. Together they promoted the worship of their god, Aten; symbolized by a sun disk. Akhenaten was a monotheist and neglected the rule of his kingdom to devote his time establishing his new diety, Aten, as the one universal god. Marked parallels between Akhenaten's beliefs and those of the Hebrew worship of Yahweh included one god, creator of all things, father of all, intangible yet ever-present.

The young king addressed his god as "Father which art in heaven," he made no graven images. He knew his god as "the God of Love," compassionate, tender, merciful, one whose kingdom was "within" the hearts of men and was "the Lord of Peace" and of truth. History suggests the Hebrews may have adopted much of his one-god religion and that this later had a great influence on Moses. Could it have been the other way around? Perhaps the God of Israel was spread beyond the boundaries of Goshen for a short time, because Egypt promptly reverted to worship of many idols and gods at the end of Akhenaten's reign. The countless gods of polytheistic Egypt are too numerous to mention. Every aspect of nature, every object was thought to be inhabited by a spirit which could choose its own form -- croco- dile, tree, man, fish, gods of fertility, of agriculture, and on and on. Polytheism seemed to have little influence on the religion of the Hebrews.

There was great opulence in the courts of Egypt at this time. For example, a daughter of Akhenaten and Nefertiti married a young king, Tutankhamun (1361 - 1352 B.C.). Our world is familiar with King Tut and the f abulous treasures found in his tomb.

But when the time of the promise drew nigh,
Which God had sworn to Abraham,
The people grew and multiplied in Egypt.
Till another king arose
Which knew not Joseph.

ACTS 7:17, 18

King Tut's successor was Sethos I who became concerned about the growing numbers of Hebrews living in the land and he began a building program which was continued by the Ramesses.

Therefore they did set over them taskmasters
To afflict them with their burdens.
And they built for Pharaoh treasure cities
Pithom and Raamses.

EXODUS 1:11

The Hebrews were a ready made source of labor. They were organized into small groups and placed under task masters to dig out mud which over- flowed from the Nile River and make bricks to build the new cities. Today mud bricks are made the same way, but it is becoming increasingly difficult to obtain the raw material since the Aswan Dam reduces the flow of silt. Flooding and drought are now controlled by the high dam.

The more work imposed upon the Hebrews, the more they multiplied and grew. Pharaoh then turned to the ·Hebrew midwives, ordering them to kill all male children at birth. This the midwives would not do, so it fell to Egyptian authorities ·to enforce this edict.

God will not be circumvented. This time he chose a Levite family for his purpose. One who already had a girl and a boy born before the order to kill all newborn males became effective. His mother had the insight to perceive this was no ordinary child and took precautions to hide him for three months, at which time she placed him in an ark and left him at the edge of the River Nile.

He was in God's hands. Miriam, his sister, watched from a distance as the daughter of Pharaoh came to wash herself at the river and discovered the child and desired it for her own. Conveniently, Miriam just happened to know someone who could nurse it for her, so his own mother cared for hi m for the first f ew year's of his life.

Pharaoh's daughter named him "Moses" because she said, I drew him out of the water. "Moses" has a num ber of meanings. The Hebrew Moshah or Mosheh translates "to draw out;" Moses in Egyptian means "to be born" and Mase means "child"; all of which is apt. Regardless, he was destined to become one of the greatest leaders of all times. His childhood was spent in the royal household. At the Egyptian court, Moses received training in all wisdom of Egypt which was highly advanced. He learned to write and received knowledge in the sciences of that day, which included magic, in which the Egyptians excelled. He was probably schooled in mathematics, religions and architecture. All of this to prepare him to become an official of Egypt.

When Moses was forty years old, he went one day to see his people and espied an Egyptian beating a Hebrew unmercifully. Hating the oppression of his people, he killed the Egyptian. It was seen and reported to Pharaoh who sought to slay Moses. Moses fled for his life and did not stop until he came to Midian. The Midianites were descendants of A braham through Keturah, his second wife, taken in his old age after the death of Sarah. They were desert dwellers who lived south of the Dead Sea in Arabia and in Sinai. It was at the home of Jethro, a Priest of Midian, who lived in Sinai that Moses stopped. Jethro believed in the God of Abraham and it was to this priestly man that God directed him. Moses married Zipporah, Jethro's daughter, and tended the flocks of his father-in-law for forty years.

> And it came to pass in process of time,
> That the king of Egypt died:
> And the children of Israel sighed
> By reason of bondage, and they cried,
> And their cry came up unto God
> By reason of the bondage.
> And God heard their groaning,
> And God remembered his covenant
> With Abraham, with Isaac, and with Jacob.
>   EXODUS 2: 23, 24

In all likelihood, this new king was Ramesses II (1304 - 1237 B.C.). He has been called "the greatest boaster in Egyptian history." He built some of Egypt's most imposing structures (with slave labor). In front of one of these he placed no less than six statues of himself. He erased his predecessor's names from records of royal achievements and inserted his own. He erected the memorial temple "The Ramesseum" at Thebes. Statues and inscriptions extolling his exploits have been unearthed from Egypt to Syria. And as fate would have it, the mummified face of Pharaoh Ramesses II stares from a case in the Egyptian Museum in Cairo today!

No w the time was right to use Moses as God had predestined. Moses was tending Jethro's flock on the backside of the desert, at the foot of Mt Horeb, when God called out to him from a flaming bush; a bush that burned but was not consumed. Here the Lord unfolded his purpose to Moses.

> **Now therefore, behold, the cry of the children of Israel**
> **Is come unto me.**
> **I have also seen the oppression**
> **Wherewith the Egyptians oppress them.**
> **Come now therefore, and I will send thee unto Pharaoh**
> **When thou hast brought forth the people**
> **Out of Egypt**
> **Ye shall serve God upon this mountain.**
>
> **EXODUS 3:9-12**

Moses doubted his ability to carry out such an awesome commission. Confronted by the Lord, he had to express his inadequacy. How could he explain to his people that God had really sent hi m and how could he make them understand that he was truly representing the God of their fathers. The Lord replied "I A m that I A m." Tell them this is my name forever and this is my memorial unto all generations.

From the beginning, God's people knew his personal name as Yahweh. To them this name was divine, so the use of the word Lord was substituted because Yahweh was too holy to be used commonly. Yahweh is related to the Hebrew verb "to be" or "am", but it goes beyond existing. He is an eternal "I Am;" one who always was and always will be; their provider, redeemer and judge. All of this the people would understand when Moses told them he was sent by "I am."

The Lord instructed Moses in all that would transpire before the exodus; still Moses doubted. Patiently, the Lord showed signs and wonders to Moses, explaining how he could work miracles before the Pharaoh. He also made Aaron, older brother of Moses, his spokesman and gave him a rod by which he would do signs before Pharaoh.

And the Lord said unto Moses,
When thou goest to return unto Egypt,
See that thee do those wonders before Pharaoh,
Which I have put in thy hand:
But I will harden his heart,
That he shall not let the people go.
And thou shalt say unto Pharaoh,
Thus saith the Lord, Israel is my son,
Even my first-born:
And I say unto thee, Let my son go,
That he may serve me:
And if thou refuse to let him go, behold,
I will slay thy son, even thy first-born.

EXODUS 4:21 - 23

It came to pass that the Pharaoh did indeed refuse to let the children of Israel depart. When Moses and Aaron came before the Pharaoh to request he let the people go, he not only refused but increased the workload and the suffering of the Israelites. Then Moses turned to God questioningly and in despair.

And God spoke unto Moses, and said unto him,
I am the Lord and I appeared unto Abraham,

Unto Isaac, and unto Jacob, by the name of God
Almighty,
But by my name JEHOVAH was I not known to them
Ye shall know that I am the Lord your God,
Which bringeth you out from under the burdens of the
Egyptians.

                                                    EXODUS 6:2-7

Jehovah: the provider, the redeemer, the victor; the peace; the one who is all things to his people. Moses would learn to trust and to lean on Jehovah for all things in the years ahead. First he must f ace the Pharaoh again. God sent ten plagues, and until the very last one, Pharaoh's heart remained hard. First, for seven days, God turned the rivers to blood, the fish died and the river stank and all water in ponds, pools and vessels was also turned to blood. When the Pharaoh refused to let the people go, the rivers brought forth frogs in such numbers they were under foot, in the beds, ovens, everywhere! The Pharaoh called for Moses to remove the frogs, but when the frogs were gone, Pharaoh's heart was again hardened and so it went through plagues of dust turned to lice and plagues of flies.

From this time on the land of Goshen would be spared the plagues of death to cattle, boils upon mankind, devastating hail that killed everything it hit; man, beast, trees, flax and barley. Only the wheat and rye were spared because they were not yet grown. After this, the Lord sent locusts to eat all that remained. Then three days of darkness so thick it could be felt. Nothing in the land moved save the

Israelites for there was light in the land of Goshen. One last plague remained. The Lord instructed Moses and Aaron in preparation for this one. The Israelites were sent out to borrow jewels of silver and gold from the Egyptians. By this time Moses had made a great impact upon all of the people and they willingly lent their jewels to the children of Israel. The Lord had said about midnight he would pass through the land and the first born of the pharaoh and of all the people in the land, all of the servants and all of the beasts, would die. Only the first born of the Israelites would be spared. Their protection would be the blood of a sacrificial lamb. Every family must choose a lamb, without blemish, and sprinkle its blood upon the door post of their home. They were instructed to roast the lamb, eat it with unleavened bread and bitter herbs as they stood, ready to depart.

And it came to pass, that at midnight
The Lord smote all the first born in the land of Egypt.
And Pharaoh rose up in the night, he,
And all his servants, and all the Egyptians;
And there was a great cry in Egypt,
For there was not a house where there was not one
dead.
EXOD 12:29 - 30

These plagues may have occurred over a period of as much as a year. Natural disasters could account for many of them, beginning with unusually high flooding of the Nile, bringing down red earth and microcosms which could set off a chain of events such as dead fish, pollution, frogs coming forth from the river, lice and fleas.

Elements of nature such as severe hail and thunderstorms are plausible, but this in no way diminishes God for all the forces of nature are at his command.

With the passing of the Death Angel, Pharaoh and all of the Egyptians urged Moses and his people to take everything they possessed and depart. They left in such haste, they took their dough before it had risen, gathered their belongings, their herds and cattle, and the borrowed jewels of the Egyptians, and they departed Rameses. There were about six hundred thousand men, besides women and children. A mixed multitude went with them, flocks and herds, even very much cattle. And Moses took the bones of Joseph with him as Joseph had prophesied. It has been estimated the total of men, women and children would have been over two million.

> And it came to pass at the end of the
> Four hundred and thirty years,
> Even the selfsame day it came to pass,
> That all the hosts of the Lord
> Went out from the land of Egypt.
>
> EXODUS 12:41

From this time forth, the Passover has been observed yearly by the Hebrews as a memorial to the Lord and in remembrance of the night they were spared and brought forth out of bondage in the land of Egypt.

The Lord led the people through the way of the wilderness of the Red Sea.

> God led them not through the way

Of the land of the Philistines
Although that was near; For God said,
Lest the people repent when they see war,
And they return to Egypt.

EXODUS 13:17

The shortest, most travelled way would have been by the shore of the Mediterranean Sea. The Egyptians had established strongholds along this coast; great fortresses and palaces similar to those in Egypt. Excavations have located six of these from the Nile Delta to Gaza. History reveals that about the time of the Exodus this area was invaded by "Peoples of the Sea," chief among them the Philistines. They were defeated by the Egyptians who settled them as mercenaries in their own strongholds. If God had led his people this way they would have had to face a part of the pharaoh's army and the Philistine mercenaries. After generations of bondage, they had become too brow-beaten and intimidated to face aggression. God had foreseen and prevented this confrontation.

God's way would put them in a situation they could not run from. He led them on a course that put them between the Red Sea and the wilderness. Perhaps near the site of present day Suez. Then the Lord again hardened the heart of the pharaoh, who pursued them with a great army and all his horses and chariots. The children of Israel were sore afraid but Moses assured them the Lord would fight for them.

And the Lord said unto Moses
Lift up thy rod and stretch thine hand over the sea,

And divide it, and the children of Israel
Shall go on dry ground
Through the midst of the sea
And the Egyptians shall know
That I am the Lord.

EXODUS 14:15, 18

And Moses stretched out his hand over the sea and the Lord caused the sea to go back by a strong east wind that blew all night and the waters were divided. The children of Israel crossed on dry ground but when the Egyptians pursued them, their chariots lost their wheels and while they were bogged down the sea returned in strength, and although the Egyptians fled, the Lord overthrew them in the midst of the sea as the waters returned and covered the chariots and the horse men and all the army of the Pharaoh that came in the sea.

Thus the Lord saved Israel that day
Out of the hand of the Egyptians;
And Israel saw the Egyptians
Dead upon the seashore.
And Israel saw the great work
Which the Lord did upon the Egyptians;
And the people feared the Lord,
And believed the Lord, and his servant Moses.

EXODUS 14:30, 31

An earthquake in 1755 sent a devastating 40-foot wall of water into Lisbon, Portugal killing an estimated 60,000 people. The Alaskan earthquake of 1964 greatly influenced tides as far south as the California coast. Only modern-day communications and forewarning prevented untold deaths. It is known that the Red Sea is a part of the tremendous geological fault or rift extending from the Beka'a Plain, which divides the Lebanons from the Anti-Lebanon Range in Syria, south through the Jordan and the Gulf of Aquabah and on into Africa. The Lord who created the universe still has control of elements on this earth and orders them as he will. An earth-quake could very well have contributed to the parting of the sea.

Moses led the multitude of Israel into the wilderness of Sinai, encamp-ing where there were wells of water. But the people murmured against Moses and Aaron that they were being killed by hunger. The Lord heard their grumbling and said:

> I have heard the murmurings of the children of Israel
> Speak unto them saying
> At even ye shall eat flesh and in the morning
> Ye shall be filled with bread;
> And ye shall know that I am the Lord your God.
>
> EXODUS 16:12

When evening came, quails came up and covered the camp and in the morning the dew lay all about. When the dew was gone; small, round, white particles like coriander seed remained. It tasted like wafers made with honey. For all the time the children of Israel wandered in the Sinai wilderness, God supplied this substance which they called "manna." He directed them to gather it fresh six mornings of each week. On the sixth day they were to gather a double portion, for one day of each week was to be set aside as a sabbath to the Lord.

When the people did not heed the Lord, but gathered more than they could eat during the week, by morning it stank and bred worms. Only on the Sabbath would the manna remain fresh for more than one day.

Quails in Sinai are not uncommon, even today. Twice a year the quails' migration route takes them across the region through which the Israelites travelled. Annual exports from Egypt during the past one hundred years have been between two and three million birds, although their numbers are becoming depleted through the heavy toll this has extracted and measures have been taken to control their slaughter.

As for the manna, nobody knows just what it consisted of but with God nothing is impossible. He had the material at hand in the very air itself to manufacture carbohydrates and starches. All food molecules in this class have a structure built on CH_2O - a "hydrate of carbon" or carbo-hydrate. Hydrogen (H) and oxygen (0) and carbon (C) are all elements found in our atmosphere. A scarcity of trees to utilize carbon dioxide and millions of people exhaling it would build up an excess of carbon. In addition to this, Landsat photos show evidence of carbon vapors in areas where oil deposits exist, such as those in the Sinai. Granted it would be a complex task for man; but for God, who originated it all, a subtile change in atom combinations would be plausible. Certainly not out of line for a God who created the world from things unseen.

And the congregation pitched in Rephidim
And there was no water for the people to drink
And the Lord said unto Moses, go before the people.
Take thy rod in hand and go. Behold,
I will stand before thee there upon the rock in Horeb,
And thou shalt smite the rock
And there shall come water out of it,
That the people may drink.

EXODUS 17:1- 6

The children of Israel travelled the mountain route to avoid the highways controlled by Egyptians and Philistines. They entered the territory of the Midianites, the area that Moses knew so well from herding the sheep of his father-in-law. He was familiar with the high red granite mountains. The mountain brooks in southern Sinai carried rainwater down to the coastal belt where it was absorbed by the porous sand and the wells dug here gave forth an abundance of sweet water. There was also moisture in the mountain clefts year around. What Moses could not see, but God was aware of , was vast underground reservoirs of water just waiting to spring up. Aerial photos of this area today reveal the existence of this primeval underground water supply.

Then came Amalek and fought
With Israel in Rephidim.

EXODUS 17:8

The Amalekites, descendants of Esau's grandson Amalek, were camel-riding desert nomads, who had spread from Edom across the Sinai Peninsula to the Red Sea. They were swift moving, battle trained fighting men ready to fight for and protect their control of the water wells, the oases and the grazing lands of Sinai. This was the first battle the children of Israel would face. Untried, unfamiliar with warfare, it would have been no contest without the Lord. Moses chose Joshua to lead the men in battle and they prevailed as long as Moses held up the rod of God. When his arms grew tired and he had to lower the rod, the Amalekites prevailed, so Aaron and Hur held up Moses' hands all day and they won the battle. God gave them the victory.

> And the Lord said unto Moses
> I will utterly put out the remembrance of Amalek
> From under heaven.
> EXODUS 17:14

In the third month the Israelites camped before Mt Sinai, known today as Jabol Musa, the Mount of Moses. A gaunt, imposing, wind-tortured peak of 7,497 feet, surrounded by other peaks equally as rugged and a mountain also called Mt Horeb. Moses had come full circle, because it was at the foot of this same mountain that he had been called by God from a burning bush. Here, according to God's word to Moses, the children of Israel prepared to hear and see their Lord.

And it came to pass on the third day in the morning,
That there were thunders and lightnings
And a thick cloud upon the mount
And the voice of the trumpet exceeding loud;
So that all the people that was in the camp trembled.
And Mount Sinai was altogether on a smoke,
Because the Lord descended upon it in fire...

And the whole mount quaked greatly.
EXOD 19:16-18

The people drew away from the mount in terror. Only Moses could go upon the mountain and into God's presence. It was here he received the ten commandments, the judgments and laws which are still the foundation of the Hebrew religion and government to this day. The first four command- ments concern men's relationship to God (Thou shalt have no other gods before me;) the remaining six, their relationship to one another. The judg- ments and laws were similar to other ancient law-codes of Western Asia (notably that of Hammurabi, king of Babylon in 1690 B.C.) with one important exception: The laws given to Moses rest on the authority of God, not on a king; and legal, moral and religious laws are inseparable.

The Lord called Moses up into the mount and the glory of the Lord covered Moses for forty days and forty nights, during which time he was given the ten command ments on two tablets of stone written with the finger of God and all the details for a tabernacle wherein the Lord's presence would abide with the people.

When the people saw that Moses did not come down from the mount, they appealed to Aaron to make them gods. Already these fickle children of Israel were ready to doubt God. Aaron readily obliged them by melting their golden earrings and moulding them into a golden calf. And the people said:

These shall be thy gods, 0 Israel,
Which brought thee up out of the land of Egypt.
EXOD 32:4

The Lord looked down upon them as they worshiped and sacrificed to the heathen Egyptian idol they had formed; as they corrupted themselves in an unholy, licentious orgy, and his wrath waxed hot against them. Only Moses' intervention saved the people from certain death. But when Moses returned from Mount Sinai, with the tablets of God and he saw the calf and the dancing, his anger was so great he cast the tablets out of his hands and broke them.

Moses went again upon Mount Sinai for another forty days and nights and he did neither eat bread, nor drink water.

And it came to pass
When Moses came down from Mount Sinai
With the two tables of testimony in Moses hand,
When he came down from the mount,
That Moses knew not that the skin of his face
shone while he talked with him.
And till Moses had done speaking with them,
He put a veil on his face.
EXOD 34:29-33

Moses spoke to all the congregation, instructing them on the sabbath day and the tabernacle, its furnishings and the priests who would serve the Lord therein. Then the people who were wise-hearted, willingly gave gold, silver, brass, fine linen, goats' hair, rams' skins dyed red, badger skins and shittim wood, oil, spices and sweet incense for the tabernacle. (It is interesting to note that the gold and silver jewelry borrowed from the Egyptians at God's bidding was destined to become a part of his tabernacle.) And the people gave of their individual skills and talents in the construction of each article just as the Lord had specified.

> **And Moses did look upon all the work,**
> **And, behold, they had done it as the Lord had**
> **commanded**
> **And Moses blessed them.**
> **EXODUS 39:43**

On the day appointed by the Lord, Aaron and his sons were anointed and sanctified to serve the Lord. The tabernacle was erected, the ark of the testimony was brought into the tabernacle and the mercy seat was set above the ark. Then the veil was hung to separate this portion, the Holy of Holies, from the rest of the tabernacle. Only the high priest could enter this holy section of the tabernacle, and then only once a year to seek atonement for the people. Before the veil was placed the table for bread, the candlestick, and the golden altar of incense. A hanging was erected at the door of the tabernacle. Outside this door was the altar of burnt offering and the laver of water to wash their hands and feet and it was imperative that the priests wash before entering the tabernacle.

> **Then a cloud covered the tent of the congregation**
> **And the glory of the Lord filled the tabernacle.**
> **EXODUS 40:34**

The priests observed all the laws that the Lord had given Moses concerning burnt offerings, meat offerings, peace offering, sin offerings and laws made for the congregation and for the priests. Blood sacrifices of bullocks, rams, lambs, goats and pigeons were continually offered to the Lord for the life of the flesh is in the blood and was given on the altar to make atonement for their souls.

> Now when these things were thus ordained,
> The priests went always into the first tabernacle.
> Accomplishing the service of God.
>
> HEBREWS 9:6

The Lord understood these people. He knew they would never be faithful to him without established laws and rituals. This, in spite of the fact that his presence was manifest by the glory cloud that rested on his tabernacle.

Neither did they fully understand the significance of the tabernacle and the articles of worship therein, nor that it was only a pattern or shadow of the Lord's final plan of salvation for mankind.

> For the law having a shadow
> Of good things to come,
> And not the very image of the things,
> Can never with those sacrifices
> Which they offered year by year continually
> Make the comers thereunto perfect.
>
> HEBREWS 10:1

It was at this time that all of the tasks associated with the tabernacle were assigned to the tribe of Moses and Aaron, the

Levites. From thirty to fifty years of age they would serve the Lord. Specific tasks were assigned to certain ones from assembling and dismantling the tabernacle to the offering of sacrifices.

> Thus shalt thou separate the Levites
> From among the children of Israel;
> And the Levites shall be mine.
>
> NUMBERS 8:14

On the day that the tabernacle was first reared, God's presence was with it in a cloud by day and the appearance of fire by night. So it was for all the years they remained in the wilderness. Whether it was for two days, or a month, or a year, that the cloud tarried upon the tabernacle, the people remained in their camp. When the cloud was taken up, they travelled. On the second month of the second year they journeyed out of the wilderness of Sinai and the cloud rested in the wilderness of Paran at Kadesh-barnea, an eleven day journey from Mount Sinai.

Moses, by the command of the Lord, sent out twelve men, leaders from each tribe, to spy out the land of Canaan. They searched the land from the Wilderness of Zin to Hebron, a distance of approximately 70 miles. When they came to the brook of Eshcol, they gathered fruit in abundance, pomegranites, figs and huge clusters of grapes. The promised land was indeed fruitful. But there was also a fearful array of people already settled in the land and after forty days of searching and spying, the leaders returned with conflicting reports. Ten of the leaders convinced the people that the heathen peoples were too strong and too numerous to be conquered. They found the Amalekites in the south, Hittites, Jebusites and Amorites in the mountains and Canaanites by the sea and reported:

The people is greater and taller than we;
The cities are great and walled up to heaven;
And moreover we have seen the sons of Anakim there.
DEUTERONOMY 1:28

Moreover, the sight of the Anakim had struck terror in them because the Anakim were a race of giants. Only Joshua and Caleb had the wisdom to know that the Lord was with them and the land could be theirs. Moses and Aaron also believed and begged the people to have faith in God, but they would not. Instead, they turned in complete rebellion against Moses, preparing to stone him to death. God intervened and in his anger would have killed all of the people but for Moses, who again pleaded for their lives. The Lord pardoned them for Moses' sake but doomed those over twenty years old to die in the wilderness. Only Joshua and Caleb were spared this sentence. For forty years, a year for each day their leaders had searched the promised land, they were destined to remain in the wilderness. Only then would the Lord bring the children into the promised land. A land that could have been theirs in one year!

As the Lord had proscribed, they wandered for forty years in the wilderness until all the unbelievers had perished. Apparently much of that time was spent around Kadesh-barnea which is still an important oasis on the northeastern edge of Sinai. It was an important staging area for cross-country traders and nomads, providing an ample water supply. A t the end of this time, preparing to move toward Canaanland, Moses sent messengers to the King of Edom requesting permission to pass through his country, but he forcefully refused them passage under any circumstances. The Edomites, descendants of Esau, Jacob's brother, were destined to be a thorn in the side of the Israelites. Entry through Edom would have been a direct route. Bozrah (identified today with Buseirah) in Jordan; almost due east of Kadesh-barnea) was the home of Edomite kings and located on the King's Highway, the main caravan route from Mesopotamia to Egypt. It's name means fortress and it was guarded on three sides by steep ravines. Undoubt- edly it was a wise move to proceed toward the Promised Land from the east, a circuitous route through the territory of Moab, which occupied most of the land east of the Dead Sea, and Ammon to the north of Moab and east of the Jordan River.

As they came to Mt Hor (possibly Jabal Harun), the Lord called Moses, Aaron and Eleazor, son of Aaron, to the top of the mount and Aaron died there. Only Moses and Eleazor came down from Mt Hor. They journeyed from Mt Hor to by-pass the land of Edom until they came to the land of the Amorites. Again, Moses sent emissaries to Sihon, an Amorite king who had conquered Hebron, an ancient city of Moab. This king also ref used them passage through his borders and, gathering his people together, attacked the Israelites. Forced to fight, the Israelites obtained a great victory.

> Thus Israel dwelt in the land of the Amorites.
> NUMBERS 21:31

From here, the children of Israel moved into the plains of Moab by Jericho. Having observed the great victory of the Israelites over the Amorites, Balak, king of Moab, was afraid, and with good reason. The Lord was wit h the Israelites because it was fulfilling his word to bring them into the Promised Land. He gave them victory over the Midianites, the Amorites and the kingdom of Og. After that, the tribes of Reuben and Gad looked on the lands they had conquered east of the Jordan and saw it was suitable for the multitudes of cattle which they owned. They petitioned Moses for this land, agreeing to leave their families and their possessions here, but going on themselves with the rest of the people to fight with them until all be settled on lands of their own.

> We will pass over armed before the Lord
> Into the land of Canaan.
> That the possession of our inheritance
> On this side Jordan may be ours.
> NUMBERS 32:32

Moses agreed, giving the tribes of Gad, of Reuben and half the tribe of Mannaseh the lands on the east bank of the Jordan. Here they all prepared for the final assault upon Canaan.

Moses himself was not destined to set foot in the Promised Land, but spoke to the people for the last time, warning them again not to mingle with the inhabitants of the land lest they accept their heathen practices and worship, but to utterly drive them from the land; to refrain from idol worship, to keep the command ments and laws given them at Mt Sinai, to remember the covenant of the Lord and he left them with a final warning to seek the Lord with all their heart and soul for if they forget Him who brought them out of Egypt:

> The Lord shall scatter you among the nations
> And you shall be left few in number
> Among the heathen,
> Whither the Lord shall lead you.
> Know therefore this day,
> And consider it in thine heart,
> That the Lord he is God in heaven above,
> And upon the earth beneath
> There is none else.
> DEUTERONOMY 4:27 & 39

For forty years Moses had faithfully led these willful, rebellious people. Now he went upon Mt Nebo, which is in the land of Moab, near Jericho, and looked upon the Promised Land. His view covered the dark mass of the Judean hills and the Jordan River as it followed its serpentine path to the Dead Sea. Jericho was a lush, green spot, standing out from its seer surroundings and Jerusalem a blur in the distance. After that glimpse, Moses died according to the word of the Lord and God buried him in the land of Moab.

And there arose not a prophet since
In Israel like unto Moses
Whom the Lord knew face to face.

DEUTERONOMY 34:10

CHAPTER VI

THE PROMISED LAND

The Lord had promised Abraham "I will make of thee a great nation" and his word will always be fulfilled. He alone who sees the end from the beginning, knew that Jacob's sons would not have remained together in

Canaan to form a nation, but would each have gone their separate ways, inter mingling with the Canaanites and losing their identity. In his infinite wisdom , he sent Joseph ahead into Egypt to prepare the way for them all. Only in the cradle of the Nile and under bondage could they have remained together and grown to become a nation; a chosen people, whom Moses led to the Promised Land; a people who were purged during their forty year sojourn so that a new generation, born free in the wilderness was ready to fight for their heritage.

It now f ell upon Joshua to assume the leadership of this people. The first thing to be faced was Jericho, a formidable, walled city. Joshua sent spies to the city who went to Rahab, a harlot. She hid them from the king, knowing their God was almighty. For this they promised to spare her life and returned to report she had told them that all the inhabitants were afraid of them, having heard of the miracles God had performed for them.

The priests led the way with the ark of the covenant and the people crossed over the Jordan River on dry land because the Lord had once again dried up the waters as a sign that he was with them.

> On that day the Lord magnified Joshua
> In the sight of all Israel.
> And they feared him, as they feared Moses,
> All the days of his life.

JOSHUA 4:14

The story is familiar to everyone how the Israelites compassed the city of Jericho each day for six days and the seventh day they compassed it seven times, the priests blew their trumpets, the people shouted and those great walls fell flat. The people utterly destroyed the city, sparing only Rahab and her family. And they burnt the city with fire. The capture of Jericho was followed by the battles of Ai and a treaty with Gibeon. Ai was not defeated the first time, but by strategy, and God's help, the city was captured the second time. The people of Gibeon, a great fortified city atop a ridge, who controlled the whole region, were nonetheless afraid of facing the Israelites who had the power of God on their side so they formed an alliance with them. When Adonizedec, king of Jerusalem, heard of this alliance he gathered together four of his allies, kings of Hebron, Jarmuth, Lachish and Eglon. Even together they could not stand against Joshua and his army. Then Joshua moved against Makkedah, Libnah, Lachish, Eglon, Hebron, Debir, in turn, and the Lord delivered them all into his hands.

And all these kings and their land
Did Joshua take at one time
Because the Lord God of Israel
Fought for Israel.
                                        JOSHUA 10:42

Then the kings of the Canaanites on the east and on the west, the Amorites, the Hittites, the Perizzites and the Jebusites and the Hivites went out with much people to conquer the Israelites but the Lord delivered them into the hands of Israel. Of the cities only Razor did Joshua burn, and of the cities only Gibeon made peace with them.

So Joshua took the whole land,
According to all that the Lord said unto Moses;
And Joshua gave it for an inheritance unto Israel
According to their divisions by their tribes.
And the land rested from war.
                                        JOSHUA 11:23

In the 1950's, the Israeli archeologist, Dr Yegael Yadin, Director of the Institute of Archeology at the Hebrew University of Jerusalem found indisputable evidence of a violent destruction of the city of Razor (Tel el-Qedah) around 1250 - 1255 B.C. which he unhesitatingly credited to Joshua. His excavations showed it had been a huge city of 30,000 - 40,000 people and was not rebuilt again until the time of King Solomon in the Tenth century B.C.

There is contention among archeologists concerning the dating of some excavations. Jericho is a classic example. The first explorations around 1900 A.D. revealed traces of two rings of fortifications consisting of thick walls of sun-dried clay bricks. In the 1930's a larger expedition, directed by Professor John Garstang, studied four successive building stages, the last of which had been violently destroyed and burned (possibly by earthquake and fire. The period of this destruction he placed at the time of the Israelite invasion of Canaan. But in the 1950's, Dame Kathleen Kenyon again excavated Jericho for the British School of Archeology in Jerusalem and her conclusion was that the city had been destroyed much earlier than Professor Garstang's findings showed it to be. Dating is not an exact science in archeology and much of it is done by identification of pottery and the periods it is believed to belong to. But the fact remains that the walls of Jericho did come tumbling down!

And for those who doubt that the Lord God of Israel delivered the cities into the hands of Joshua, let them look again at the modern-day history of Israel. On 29 November 1947, the United Nations Assembly adopted its Partition Resolution whereby Israel was divided between the Jews and the Arabs and two states established. The Arabs rejected this decision but on 4:30 P.M. Friday, 14 May 1948, the evening before the British forces would leave the country, Israel declared the establishment of the State of Israel. At midnight, less than eight hours after Israel's declaration, the neighboring Arab countries announced their armies had invaded the newly established State of Israel. Seven Arab countries had banded together - Iraq,

Lebanon, Syria, Jordan, Egypt, Saudi Arabia and Yemen. The War of Independence lasted until 20 June 1949 when the Israel - Syria Ar mistice Agreement was signed. Similar agreements had been signed earlier with Egypt, Lebanon and Jordan. Consider if you will a newly formed state facing war against seven established nations at one time and winning without the miraculous intervention of the Lord.

Again, on 2 2 May 1967, Egypt's Nasser blocked the Straits of Tiran to Israel shipping. On 31 May, King Hussein of Jordan joined Egypt and Syria. The Six-Day War began on 5 June 1967. On the third day, the Jews captured Jerusalem and in the afternoon Hebron, Nablus (Shechem) and Jericho. Jerusalem, Samaria and Judah passed to Israeli control in this six-day period. God's covenant people had won again and God's promise to Abraham still stands:

> For all the land which thou seest,
> To thee will I give it,
> And to thy seed forever.
> GENESIS 13:15

When Joshua became old and stricken in age, there still remained much land to be possessed - all the borders of the Philistines (which included Gaza, Goth and Ashdod - recently captured by the Philistines from Egypt); from the south all the land of the Canaanites, and all Lebanon. The land they did possess was divided among the tribes and Hebron was given to Caleb for his faithfulness to the Lord.

And the whole congregation of the children of Israel

Assembled together at Shiloh
And set up the tabernacle of the congregation there.
And the land was subdued before them.

JOSHUA 18:1

Joshua sent the Reubenites, the Gadites and the half tribe of Manassah back across the Jordan River to their families. They had faithfully remained until all of the tribes had been assigned territories.

Although the Promised Land belonged to the children of Israel, there were still Canaanites in the land. Joshua faithfully served the Lord and Israel followed his leadership until his death at one hundred and ten years. Before he died, Joshua saw fit to warn the people for a last time for he sensed the waivering and the willingness of the people to accept the strange gods of the Canaanites.

Choose you this day whom ye will serve,
Whether the gods which your fathers served
That were on the other side of the flood,
Or the gods of the Amorites,
In whose land ye dwell;
But as for me and my house,
We will serve the Lord.

JOSHUA 24:15

At his death, Israel was left without a leader who could inspire the people to be faithful to their God The tribes were now dispersed and occupied with their own lands but there were still groups of Canaanites living among them. The military had been disbanded, further weakening them in the sight of their enemies. When the

Israelites accepted the gods of the people around them, it provoked the Lord to anger and he delivered them into the hands of spoilers.

The first strike came from the king of Mesopotamia and he ruled them for eight years. When the children of Israel cried to the Lord, he sent a deliverer - Othniel, Caleb's younger brother, who led the people in regaining their freedom, which they kept for forty years.

Again, the children of Israel did evil in the sight of the Lord who raised up Moab against them for eighteen years. This time when the Israelites repented, the Lord sent Ehud, a Benjamite, to deliver the m from Moab. And the land had rest for eighty years.

The next time the Israelites strayed from God, he allowed the Canaanites to plague them with a mighty army led by Sisera who had nine hundred chariots of iron under his command. For twenty years, the people were oppressed by Sisera until they went to Deborah, a prophetess of God from the hill country of Ephraim. She it was who judged Israel at this time. Deborah called for Barak, saying the Lord commanded him to go to Mt Tabor with ten thousand men of the tribes of Naphtali and Zebulun and there he would deliver the Canaanites into his hand. Barak was afraid and would not go without Deborah. She went, but not before warning Barak that the honor of the battle would not be his but would belong to a woman. Barak assembled his men on Mt Tabor where they had a fine vantage point and where the iron chariots of Sisera could not go, forcing the Canaanite army to detour around by the waters of Megiddo at the western end of the Valley of Jezreel. As the chariots of Sisera approached the mountain, the troops of Barak rushed down upon the enemy, creating confusion among the horses and as the frenzied horses ran amok, chariots crashed into each other, overturned or ran down their own troops. The enemy abandoned their chariots and fled on foot with Barak's men in pursuit.

> And all the host of Sisera
> Fell upon the edge of the sword
> And there was not a man left.
>
> JUDGES 4:16

Except for Sisera who fled to the tent of Jael, the wife of Heber the Kenite, whom Sisera took for a friend. She gave him cover in her tent, but when he fell asleep from exhaustion she took a tent peg and drove it through his temple. So he died and Deborah's prophecy was fulfilled. This was the last battle the children of Israel fought against the Canaanites. The Song of Deborah, written in commemoration of this battle, is one of the most powerful poems in the saga of the Israelites. It also makes evident the fact that not all the tribes supported this battle. The tribes of Judah and Simeon were too far off in the south and were not even contacted, but Rueben and Dan were called and did not come. Neither did Asher respond. The Song of Deborah has praise for those who did volunteer: namely, Issachar, Ephraim, Benjamin, Manasseh, Zebulun and Naphtali.

Forty years passed and then because they did evil in the sight of the Lord, Israel was delivered into the hands of the Midianites. The Midianites, together with Amalekites, came up from the Arabian desert in large numbers and they plundered the crops and stole the animals of the Israelites.

> For they came up with their cattle and their tents,
> And they came as grasshoppers for multitude;
> For both they and their camels were without number:
> And they entered into the land to destroy it.
> And Israel was greatly impoverished
> Because of the Midianites;
> And the children of Israel cried unto the Lord.
>
> JUDGES 6:5 &:. 6

The Lord heard their cry and raised up Gideon to rescue them in this time of trouble. He was secretively threshing wheat by the winepress to hide it from the Midianites when the angel of the Lord appeared before him. God has a way of doing much with the humble and the meek. Gideon had trouble believing the Lord had picked hi m as a leader of the people, for he was of the tribe of Manasseh, the smallest of the tribes; from one of the poorest of families within the tribe, and even the least of those within his family. Yet the Lord said:

> Surely, I will be with thee
> And thou shalt smite the Midianites as one man.
>
> JUDGES 6:16

Gideon knew the right priorities. First, he tore down his father's altar to Baal and the grove that was planted in its honor. In its place he built an altar to the Lord God of Israel and sacrificed his father's young bullock thereon. Then the spirit of the Lord came upon Gideon, and he blew a trumpet calling the people to battle. The first to respond were the men of Abiezer, his own clan. The call went out to all Manasseh and they respond ed. Also to Asher, Zebulun and Naphtali who gathered their men to battle, until the men numbered thirty-two thousand. Gideon assembled his forces along the southern edge of the Valley of Jezreel. The enemy was encamped in the valley itself -- a great number made up of the "children of the east" from the deserts of Arabia; Amalekites from Sinai and the Negev and Midianites from the wilderness of Moab, south of the Dead Sea. Yet the Lord told Gideon his army was too large -- there would be no glory for the Lord in their victory. So Gideon told all his men that whosoever was fearful and afraid could return home. Only ten thousand stayed with Gideon, but the Lord had still another test for the men which would prove who were the best qualified and only three hundred men remained. Gideon, like Deborah, planned his battle by sowing confusion in the enemies midst. Camels were not like horses and chariots. Camels would not panic nor stampede at the sound of trumpets. Camel herds would not move without a command from their masters. If the Israelites attacked during daylight they would have no chance of success. So at midnight, Gideon and his three hundred men, crept up to the edge of the enemy camp. He divided his men into three equal groups and every man took his place around the camp. Each man carried a trumpet in his right hand and a pitcher concealing a flaming torch in his left. When Gideon blew his trumpet and broke his pitcher so that the light shone forth and cried "The sword of the Lord and Gideon" each man did the same and stood still, every man in his place. Confusion and terror struck the enemy camp, they believed they were under a massive attack. In the darkness of the camp, they could not distinguish friend from foe and every man's sword was wielded indiscriminately against another. Then began a panic flight which was quickly followed by the rest of the thirty two thousand who had not seen battle. Gideon sent messengers to Ephraim and they joined in the chase until all of the Midianites were subdued and there was peace once more until Gideon's death. Then the people began to worship Baalim and made Baalberith their god. And they waxed more evil yet in the sight of the Lord.

> And served Baalim and Ashtaroth,
> And the gods of Syria, and the gods of Zidon
> And the gods of Moab and the gods of the children of Ammon
> And the gods of the Philistines
> And forsook the Lord, and served him not.
> And the anger of the Lord was hot against Israel
> And he sold them into the hands of the Philistines
> And into the hands of the children of Ammon.
>
> JUDGES 10:6 - 7

The battles of Barak and Gideon were both fought in the Valley of Jezreel and place names are the same today as they were then. Waters still flow from the spring Ein Harod and the Kishon Stream, Megiddo is still at the southern end of the valley and Mt Tabor looms over it all.

The next time war came, it was to the children of Israel on the other side of the Jordan in Gilead, the land of the Amorites. These tribes were distressed until the people turned again to the Lord and put away the strange gods among them. The Amorites gathered in Gilead and the Israelites encamped in Mizpeh and the Lord called out Jephthah, a Gileadite, and when the spirit of the Lord came upon Jephthah he fought against the Amorites and subdued them with a very great slaughter.

The children of Israel had degenerated into a low state of religion and morality. Without a central government or a strong religious figure, it was inevitable that they would sin again against the Lord.

In those days there was no king in Israel,
But every man did that which was right
In his own eyes.

JUDGES 17:6

For forty years, the land was ruled by the Philistines. The angel of the Lord appeared to a childless woman of Dan, foretelling she would have a son who would be dedicated to God (a Nazorite), one who would deliver Israel from the Philistines. This son was named Samson and when the spirit of the Lord moved upon him he fought the Philistines single-handedly with a great super human strength.

Morally, he was of weak character, but God had destined him to deliver the Israelites, and in the end he gave his life in exchange for about three thousand Philistines.

The last and one of the greatest of the judges, or prophets of Israel was Samuel. The leadership of Israel had passed to the priesthood. Eli ministered at Shiloh where the Ark of the Covenant was located. Hannah, a childless wife of a Levite, vowed if the Lord would but bless her with a son she would give him to the Lord.

> **Samuel ministered before the Lord,**
> **Being a child, girded with a linen ephod.**
> **And the child Samuel grew on,**
> **And was in favor both with the Lord, And also**
> **with men.**
> **ISAMUEL 2:18 &: 26**

When Eli grew very old, the Lord called to Samuel and he answered "Here am I." Thus the pattern was set for his lifetime. The Lord spoke to him, and all Israel from Dan to Beersheba (from the north to the south) knew Samuel was a prophet of the Lord.

When Eli was ninety-eight years old, the Philistines attacked Israel and the Israelites lost about four thousand troops. Knowing the Philistines would attack again, the Israelites brought the Ark of the Covenant out of Shiloh. The two sons of Eli, wicked, corrupt men who did not walk in the ways of the Lord, accompanied the ark. But again, Israel was smitten and the Ark of the Covenant was taken. Also Eli's sons were killed. When this was related to Eli, he was shocked and grieved to hear of the death of his sons but when he heard the ark was taken, he fell backward, broke his neck, and died.

The Philistines brought the Ark of God from Ebenezer to Ashdod. They brought it into the house of Dagon, their god. In the morning Dagon had fallen upon his face to the earth before the Ark of the Lord. The people set Dagon upright and in his place. When the people awoke the next morning, they found Dagon fallen before the Lord, with his head and his hands cut off. Seeing this, none dared enter the house, but the people felt the heavy hand of the Lord upon them and they carried the ark to Gath.

> **The hand of the Lord was against the city**
> **With a very great destruction,**
> **And he smote the men of the city,**
> **And they had emerods (hemorrhoids)**
> **In their secret parts.**
> **I SAMUEL 5:9**

Therefore, they sent the ark of God to Ekron and that city experienced the heavy hand of God just as the others had. The ark was in the land of the Philistines for seven months and the people cried to be delivered from it. The priests and diviners saw fit to send it back to Israel with a trespass off ering to the God of Israel of

> **Five golden emerods and five golden mice,**
> **According to the number of the Lords of the**
> **Philistines,**
> **For one plague was on you all, and on your lords.**
> **I SAMUEL 6:4**

Why the golden mice? Could the plague they experienced have been similar to the bubonic plague that devastated Europe and which is primarily a rodent disease?

The priests directed that the ark be placed on a new cart and the golden of f erings placed in a cof f er beside it and that two milk cows that had known no yoke be separated from their calves and tied to the cart. If the cows took the ark to Israel, it would be a sign to the Philistines that the Lord God of Israel was responsible for all the evil that had befallen them the past seven months.

> **And the men did** so; **and took two milch kine,**
> **And tied them to the cart,**
> **And shut up their calves at home.**
> **And the kine took the straight way to Bethshemesh,**
> **Lowing as they went.**
> **And turned not to the right hand or left.**
> **I SAMUEL 6:10-12**

No power on earth could have moved those cows to leave their calves of their own volition. The Philistines hitched the cows to the cart but did not force them in any way to move. Their calves were restrained from following, yet those cows were drawn down the highway to Bethshemesh, lowing, crying out for their calves with every step they took. What else but the Spirit of God could have directed the cows as they brought the ark over the border of the Philistines and into Israel?

And as if that was not enough proof that God had brought about their suff ering, notice that these were cows that had never known a yoke. Yet they moved in unison as an experienced team, not balking at the yoke, not going their own ways, but together travelling straight down the highway.

The men of Kirjath jearim fetched the ark to the house of Abinadab. The ark was not returned to Shiloh, nor is there further mention of Shiloh being used by Samuel. Shiloh had been the spiritual center of Israel from the days of Joshua and it seems strange that it should cease to be a place of worship and judgement for Israel. Archeology may supply this answer. It appears to have been burnt at about the time the ark was taken to battle against the Philistines. Perhaps when the Philistines captured the ark, they invaded and burnt Shiloh as well.

Samuel led the people from their worship of Ashtaroth and other strange gods and when they turned again to the Lord, he delivered them and the hand of the Lord was against the Philistines all the days of Samuel.

CHAPTER VII

KINGS

Samuel judged Israel in Bethel, Gilgal and Mizpeh each year, but he dwelt in Ramah, his birthplace and the burial place of Rachel, and there he built an altar to the Lord. When he was old he made his two sons judges over Israel. His sons were like Eli's sons. They took bribes and perverted judgement. Then the elders of Israel came to Samuel, requesting a king like other nations. Samuel was incensed for the Lord's sake, but the Lord spoke to him.

They have not rejected thee, but have rejected me.
That I should not reign over them.
I SAMUEL 8:7

Therefore, Samuel warned the people that the costs would be heavy; levies on people and lands and imposition of taxes to maintain a kingdom. Nevertheless, the people desired a king, so the Lord Himself chose their first king; Saul, a choice young man, tall, well-built, a goodly man of the tribe of Benjamin. Samuel anointed Saul and the spirit of the Lord came upon him. Samuel called the people together at Mizpeh and presented Saul to them, the Lord's chosen one and the people cheered. But the children of Belial said "How shall this man save us?"

In spite of being anointed and presented to Israel as their king, Saul returned home and waited for a sign from the Lord. The time came when the Ammonites camped against Jabesh-gilead, across the

Jordan River, and threatened to thrust out the right eye of every man unless Israel came to their rescue. The people of Israel remained unconcerned until the messenger brought word of this to Saul. Then the spirit of God came upon Saul and he acted boldly by cutting up his oxen and sending the pieces out to all the people, threatening them if they did not come to battle with him and Samuel, the same thing would happen to their oxen! The people came, three hundred thirty thousand men and they came against the Ammonites with a resounding victory. Now the people were ready to accept Saul as their king and all the people went to Gilgal and there they made Saul king before the Lord.

When Saul had reigned over Israel for two years, a mighty army of Philistines camped in Mich mash and the people of Israel were so frightened, some of them fled across the Jordan River. Samuel had told Saul to wait seven days until he arrived , but Saul impatiently off ered the burnt off ering to the Lord in Samuel's stead. This was the first outward sign of disobedience to the Lord and it forfeited his right to establish his kingdom in Israel through future generations. Still the Philistines remained. As Saul tarried at Gibeah, Jonathan, son of Saul, and his armor-bearer slipped away and to the back of the Philistine garrison. Climbing sheer cliffs, they took the garrison by surprise and killed the men who were manning it. God entered the battle with an earthquake "and the earth quaked so it were a very great trembling" and the Philistines fled.

Routing the Philistines allowed Saul to take over the Philistine fortress at his home town, Gibeah of Saul, five kilometers north of Jerusalem. Gibeah is the modern Tell-el-Ful beside the main road from Jerusalem to Nablus

{Shechem). In the mid-1960's, King Hussein of Jordan started to build a palace on the summit, for this area was then under Jordanian rule. The Six-Day War in June 1967 put an abrupt end to its construction. The unfinished royal palace is now in Israeli territory -- just as King Saul regained it from the Philistines in his day.

Saul continued to f ight against the enemies surrounding Israel; Moab, Ammon, Edom and the Philistines.

> Now go and smite Amalek
> And utterly destroy all that they have,
> And spare them not,
> But slay both man and woman,
> Infant and suckling, ox and sheep, camel and ass.
> I SAMUEL 15:3

Saul gathered his army and marched on the Amalekites, pausing to warn the Kenites (related to Moses through the Midianites) who departed. Saul gained a great victory over the Amalekites, but he spared king Agag's lif e and took him captive. Also he brought back the best of the sheep and the oxen and the lambs in direct violation of the Lord's command. The Lord had no pleasure in the sacrificial animals Saul had brought back and it repented him that he had made Saul king.

Behold, to obey is better than sacrifice,
And to hearken than the fat of rams.

I SAMUEL 15:22

Samuel departed from Saul, although he grieved for him. Nevertheless, the Lord called him to anoint another, so he went to Bethlehem where the Lord led hi m, and to Jesse of the tribe of Judah. There seven sons of Jesse passed before Samuel but they were not of the Lord's chasing. Then the youngest son was brought in from tending the sheep. He was ruddy (red haired), of a beautif ul countenance and this time the Lord said "Anoint him, for this is he" and the spirit of the Lord came upon David from that day forward.

But the spirit of the Lord departed from Saul
And an evil spirit from the Lord troubled him.

I SAMUEL 16:14

Saul sought for one who was a talented harpist and lo and behold David was brought before him and his playing was soothing to the king.

Again, the Philistines gathered their armies against Israel and pitched their tents in the territory of Judah. Saul gathered his army toget her across the valley from the Philistines. For forty days the armies remained stalemated; each on a mountain top. Every day Goliath of Gath, a giant among men, would show himself and challenge the Israelites to send a man out to fight him. He was a terrifying figure with his tremendous size and armed as he was with a coat of mail, a brass helmet, brass greaves upon his legs and a target of brass between his shoulders, a heavy spear and sword. Altogether his armor and weapons weighed almost as much as he did.

No one would accept his challenge until, on the fortieth day, David, who was considered too young for the army, came with supplies for his older brothers. Upon seeing Goliath, he asked:

Who is this uncircumsized Philistine,
That he should defy the armies of the living God?
I SAMUEL 17:26

Refusing armor, David chose five smooth stones and with his sling in hand he went to meet Goliath who disparaged and cursed him. What Goliath did not realize was that David was in his natural element and came in the name of the Lord of hosts, the God of the armies of Israel whom the giant had defied. As David ran to meet the giant he fit a stone into his slingshot and shot it directly into the giant's forehead, the only vulnerable spot on his body. He then hastened to cut off Goliath's head with the giant's own sword. Goliath never had a chance. To both armies it looked as though all the odds were on the giant's side; he had protective armor, great strength, a sword, a shield and a spear - pitted against an unarmed, inexperienced youth. Not so, because David's expertise with the slingshot gave him every advantage for he shot before he was in range of the weapons of Goliath and he had faith that the Lord was on his side.

When the Philistines saw their champion was dead, they fled while the Israelites shouted and pursued after them, even unto Gath.

Jonathan's admiration for David was great and that day they made a covenant of friend- ship which both kept all of their lives. King Saul took David into his home, made him captain over a thousand and all was well until king Saul realized the women of Israel were honoring David's prowess above his own and from that day jealousy consumed him, and he saw David as a threat to his throne.

> And Saul was afraid of David
> Because the Lord was with him,
> And was departed from Saul.
>
> I SAMUEL 18:12

From that day forth, Saul plotted to take David's life. David and Saul's daughter Michal loved each other. Saul saw a way to use the situation and required a dowry from David of one hundred Philistine foreskins, hoping he would be killed. Instead David brought back two hundred foreskins and Saul allowed Michal to marry him. Through all of this David behaved himself wisely. Nevertheless, Saul sought continuously to kill him. Finally, David could stay no longer, he escaped only because of the help of Jonathan and Michal. First, he sought refuge with Samuel, then with Ahimelech, the priest, where he picked up the sword of Goliath and on to Gath, where he sought refuge from king Saul. He soon realized what a rash move that had been and feigning madness was able to leave. From there he escaped to the cave of Adullam. Everyone who was in distress, in debt or discon- tented found their way to David and he became captain over them. When they heard the Philistines were fighting the men of Keilah, a neighboring village, David and his army went to their rescue. Then king Saul heard of it and sent his army af ter David who evaded the king in the wilderness of Ziph for a time. Constantly harried, David sought refuge in the wilderness of Engedi, a range of steep mountains, deep ravines, tortuous, narrow paths fit only for the mountain goats which still abide in them and which accounts for their name. At the base of the mountains and on the western shore of the Dead Sea is the spring En-Gedi "spring of the kid"; also referred to today as "David's fountain", commemorating his exile in this area. The cliffs, pocked with caves, afforded excellent shelter and lookouts for David and his men. Even here, Saul pursued relentlessly. Twice David had opportunities to overcome or kill Saul, but because an anointing had once rested on king Saul and the Lord had chosen him, David would do him no harm. But because their paths had crossed, David judged it expedient to move once more. Again, he crossed into Philistine territory and king Achish of Gath assigned Ziklag to David and his men.

And it was told Saul that David was fled to Gath;
And he sought no more again for him.
I SAMUEL 27:4

For over a year David and his men raided the nations south of Judah, such as the Amalekites and Gezrites, leaving no witnesses. All this time he was deceiving king Achish who believed he was warring against king Saul and his own people. In due time, the Philistines gathered their armies against Israel again. King Achish would have included David and his men in this army but his princes did not trust David. Thus he was spared from fighting against his own people. The Philistines gathered their armies at Aphek and marched north to the valley of Jezreel (Esdraelon) where so many previous battles had been fought. This was good fighting terrain for them and for their chariots; much better than the Judean hills of Saul's people. Unaccountably, Saul came north to meet his enemy at the foot of Mount Gilboa and here he was no match for his old foe. The Philistines decimated the army of the Israelites. Three of king Saul's sons were slain, including Jonathan. King Saul himself was mortally wounded by arrows and he fell on his own sword rather than allow the enemy to kill him.

> So Saul died, and his three sons,
> And his armor bearer and all his men.
> That same day together.
> I SAMUEL 31:6

The Philistines put king Saul's armor in the house of their god Ashtaroth and fastened his body to the wall of Bethshan. When the inhabitants of Jabesh-gilead heard of it, they travelled all night and brought the body of Saul to Jabesh and buried his bones and fasted seven days for they had not forgotten Saul fought to protect them when no one else would listen to their cry for help.

An Amalekite brought the news of Saul's death to David, hoping to please him by claiming credit for killing Saul. David was grieved for Saul and for Jonathan and for Israel. As for the Amalekite, he ordered him killed.

David returned to Judah and they anointed him king. Abner, captain of Saul's army, made Ishbosheth, the son of Saul, king in his stead. David was king in Hebron for seven and a half years and Joab, his nephew by his sister, was captain over his army.

Abner and Joab and their servants met by the pool of Gibeon and they sat on opposite sides of the pool. Here it was proposed that twelve servants of Abner and twelve servants of Joab would stage a contest. Each caught an opponent by the head and thrust his spear in the other's side. And there was a very sore battle that day.

In 1956, Dr James Pritchard came upon this pool; actually not a pool, but a water system, a means of supplying water from a deep source within the city. Thousands of tons of limestone had been removed to form a deep shaft with a spiral, winding stairway leading to a tunnel that dropped down to water level twenty seven meters below the surface of the ground. While Dr Pritchard was excavating this site, he came upon numerous jar handles inscribed with "Gibeon" or "vineyard of Gibeon." Further search revealed a number of curious cellar-like cuttings in the surface limestone. They had small circular openings at the top which expanded into six feet deep tanks, in one of which was found a large storage jar of approximately ten gallons. The rock cuttings had been storage cellars for wine jars. Dr Pritchard found that even on the hottest days the temperature in these cellars remained at a constant 65° Fahrenheit, an ideal wine temperature!

> Now there was long war between the house of Saul
> And the house of David.   -
> But David waxed stronger and stronger.
> And the house of Saul waxed weaker and weaker.
>
> II SAMUEL 3:1

Then Abner came to king David and they agreed David would be king over all the land and Abner left in peace. But unknown to David, Joab and Abishai followed and killed Abner for having previously slain their brother. King David lamented the death of Abner and realized he did not have control over his nephews and in the future they would cause him further grief.

> I am this day weak, though anointed king;
> And these men, the sons of Zeruiah (his sister)
> Be too hard for me.
>
> II SAMUEL 3:39

Two of Saul's men sought to please David by killing Ishbosheth. On the contrary, David had them killed for having slain a helpless man. Then all the tribes of Israel came to Hebron and they anointed David king over Israel. David was thirty years old when he began to reign and he reigned forty years. He reigned for seven years over Judah and for thirty-three years over all Israel.

David's first action was the capture of Jerusalem. It belonged to the Jebusites and was a dividing point between Israel to the north and Judah to the south. It provided David with a royal city of his own since this land had never been possessed by any of the tribes. A capitol city set apart from the land, similar to Washington D.C.

Jerusalem was a fortress set on a hill, hitherto impregnable. But David knew there was a fresh water spring in the Kidron Valley that supplied Jerusalem with water through a secret water shaft, or gutter, that the Gebusites had dug from inside their city down to the spring outside their walls. It was through this vulnerable opening that David's men gained access to Jerusalem and ultimately captured the city.

In 1867, a British engineer, Captain Charles Warren made a survey of Jerusale m. While visiting the spring he noticed a crevice in the roof of the cavern above the spring. He wor med his way into this crevice and up an adjourning shaf t until he came to daylight. It was assumed this was the same water shaf t used by David's men, except for one problem. It had come out only half way up the hill. It was believed the walls of Jerusalem at that time had been at the top of the hill, and it was not reasonable that the Jebusites would have had its entry outside their walls. In 1961, with this in mind, Dame Kathleen Kenyon dug a great trench straight down the side of the steep hill and did find a thick city wall that dated to the proper period, about 1,000 B.C. and. as expected, it was below the entrance to the water shaf t. This confir med the biblical account and gave historians a general outline of the city limits of Jerusalem when David acquired it. This was one of the most satisf

ying acheological finds in Palestine.

David's royal city turned out to be rather small, only a dozen

acres. But it was sufficient for David to establish a holy kingdom which

had always been the Lord's intent.

And David went on, and grew great,
And the Lord God of Hosts was with him.
II SAMUEL 5:10

When the Philistines heard that David was anointed king over all

Israel, they knew he was becoming too powerful and must be stopped,

so they came to the valley of Rephraim and pitted their strength against

hi m, but David prevailed. Twice, the Philistines launched attacks

against Jeru- salem and were defeated each time. Victorious, David

continued against the Philistines and wiped out all those that remained

in the valley of Jezreel and Beth-shan and in the Sharon plain. But he

could not drive them from their coastal cities.

King David loved the Lord and greatly desired to bring the ark

of God to Jerusalem. In his eagerness and over-zealousness, David

gathered together 30,000 chosen men of Israel to bring the ark to

his city. They set the ark of God upon a new cart and brought it out

of the house of Abinadab in Gibeah and Abinadab's sons drove the

new cart. David and all of Israel played upon musical instru ments

and everyone rejoiced until the cart shook and the ark appeared

unsteady. Uzzah, a priest, touched the ark to steady it and God smote him for his error. The priests, of all people, knew the ark of God was holy and untouchable, but it had become too com mon-place during the time it had resided at Gibeah.

For three months the ark remained where Uzzah had stopped, until king David and the people understood God's holiness and this time the move was planned. Off erings were properly made to the Lord.

And David danced before the Lord with all his might;
And David was girded with a linen ephod
So David and all the house of Israel
Brought up the ark of the Lord
With shouting and with the sound of the trumpet.
II SAMUEL 6:14 - 15

And they set it in the tabernacle, in the tent that had been pitched for it. All the people participated in the peace offering that day. Only Michal, Saul's daughter, disapproved of David's dancing before the Lord.

Priests were appointed from among the Levites to minister before the ark, to make offerings, to make music and to thank and praise the Lord continually. Still David was not satisfied. As he sat in his house of cedar he thought of the ark resting under a tent and desired to build a house for the Lord. This was not to be, for the Lord saw fit to give this task to his son.

He shall build a house for my name.
And I will stablish the throne of his kingdom
Forever.
II SAMUEL 7:13

With this promise, the Lord assured David his kingdom would be an everlasting kingdom and the throne of David established forever.

From this time, David was victorious over his surrounding enemies. First he conquered Moab and they became his servants; then Syria to the north was overcome and he put garrisons in Syria and they became his servants. Also Edom. He conquered and placed garrisons within their nation. Finally, the Ammonites were subdued. They had constantly harrased the tribes east of the Jordan River and they also controlled the "King's Highway." With these victories, David had subdued all the neighboring nations; further- more, they had become his vassals, rendering tribute and protection from outlying countries.

Thus David ended his campaigns. The mountains and the fortified cities built on them were Israel's strength. East of the Jordan, it was the mountains of Gilead; west of the Jordan, the Hebron Hills, Jerusalem, Shechem and Galilee.

With many of the surrounding nations subdued, David sent Joab and his army to fight the Ammonites, but he remained at home. As he looked down from his roof top, he espied Bathsheba washing herself and he had her brought to him. When she found herself with child, she informed David who sent for Uriah, her husband, to come home from battle. Uriah was too loyal to David and the army to go home to Bathsheba. When this ploy failed, David instructed Joab to put Uriah on the front battle lines. It was only a mat ter of time until Uriah was killed.

And when the mourning was past,
David sent and fetched her to his house.
And she became his wife
And bare him a son.
But the thing that David had done
Displeased the Lord.

II SAMUEL 11:27

This dishonorable deed was uncharacteristic of David, but he seemed uncon- scious of his great transgression until the Lord sent Nathan the prophet to point out his sin and the Lord's great anger. David repented mightily and the Lord forgave him but that did not stop the reaping of a bitter harvest. His sinful actions had repercussions that effected all of his family. Although Bathsheba's first child died, she bore another and called him Solomon and the Lord loved him. There were further consequences, perhaps because of loss of respect for their father.

Amnon, son of David, raped his half-sister and David did nothing. Her brother, Absolom, hated Amnon but held his peace for two years, then killed his half-brother. For the next three years Absolom was in exile in Geshur. David sent Joab to bring Absolom home and then refused to see him for another two years. As bitterness grew in Absolom, he wooed the people and turned them against king David and set up his own kingdom in Hebron. When David saw that the men of Israel had chosen Absolom, he fled from his throne and Jerusalem to allow the Lord to work it out. Then David's army, men who were still loyal to him, went to battle against Absolom's army. David commanded Joab to spare Absolom but Joab disobeyed, for he took the life of David's son and redeemed the throne for David. Later, when David was old and feeble, Adonijah, brother to Absolom, plotted to seize the throne. This time David called Bathsheba and swore:

> **Assuredly, Solomon thy son shall reign after me,**
> **And he shall sit upon my throne in my stead,**
> **Even so will I certainly do this day.**
>
> **IKINGS 1:30**

So Solomon rode upon the king's own mule and Zadok the priest and Nathan the prophet anointed him king.

Although there was much strife within David's own household, he loved and exalted the Lord all the days of his life and his greatest desire was to give glory to God. He left a pattern for the temple and much gold and precious stones for the fittings and vessels of the house of the Lord which Solomon would build and he also bequeathed a nation at peace with its neighbors.

Solomon began his reign during this peaceful period and he asked the Lord for an understanding heart to judge the people. This pleased God so much he gave him wisdom , understanding, riches and honor. The people saw that God was with him because of the wise judgements he made. Solomon reigned over all Israel from the river to the land of the Philistines and to the border of Egypt and his fame spread far and wide for he was wiser than all men.   .

King David had purchased a piece of property just outside Jerusalem; a threshing floor on which to build an altar to God. Solomon chose this site for the temple and requested king Hiram of Tyre to furnish cedars of Lebanon and servants knowledgeable in woodcraft for the building of the Lord's temple.

**And the king commanded, and they brought great
stones,
Costly stones and hewed stones,
To lay the foundation of the house.**

I KINGS 5:17

Josephus, the great historian of the first century A.D., gave details in the way Mount Moriah was flattened. A rocky hill, difficult to climb just east of Jerusalem - that was David's threshing floor and also the mount on which Abraham had offered Isaac as a sacrifice to the Lord. According to Josephus, Solomon had a great wall built around the summit of the mount. The slopes below this wall were covered with enormous blocks held together with lead and the interior reinforced with iron. The rough surface within the wall was levelled and the rock foundation smoothed to make a perfectly flat platform. This platform is intact today, and even part of Solomon's wall remains. Some of the blocks forming the base are approximately thirty feet long and three feet thick. This temple site was connected to the city by a huge bridge that spanned the valley.

The temple itself was ninety by thirty feet by forty five (6 0 x 20 x 30 cubits), built of pre-cut stone so that no axe or hammer was used on the build- ing. These stones were covered with cedar, intricately carved. The interior of God's house was inlaid with gold. The doors were made of olive trees carved with cherubim, palm trees and open flowers, overlaid with gold. Two cherubim, with wing spans that touched the walls, guarded the ark of God. The pillars of the porch were cast of brass and the tops were decorated with wreaths and chainwork. Solomon had a laver for water (a molten sea) forty five f eet in circumference made of brass and set upon twelve oxen. The temple was surrounded by three floors of rooms, thirty on each floor for the priests living quarters. The whole temple was built with superb craftsmanship, all fit to- gether so precisely that there was no need of tools. The vases, tables, candelabra, vessels, ladles and spoons were all made of gold. The veil that separated the inner sanctum, the "holy of Holies", from the rest of the temple was as thick as a hand's breadth and woven in white, scarlet, blue and gold. In all, seven years was spent in the building and finishing work of the temple.

Then the ark of the Lord was placed in the temple and Solomon and all Israel assembled and a glory cloud filled the house of the Lord. Solomon stood before the altar and spread his hands to heaven.

But will God indeed dwell on the earth?
Behold, the heaven and heaven of heavens
Cannot contain thee,
How much less this house that I have builded?
I Kings 8:27

And the king and all Israel offered sacrifice before the Lord.

But Solomon was building his own house thirteen years,
And he finished all his house.

I Kings 7:1

The Phoenicians occupied a narrow, coastal region from 1200 B.C. onward in what is today Lebanon. The peoples were Canaanites, experienced seamen, skilled architects and traders whose principal cites were Tyre, Sidon and Byblos. It was from Hiram, king of Tyre, that Solomon turned to for help in his building programs.

He also formed an alliance with Hiram that proved advantageous to both nations. King Solomon made a navy of ships in Ezeon-geber on the shore of the Red Sea in the land of Edom (modern Eilat). King Hiram sent his ship building experts and experienced seamen to man the ships. Thus they gained new markets in the Far East and in Africa which brought them spices, gold and other luxuries. Israel lay between Egypt and Mesopotamia and also be- tween the Mediterranean and the Red Sea. Solomon grew rich from the bene- fits of trading and toll charges. Evidently, the ships of Solomon travelled extensively, for:

When the queen of Sheba
Heard of the fame of Solomon
Concerning the name of the Lord
She came to prove him with hard questions.

I Kings 10:1

Not only did the ships travel far but people recognized that the Lord was blessing Solomon in all that he did.

The queen of Sheba travelled about 1,500 miles over rugged desert terrain with a camel caravan loaded with costly gifts and an abundance of spices to see first hand if the reports were true. She left impressed that the half had not been told. King Solomon exceeded all the kings of the earth for riches and for wisdom.

> Now the weight of gold that came to Solomon in one year
> Was six hundred three score and six talents of gold.
>
> I Kings 10:14

With this abundance of riches flowing into Israel, Solomon spent lavishly. He built a house for his wife, Pharaoh's daughter; a great ivory throne overlaid with gold for himself, mounted above six steps guarded by fourteen statuesque lions; all the vessels and cups within the palace were of gold. He gathered together twelve thousand four hundred chariots, horses and horsemen which he assigned to Jerusalem and to Razor, Megiddo and Gezer, cities especially rebuilt at this time.

All three cities have long histories, even before the arrival of the Israelites from Egypt. All have been given special attention by archeologists and from each of them comes evidence of Solomon's influence. Megiddo was first excavated in the 1 930's by the Oriental Institute of the University of Chicago. They found evidence that Megiddo had been destroyed by fire around 1100 B.C., rebuilt in the tenth century with a stout, solid wall with a gate of distinctive design. It was a triple gate with a square tower on each side of the entrance and three chambers set between four piers which jutted out from either side of a long passageway. This unique gateway was believed to be of the Solomonic period.

In 1955, Dr Yadin excavated Razor. At a level believed to be tenth cen tury, he discovered a gate similar to the one found at Megiddo. Further excava tion confirmed that these unusual gates were identical. This excited Dr Yadin to such an extent that he checked reports on the excavation of Gezer which was begun in 1909 but never completed. This report did not include a gateway, but Dr Yadin predicted there should be a gate the same as those at Hazor and Megiddo. Several years later, 1965 to 1971, the Hebrew Union College of America found that Dr Yadin had been correct, there was an identical triple gate.

Still, Dr Yadin was not completely satisfied. Gezer and Razor had case- mate walls, but the one at Megiddo was solid. Dr Yadin returned to Megiddo to see for himself. His detailed exploration revealed that the solid wall had indeed been built over a casemate wall. This unique gate, found in each of the cities Solomon had built substantiates the Biblical account of Solomon's cities, indicating all were designed by the same architect.

Solomon's downfall came because he did not heed God's warning not to take wives from heathen nations. Solomon loved many strange women besides the daughter of Pharaoh; hundreds of wives, princesses and concubines. These wives influenced him to worship their gods: Ashtoreth, the goddess of the Zidonians; Milcom of the Ammonites; Chemosh of Moab; Malech of Ammon. He built places of worship for all these strange, heathen gods and personally burnt incense and sacrificed to them. Worship of these gods included perverted and gruesome practices - child sacrifice, fertility rites, prostitution and sexual deviations.

The Lord was angry with Solomon for breaking his covenant and statute. As a result, Israel would be divided and its power and glory would be no more. Because of his promise to David, the Lord did not remove Solomon from the throne; it remained for his son to see the kingdom rent and torn from him.

Jeroboam, Solomon's servant, was a mighty man of valor and Solomon made him ruler over the house of Joseph. Ahijah, a prophet, foretold that the Lord would take the kingdom from Solomon and give ten tribes to Jero- boa m because the people worshipped false gods according to Solomon's example.

> **And unto his son will I give one tribe,**
> **That David my servant may have a light**
> **Always before me in Jerusalem,**
> **The city which I have chosen me**
> **To put my name there.**
>
> **IKings 11:36**

At Solomon's death, Rehoboam, his son, reigned in his stead. Then the people of Israel sent for Jeroboam and they confronted Rehoboam requesting him to lower the heavy taxation Solomon had imposed upon the people in his latter days. Ignoring the counsel of the old men of his court, Rehoboam listened to the rash advice of his contemporaries and advised the people to expect even heavier taxation. So Israel rebelled against the house of David and the people made Jeroboam king over them. Only the house of Judah and of Benjamin remained subject to Rehoboam, son of Solomon.

Jeroboam built Shechem in Mount Ephraim and dwelt there. But in his heart he knew the people would return to sacrifice in the house of the Lord at Jerusalem and become again one nation. Therefore, he made two calves of gold and he set them in Bethel and in Dan, telling the people:

> It is too much for you to go up to Jerusalem.
> Behold thy gods, 0 Israel,
> Which brought thee up out of the land of Egypt.
>   I KINGS 12:28

And the people came to worship and to sacrifice before the golden calves.

Even though the Lord promised to be with Jeroboam if he would walk with Him, Jeroboam continued in his evil ways, making the lowest of the people priests qf the high places.

The Lord sent prophets to warn that Israel would be rooted up and scattered beyond the river because of Jeroboam's sins and those of the people. They did not heed because they could not . see immediate doom for the nation. Nineteen kings reigned over Israel and none were godly, although some were more evil than others. Jeroboam was succeeded by his son Nadab who ruled for only two years before being assassinated by Baasha. After him Elah ruled and was also murdered by Zimri who committed suicide. Omri ruled in his stead.

> Omri wrought evil in the eyes of the Lord
> And did worse than all that were before him.
>
> I KINGS 16:25

Yet Omri restored Israel to a strength it had not known. He established a firm government and is best known for the magnificent palace he built on the summit of a hill protected by a massive wall and fortifications. This fortress gradually gave its name to the surrounding area - Samaria. One hundred and fifty years later, Assyrian writings would refer to this land as "the land of Omri." Omri has the distinction of being the first king of either Judah or Israel to be named in available records of other nations because of his control of the caravan route along the King's Highway through the land we know as Jordan. This record is in the famous Moabite Stela of king Mesha. This stela is black basalt inscribed with an account of Mesha's struggle against Israel. It was found in 1868 in an Arab village (Biblical Dibon) east of the Dead Sea. It is now on display in the Louvre in Paris.

Religious life reached an all-time low during the reign of Omri's son, Ahab, and his evil wife Jezebel who brought Ba-al worship from Phoenicia to Israel.

**And Ahab did more to provoke
The Lord God of Israel to anger
Than all the kings of Israel
That were before him.**

I KINGS 16:33

King Ahab, like his predecessor Solomon, was a great builder. Excavations at Megiddo revealed a vertical shaft inside the city walls that led down to water level eighty feet below. Access was by steps cut in the side of the shaft. King Ahab is credited with this protective water system. After completing the water system at Megiddo, Ahab turned to Razor. Dr Yadin, again following the Bible, believed Ahab would install a similar system in Razor. By patience and intuition, Dr Yadin did find one. Today visitors to this site still climb down to the ancient water source. Even today this is considered an astonishing engineering feat.

The Bible refers to the ivory house which king Ahab made. This has been passed over lightly as fable or exaggeration, but when archeologists started uncovering hundreds of fragments of carved ivory at the site of Ahab's palace, this fable became altogether real. These carved scraps were Phoenician in style and had been inlays for walls and furniture. The motifs were varied: floral designs, pagan gods and animals, cherubim, sphinxes and hu man figures. The most impressive was that of a "woman in the window," complete enough to show the woman's elaborate hairdo and adornments. This is an apt reminder of the fate of Jezebel herself .

During Ahab's reign, God raised up a powerful prophet, Elijah, who remained an implacable foe of Ba-al worship. As with other true prophets, he spoke not of himself but by the unction of the Holy Ghost and his actions and life were ruled accordingly.

> For the prophecy came not in old time
> By the will of man.
> But holy men of God spoke
> As they were moved by the Holy Ghost.
>   II PETER 1:21

Jezebel had brought hundreds of prophets of Ba-al worship to Israel and Ahab had abetted her in exploiting this Phoenician god. Still the Lord did not forsake his people. He sent Elijah to Ahab foretelling no rain for three years. Ba-al was worshipped as a weather god, one who watched over their crops. This demonstration of drought throughout the land proved that the Lord God was almighty and Ba-al powerless. For three years Ahab searched for Elijah knowing only he could intercede with God. Only at the Lord's appointed time did Elijah appear to Ahab, challenging the prophets of Ba-al; one man against four hundred and fifty. The prophets of Ba-al placed their sacrifice upon the altar and cried unto their god to send fire to consume the sacrifice; they travailed and cut themselves till the blood gushed but their god did not respond. Then Elijah prepared his sacrifice and spoke to the God of Israel.

The fire of the Lord f ell on Elijah's of fering and at that moment the people fell on their faces and worshipped the Lord. Then came the rain, but even this was not enough to keep the fickle Israelites f aithful, although God had seven thousand faithful souls who did not bow to Ba-al.

Elijah chose a disciple, Elisha, who was blessed wit h a double portion of the power God had given Elijah. He alone was present to see the Lord take Elijah into heaven by a whirlwind and he saw him no more. Only the mantle that f ell from Elijah remained. Elisha took this mantle and walked back to the Jordan River and smote the waters wit h the mantle as he had seen Elijah do and the waters parted. Elijah had done miracles by the power of God during his lifetime, but Elisha did twice as many.

Jehoshaphat, king of Judah, formed an alliance with king Ahab and together they went to battle against the king of Syria to reclaim Ra moth-gilead. During this battle Ahab was mortally wounded. Two of Ahab's sons reigned af ter him, the last did not worship Ba-al as his mother did, but clung to worship of the golden calves. Jehu, captain of the army, rose up against him, primarily leading a revolt against Jezebel who remained the power behind the throne. That day all of Ahab's kin were slain.

And when Jehu was come to Jezreel,
Jezebel heard of it;
And she painted her face,
And tired her head (dressed her hair),
And looked out at her window.
II KINGS 9:30

Jezebel was thrown from her window, died, and was eaten by the dogs in fulfillment of prophecy.

Jehu reigned for twenty-eight years and destroyed Ba-al worship, yet the golden calves remained. During his reign and that of his son, Syria oppressed Israel, which had become a weak nation. The nation continued to serve the golden calves and one after another their kings were assassinated as moral decay and political chaos reigned. Idol worship was prevalent through- out the land. While the Israelites denied the Lord, he sent a powerful nation against them.

Assyria brought the kingdom of Israel to an end forever around 720 B.C. This was not done overnight. The Lord allowed time for his prophets to admonish and warn of impending disaster, but the people would not heed. Assyria's growing strength became evident with the rule of king Ashurnasirpal II about 880 B.C. He moved his army across Syria to Lebanon but did not directly effect Israel. His son, Shalmaneser III (859 - 824 B.C.) did threaten king Ahab, but only slightly; he took tribute and for one hundred years Assyria campaigned elsewhere. Then Tiglath-Pileser III (known as "Pul" in the Bible) swept through Syria and into Israel. He destroyed Hazar and Megiddo, then spared Samaria and placed Hoshea on the throne as a vassal king. The rest of Israel he divided into three provinces. Large numbers of Israelites were deported and scattered throughout the Assyrian empire.

Israel's final death throes came when Sargon II captured Samaria and all of Israel went into Assyria's melting pot. Samaria was repopulated with other foreigners from Syria, Babylon and Arabia.

> For so it was that the children of Israel
> Had sinned against the Lord their God
> Until the Lord removed Israel out of his sight,
> As he had said by all his servants, the prophets,
> So Israel was carried away out of their own land
> To Assyria unto this day.
>
> II KINGS 17:7 & 23

Judah also had nineteen kings and one queen. All of the kings were of the house of David. Rehoboarn and the nation of Judah did evil in the sight of the Lord and provoked him to jealousy. Shishak, king of Egypt came against Jerusalem and stripped the treasures and gold from the house of the Lord and from the king's house. How soon the mighty nation had fallen. Only for David's sake-, did his son and the sons that came af ter continue to rule in Jerusalem. Abijam, son of Rehoboam, was a sinful king, but his son Asa was right with the Lord. He removed the sodomites and the idols from the land and refurbished the house of the Lord. There was war between Asa and Baasha, king of Israel, so Asa formed an alliance with the king of Syria which kept Israel at bay. In the fourth year of Ahab's reign in Israel, Jehoshophat took the throne of Judah and he followed the Lord as had his father. Yet the people continued to burn incense in the high places to other gods. He was succeeded by his son, Jehoram, who followed the ways of Israel for the daughter of Ahab,

Athaliah, was his wif e and she brought all of the evils of Jezebel with her. Their son, Ahaziah, was the next king of Judah and ruled only one year before he was murdered. Upon his death, Athaliah destroyed all of the royal line to the throne, she thought, although one child, Joash, was hidden in the house of the Lord for six years while the ungodly daughter of Jezebel ruled Judah. Then the priests and the military brought Joash from his hiding place and crowned him king and slew Athaliah. Joash did all that was right with the Lord as long as Jehoiada, the priest, instructed him. They repaired the temple and again its glory was short-lived for Syria threatened

Jerusalem and Joash stripped all of the goold and treasures from the king's house and from the house of the Lord as ransom for Judah's safety. Amaziah,

Azariah, and Jotham ruled Judah, following the Lord as Joash had. Yet the high places remained. Then Ahaz ruled and followed Israel's heathen gods. The kings of Israel and Syria came against Judah and Ahaz turned to Tiglath-pileser for help. The king of Assyria responded and took Damascus, then swept through Israel and established Assyrian provinces at this time. Because Judah had placed herself under Assyrian protection it was spared, but a heavy tribute was extracted from Judah. King Ahaz became a vassal king who accepted the Assyrian gods as his own. His son, Hezekiah restored the nation to Godly rule although forced to continue tribute to the Assyrian king until the next king of

Assyria, Sennacherib, came to power. It took Sennacherib three years to consolidate his kingdom and during this time, Hezekiah sought to escape the vassalage imposed upon them. Isaiah, a great prophet, warned against this, foreseeing the danger. When Sennacherib had consolidated his own power he came against the cities of Judah. To quote Sennacherib's account, he beseiged forty-six cities and conquered by use of dirt ramps and battering rams. A crucial battle was at Lachish. Sennacherib placed a series of wall reliefs in his palace at Ninevah portraying this battle. These reliefs are now displayed in the British Museum as well as other battle scenes. They show Sennacherib himself sitting on an ivory throne watching the destruction of Lachish. Archeological excavations at Lachish confirm their battle strategy as it still shows traces of the earthen ramp against the walls of the city.

As Lachish was being destroyed, all who could, fled the country for the dubious safety of Jerusalem. Assyria sent messengers to speak to the representatives of Hezekiah, who listened from the walls of Jerusalem, exorting all of the people to surrender because the God of Israel could not save them. Then king Hezekiah turned to the prophet Isaiah for counsel, Isaiah spoke as the Lord directed him:

Be not afraid of the words which thou hast heard.
With which the servants of the king of Assyria
Have blasphemed me.
Behold I will send a blast upon him,
And he shall hear a rumor,

And shall return to his own land;
And I will cause him to fall
By the sword in his own land.

II **KINGS 19:6, 7**

Sennacherib never laid siege to Jerusalem. History cannot account for Sennacharib's actions. The Bible says the angel of the Lord smote 185,000 Assyrians in the night, so Sennacherib returned home. History does record that two of his sons killed him in his temple at Ninevah and another son,

Esarhaddon, ruled. This one extended the Assyrian empire to include Lower Egypt and once again Judah became a vassal state.

During this period Hezekiah apparently extended the walls of Jerusalem for excavations indicate a large population increase around 700 B.C. This could be explained by an in-pouring of refugees, necessitating the expansion.

Ye gathered together the waters of the lower pool
And ye numbered the houses of Jerusalem.
And the houses have ye broken down
To fortify the wall.

ISAIAH 22:9-10

Hezekiah apparently constructed the Siloam Tunnel which diverted the waters of the Gihon Spring to a reservoir inside the city walls. A long underground tunnel still exists leading from the Gihon Spring, chiseled through solid rock and leading to an open pool inside the city.

At Hezekiah's death, his son Manasseh became king and ruled for fif ty-five years. He brought a degradation to Judah worse than all that Ahab and Jezebel had done to Israel, for he built altars and set up idols in the Lord's house and in its outer courts. Even his own son was made to pass through the fire of Molech and he practiced witchcraf t and introduced it throughout the land.

Assyria had f inally over-extended her rule and as her power waned, that of Babylon grew and became the next great adversary of Judah.

Amon ruled only two years after Manasseh and was as evil as his father had been. So much so, that his own servants murdered him. The people made the king's son Josiah to rule in his stead. He was a Godly king who did everything possible to restore the people to God. During renovation and cleansing of the temple, a scribe found the book of the law and king Josiah had it read to all the people. Then, for the first time in many years, the people understood how far away from God they had gone. King Josiah had all the heathen altars, idols and practices torn down and abolished.

> Nevertheless the priests of the high places
> Came not up to the altar of the Lord in Jerusalem.
> But they did eat of the unleavened bread
> Among their brethren.
>
> II KINGS 23:9

Josiah died in a battle against Egyptian pharaoh Necho at Megiddo, that fateful battleground, as the pharaoh came to Assyria's aid against Babylon. For the Lord had said to Josiah:

> Because thine heart was tender
> And thou humbled thyself before the Lord •••.
> I will gather thee unto thy fathers,
> And thou shalt be gathered unto thy grave;
> And thine eyes shall not see all the evil
> Which I will bring on this place.
>
> II KINGS 22:19 - 20

Joash's faithfulness was not enough to turn the wrath of God from all that Manassah had done and Judah remained to be punished.

Pharaoh made Jehoiakim, son of Josiah, a vassal king and taxed him heavily. After eleven years Nebuchadnezzar, king of Babylon, came into the land and made him his servant until king Jehoiakim turned against him to defect to Egypt. Judah again had fallen away from the Lord for Jehoiakim and his son Jehoiachin were evil kings. By this time Nebuchadnezzer had become invincible; Egypt could no longer contend with him. The king of Babylon took Jehoiachin captive to Babylon in 597 B.C. together with his mother, his servants, and his princes and his officers (in all, about 10,000 people). Excavations at Babylon included the finding of about two hundred clay tablets, apparently records of the king's storehouse, for several of them list rations of grain and oil supplied to Jehoiachin, king of Judah. These were the first captives taken from Jerusalem, but they would not be the last.

Zedekiah ruled in Jerusalem for ten years and rebelled against the state of vassalage they were subjected to. Jeremiah, the weeping prophet, warned against rebellion against Babylon as it was God's will that the Babylonian yoke be placed on Judah as punishment for their sinful natures. Nevertheless,

Zedekiah rebelled and Nebuchadnezzer laid siege to Judah, picking off the fortified cities, one by one, until only Jerusalem remained. After a four month blockade, famine prevailed in Jerusalem; the city was broken up and all the men of war fled in the night and the Babylonian army pursued and overtook them in the plains of Jericho. Zedekiah was forced to watch the murder of his sons and then they blinded hi m , bound him and carried hi m to Babylon. The walls of Jerusalem were broken down, the house of the Lord and the king's house were burnt, every building was destroyed and burnt, leaving nothing but shambles. The elite of the people were taken captive; all the intellectual, royal, political and religious leaders were taken to Babylon. Only the poor of the land remained.

For David's sake the nation of Judah was not utterly destroyed as was Israel. Jeremiah had prophecied:

> For thus saith the Lord
> That after seventy years be accomplished at Babylon
> I will visit you, and perform my good word toward you
> In causing you to return to this place.
>
> JEREMIAH 29:10

Prophets were used in mighty ways to warn the people, prophets from all walks of lif e. It was never God's will for the nation to crumble and the people to be imprisoned and scattered among heathen nations but the prophets were hated, or ignored, as they cried out against the sins of the nation. Nevertheless, they were spokesmen directed by the Lord. Not only were their prophecies for that time but many of them are for today and remain to be fulfilled. Will this generation take heed? Has anything been learned by the mistakes of the past ?

Isaiah was a trusted advisor of king Hezekiah and prophecied until the reign of Manasseh. It may have been his intercession with God that spared Jerusalem from Sennacherib's army. Isaiah and Micah prophesied at the same time and in a similar manner; Isaiah in the king's court and Micah to the common people in both Judah and Israel. Both prophets looked ahead in time to the Messiah and to the Kingdom Age. Nobody saw the Lord more clearly than Isaiah.

> For unto us a child is born
> Unto us a son is given.
> And the government shall be upon his shoulders,
> And his name shall be called
> Wonderf ul, Counselor, the mighty God,
> The everlasting Father, the Prince of Peace.
>
> ISAIAH 9:6

Jeremiah began his ministry in Josiah's thirtieth year (626 B.C.) and continued into the early years of the Babylonian exile. Zedekiah, the last king of Judah, protected Jeremiah from the princes that would have killed him even though he would not listen to his warnings. When the noblemen of Judah were carried captive to Babylon, Jeremiah remained with the common people. When a pro-Egyptian group fled to Egypt, they forced Jeremiah to accompany them and he died in Egypt. He is famous today for his prophecy of seventy years of Babylonian exile. He was known as "the weeping prophet" and his message was of condemnation rather than salvation. No wonder the people chose not to listen even though captivity might have been avoided if they had listened.

Ezekiel prophesied in the early years of Babylonian captivity. He was of a priestly family and was exiled to Babylonia in 597 B.C. and in the latter part of his ministry became a bearer of hope and a herald of salvation. He it was who saw the vision of a valley of dry, dead bones and they were again covered with sinews and flesh and the Lord caused breath to enter into them and they lived.

> Then he said unto me, Son of man,
> These bones are the whole house of Israel:
> Behold they say, Our bones are dried,
> And our hope is lost
> Behold, 0 my people,
> I will open your graves
> And cause you to come up out of your graves
> And bring you into the land of Israel
> And ye shall know that I am the Lord.
>
> EZEKIEL 37:11-13

And again he prophesied:

Thus saith the Lord God;
Behold, I will take the children of Israel
From among the heathen
Whither they be gone,
And I will gather them on every side
And bring them into their own land
And I will make them one nation
And one king shall be king to them all.

EZEKIEL 37:21-11

Hosea was a contemporary of Isaiah and Micah and of Amos and directed his prophecies to Israel during a period of extreme idolatry and degradation. Israel's unfaithfulness to the Lord was depicted by his own marriage to a harlot.

Joel's ministry was during the time of Elisha. His prophecies were directed to Judah and covered the period of Joash. They picture events of that time as well as of the end time and portray the invasion of the Assyrians that was to come and of the coming rule of the anti-Christ in the end time. His prophecies had a double reference; to present and future. Of fateful portent was this prophecy:

And it shall come to pass afterward,
That I will pour out my spirit on all flesh
And it shall come to pass
That whosoever shall call on the name of the Lord
Shall be delivered.

JOEL 2:28,32

Amos was a shepherd in the desert of Judah and prophesied before the threat of Assyrian invasion and preached spiritual corruption, repentance or destruction. He was a great prophet of the "righteousness of God."

Jonah and Nahum were associated with Ninevah, the powerful Assyrian city founded by Nimrod, royal seat of Assyrian kings, upon whom God visited judgement. Jonah's ministry taught omission of God's judgement through repentance and Nahum's, the execution of divine judgement because of sin. The overthrow of Ninevah was a foreshadowing of coming destruction to the Gentile world and it's apostate Christendom.

Zephaniah's prophecies were similar to Joel's. "The day of the Lord" is mentioned eleven times in this book in conjunction with God's wrathful judgements in the book of Revelations.

In the end, none of the prophets were able to divert judgement on God's covenant people.

CHAPTER VIII

LIMBO

Daniel was among the first Hebrews to be removed to Babylon. In 605 B.C., Nebuchadnezzar established Jehoiakim as a vassal king in Jerusalem and to assure his hold over the Jews he took some of their choice young men as hostages. Daniel, Shadrach, Meshach and Abednego were among this first group. The king also purposed to train them in his own household. Their first test came when they refused to eat the unclean food served them. The Babylonians did not drain the blood from animals when they were slaughtered and this was in direct opposition to God's law. So the Hebrew children became vegetarians and thrived. So much so, that Daniel became a trusted advisor to all the kings that reigned during his long lifetime.

In 597 B.C., Nebuchadnezzar brought 10,000 captives from Judah because of their rebellion. Finally, in 587 B.C. after a long siege, Jerusalem was destroyed. There is no indication that the Babylonian prisoners were_ mis treated. True, they were uprooted from their own country, but many of them were awed and impressed by the splendor of Babylon and were free to establish themselves as part of the community, even to worship the God of Israel if they desired. This was the beginning of synagogues in the absence of the temple at Jerusalem. Since the people had fallen from God's grace because of their worship of other gods, no doubt some of them willingly accepted

Marduk and his host of lesser gods. Babylonian culture wrought a worldly influence upon their more provincial way of life and brought them a second language: Aramaic, Abraham's original language. Aramaic was the language of commerce and diplomacy and similar to their Hebrew language so they easily became bilingual.

There has been much controversy over when the book of Daniel was written. Those who reject the possibility of predictive prophecy discount the genuineness of this book although Jews of the pre-Christian centuries believed it to be authentic.

Nebuchadnezzar had a dream and under threat of death, demanded his wise men interpret it even though he could not remember anything about the dream. Impossible as this seemed, the God of Israel revealed it to Daniel and he related it to the king:

> Thou, 0 king, sawest, and behold a great image
> This image's head was of fine gold,
> His breast and his arms of silver,
> His belly and his thighs of brass,
> His legs of iron, his feet part of iron and part of clay.
> DANIEL 2:31- 33

Daniel interpreted the dream in this fashion: King Nebuchadnezzar and his kingdom were the head of gold. Next to come would be an inferior kingdom, then a third kingdom of brass. A fourth kingdom strong as iron would break and be broken. And in the days of the feet, he predicted the God of Heaven will set up a kingdom which shall never be destroyed.

Many years passed and another power grew in strength. The Medes, an ancient Indo-European people, allied with Babylonians in the fall of Ninevah. During Nebuchadnezzar's rule, they extended from the Persian Gulf to the Black Sea in what would become today part of Turkey, Iran, Iraq and Ar menia.

The Medes dominated the relatively small nation of Persia until the rule of Cyrus the Great, at which time they became partners in a dual nation.

Records indicate Nabonidus was the last king of Babylon, but he left its rule to his son Belshazzar as he campaigned in the Arabian desert south-east of Edom. In his absence, the empire began to crumble.

As Belshazzar and his corrupt court feasted, the golden vessels from the Lord's temple at Jerusalem were brought in to the feast that they might drink from them. In the same hour came forth a man's hand and the fingers wrote upon the plaster wall. Again, Daniel was called forth to interpret the writing.

> MENE - God hath numbered thy kingdom, and finished it.
> TEKEL (Shekel) Thou art weighed in the balances,
> And art found wanting.
> PERES (Half Shekel) Thy kingdom is divided,
> And given to the Medes and Persians.
> DANIEL 5:26 - 28

That very night the Medes and the Persians conquered the invincible city of Babylon by diverting the course of the River Euphrates and entering by the river bed while the great feast was in progress. The city surrendered peaceably.

During the rule of Belshazzar, Daniel had had a vision and when he sought for the meaning one who appeared as a man stood before him and explained:

> The ram you saw having two horns
> Are the kings of Med a and Persia
> The rough goat is the king of
> Grecia,
> And the great horn that is between his eyes
> Is the first king
>
> DANIEL 8:20 -21

This explanation was given to Daniel before Babylon was overtaken by the Medes and the Persians and Greece was named two hundred years before Alexandria the Great founded a new, powerful kingdom. During the last years of Daniel's life he was given visions that covered history from that time until now. His visions were fulfilled by the Medes and Persians (breast and arms of silver), the Greek Empire of Alexander the Great (belly and thighs of brass) and the Roman Empire (legs of iron). One vision amazingly followed each rule, power play and alliance from the death of Alexander the Great until the Maccabean rebellion. If Jewish historians had but heeded Daniel's prophecies, they would have known the time of the first coming of their Messiah. Some of Daniel's prophecies remain to be fulfilled. Maybe this generation will see them.

As Jeremiah's prophecy of seventy years of exile grew near (from 605 B.C. until 538 B.C.) Cyrus issued a decree that the temple of Israel's God be rebuilt and supplied money and materials for its accomplishment. A clay cylinder found at Babylon bares record that Cyrus granted permission for the captives to return home. The first group of exiles returned to Jerusalem to find the walls in ruins and only a few pitiful houses still standing.

In the second year of their return, the foundation of the temple was laid and as the people sang praise and thanksgiving to the Lord, the weeping of the ancients and the shouting of the younger ones intermingled. Those who had known the glory of Solomon's temple knew this building was inferior and they wept.

Enmity sprang up between Samaria and Judea primarily because the Samari tans wanted to share in building the house of the Lord. The people of Judah did not believe these people of mixed blood were worthy to build God's house and refused their help. From that time on the Samaritans did all they could to hinder the rebuilding; yet at the same time they built themselves a rival temple on Mount Gerizim overlooking Shechem (Nablus). This religious center remained until Jews destroyed it in 128 B.C.

The Samaritans pursuaded king Artaxerxes to order a stop to the rebuilding of the temple, and for fourteen years no work was done until

Haggai prophesied and stirred the people to a new commitment. They had become involved in building their own houses and had become indifferent to the completion of God's house. Once again, Zerubbabel led the people in the rebuilding program and before they could falter, the Lord sent Zechariah to reinforce their desire to see the temple completed. His prophecies also gave them a hope for the future as he related God's promises for a future world-wide reign of the Messiah and held out a vision of a coming glorious future for Israel.

Although the temple was finally restored, the ruined city walls remained crumbled and in disrepair. Only a few of the people were dedicated to the Lord. Many had married heathen women of the land, which is not bad of itself; only as it caused them to accept idol worship and the lowering of moral standards that was quickly bringing the Jewish faith to the brink of extinction. The Lord in his mercy, supplied one who could renew their faith:

> **This Ezra went up from Babylon;**
> **And he was a ready scribe in the law of Moses,**
> **Which the Lord God of Israel had given:**
> **And the king granted him all his request,**
> **According to the hand of the Lord his God upon him.**
> **EZRA 7:6**

King Artaxerxes gave Ezra, a priest and scribe in the land of Babylon, authority and assistance to return to Jerusalem where he led the people from their errors and wrong-doings and taught them how far from the Lord they had strayed.

Nehemiah, who served as cup bearer (wine taster) to king Artaxerxes heard how the Samaritans were obstructing the rebuilding of the walls and a great determination to see their completion drove him to obtain per mission

to return to Jerusalem with just that purpose in mind so that the temple of the Lord would be adequately protected.

Nehemiah told no man of his intentions, but went out secretly at night to survey the remains of the city walls.

> **Then I went on to the gate of the fountain,**
> **And to the king's pool.**
> **But there was no place for the beast**
> **That was under me.**
>
> **NEHEMIAH 2:14**

In 1960 Dame Kathleen Kenyon faced the same obstacles. A slope so covered with broken building stones and debris that excavations could only be done by shoring up each foot of the way. Nehemiah did not have time to clear this rubble and was forced to build the wall at a higher level. Gihon Spring was no longer necessary to the city since other sources of water had been discovered. The new line for the eastern wall started at the temple mount and still stands today, although much of the wall has been replaced.

Because the hand of the Lord was with Nehemiah, all of the people turned out to help with the building.

So built we the wall;
And all the wall was joined together
Unto the half thereof.
For the people had a mind to work.

NEHEMIAH 4:6

And build they did; every man, woman and child, with a prayer in their hearts and weapons handy to ward off all the enemies who opposed the completion of the wall. This monumental task was completed in fifty-two days. 445 B.C. saw God's holy city once again intact and with a population of approximately 10,000. At last the exile was behind them and just as the Israelites of old celebrated the Passover Feast to commemorate their release from Egyptian bondage, so it was again initiated to celebrate the end of the Babylonian exile.

In ten short years, Alexander the Great of Macedonia (334 - 323 B.C.) changed the course of history. A brilliant, military genius and propagator of Greek culture, he led an army that swept through and conquered Asia Minor like a tidal wave. He established the city of Alexandria in Egypt in 332 B.C. which remained a center of Greek culture from the 3rd century B.C. to the 3rd century A.D. It became the home of a large Greek speaking colony of Jews who were the first to translate the scriptures into Greek. Alexander had been a student of Aristotle and indirectly influenced by Socrates and Plato. The Hellenic influence broke down barriers between Eastern and Western civilization and split Judaism into Pro-Hellenists and less fashionable, conservative anti-Hellenists who clung to the Laws of Moses.

After Alexander's death at Babylon in 323 B.C. his empire was divided among his generals: Egypt under Ptolemies, Mesopotamia under the Seleucids, and Asia Minor under Antigonus. At first Judea fell under the rule of the Ptolemies, but in 198 B.C. the Seleucids gained control of Palestine and Syria. While this power shift took place, the Edomites moved into the southlands and became known as Idumeans.

The area vacated by the Edomites was occupied by a desert race of Arabs know n as Nabataeans. They created one of the most beautiful cities in the world, known today as Petra, a lof ty, rock-cut, rose-red city sixty miles south of the Dead Sea; inaccessible except by foot or beast and unknown to the Western world until 1812. A fantastic chasm of towering cliffs, carved into likenesses of classical temples, the so-called "Treasury of Pharaoh" carved from the rock cliffs and numerous other cavernous chambers and temples gouged into the rock, a whole city large enough to house thousands of people. Here at Petra the Nabataeans worshipped numerous gods and grew rich from their stranglehold on caravan routes and trade flowing out of India, China, Arabia and Syria to other nations. In the end they f ell under the Roman Empire. The first Hellenistic rulers had shown great favor to the Jews. Many Jews had been led to abandon their religious rites in favor of the Greek religion. But under the Syrian regime of Antiochus Epiphanes (175 - 170 B.C.) they were subjected to extreme cruelty and abominable customs so distasteful to the Jewish people that they despised him. Antiochus Ephiphanes desecrated the temple of the Lord by sacrificing a hog on its altar.

> **He that offereth an oblation,**
> **As if he offered swine's blood;**
> **He that burneth incense,**
> **As if he blessed an idol,**
> **Ye, they have chosen their own ways.**
> **And their soul delighteth in their abominations.**
> **ISAIAH 66:3**

Later Antiochus Epiphanes, a pattern or shadow of the anti-christ who is to come, entered Jerusalem again, on a Sabbath, killing all the men, capturing the women and children. The streets literally ran with blood and the city was laid waste. The remnant of the people left alive after this slaughter were forced to sacrifice to pagan idols under penalty of death. He prohibited Jewish worship and dedicated the temple in Jerusalem to Zeus and established pagan worship in it.

> **And they shall pollute the sanctuary of strength,**
> **And shall take away the daily sacrifice,**
> **And they shall place the abomination that**
> **maketh desolate.**
> **DANIEL 11:31**

The Jews rebelled against this tyrannic rule in an insurrection led by Matta- thias, an aged priest. He gathered together a group of patriots and fled to the hills where they carried on a guerrilla warfare until his death. He was succeeded by his son Judas Maccabeus who managed to regain Jerusalem and purified the temple and restored the rightful worship to the God of Abraham, Isaac and Jacob. He fought on for political independence, and when he died in battle, a younger brother took his place. The Maccabean dynasty, also known as the Hasmonean dynasty, retained independence for the Jews until 63 B.C. when Pompey's arrival overcame them. The Roman legions besieged Jerusalem, and Pompey captured the city. The last Maccabean aspirant was executed at the request of Herod and by order of Mark Antony. Coins of the Maccabean period survive to prove the autonomy of the Jewish state under its priestly rulers.

The Nabataeans had gradually pushed the Edomites northward until they occupied the southern half of Judea, an area first called Idumaea by the Greeks. The Maccabeans had conquered them and imposed circumcision and Jewish laws upon them. Still, nothing could change the feudal mistrust between the descendants of Jacob and Esau. Ironically, under the Romans, Antipater, a wealthy Idumean officer, gained great favor with the Roman Emperor and was appointed Procurator of Judea. He placed his sons in charge of Judea and Galilee.

Herod was placed over Galilee and ruled with a despotic hand from 40 to 4 B.C. The history of his rule was one of political guile and chicanery together with atrocious crimes resulting from insane jealousy, primarily against his own family. He had allied himself to the Maccabeans by marrying the princess Mariamne, but because the Jewish people favored her and her t wo sons, he had them executed. He found it expedient to please the Roman Emperors, and because it profited himself to do so, he remained loyal to them. Because of nationalistic opposition to his kingship, he was not able to enter Jerusalem until 37 B.C. During his reign he had many magnificent structures built, especially in Jerusalem; a royal palace, an imposing administration center, luxurious private homes. But none of them could compare to the temple which was built of snowy white marble. It was said that large areas of the walls of the sanctuary were covered with plates of gold which shown brilliantly in the sunlight. He also had the temple mount enlarged and the wailing wall, still standing today, was a part of this platform. Nevertheless, the Jews suspected Herod's motive in building the temple was self-aggrandisement rather than piety, which was most likely true.

All the apparent peace and prosperity; the magnificent temple and the imposing buildings of Jerusalem were but a facade for the emptiness in the hearts of the people. What had happened to the glorious beginning and potential that the nation of Israel and the throne of David had once had? The people had lost sight of the glory of the Lord. No prophet had been heard for four hundred years. It seemed impossible to sink any lower; even Herod, the present king of the Jews was their old enemy, an Edomite.

Yet they had a hope. They held to the promises delivered by the prophets of old that their Messiah, their king, t heir saviour would come again.

They were a people abiding in a state of limbo because they had been unfaithful to the one, true God; reaping the harvest they had sown through their fickleness and indifference to the Lord over the years. And yet, because Jehovah is merciful, and because there were still a few who looked for his coming, Malachi's prophecy would soon be fulfilled.

> Behold, I will send my messenger,
> And he shall prepare the way before me:
> And the Lord, whom ye seek,
> Shall suddenly come to his temple,
> Even the messenger of the covenant,
> Whom ye delight in,
> Behold, he shall come, saith the Lord of hosts.
>
> MALACHI 3:1

CHAPTER IX

PALESTINE

Palestine, officially named for the Philistines who had inhabited its coastal area, had at one time been known as the nation of Israel. Only one hundred and thirty-six miles long by sixty-nine miles wide, this minute country upon which the Lord's attention had been focused from the days of Abraham was destined for still greater things; a land cradled in the very heart of the world and containing His holy city, Jerusalem.

Under Roman sovereignty, it was directly ruled by Herod's sons. Herod Antipas ruled his tetrarchy of Galilee and Peraea from 4 B.C. to 39 A.D. He maintained friendly relations with Augustus and Tiberius, second Roman emporer, throughout his reign and succeeded in keeping an uneasy peace within Galilee. He was supported by the Herodians, the aristocracy who had prospered and attained their present standing during the reign of the first Herod.

Herod Antipas rivalled his father in a love of buildings. He established a city, Tiberias, which became one of the great cities of Palestine. Located on the western shore of the Sea of Galilee, it became Herod's capital.

Life was not as primitive two thousand years ago as is commonly believed. The Roman Empire made and maintained an excellent system of roads. Public buildings were provided, as well as local government offices, markets, town halls, baths and stadiums. For all of these, taxes were levied on income and property, sales taxes, and duties on imports. A Roman official called a censor was responsible for collections. He, in turn, auctioned these tasks to the lowest bidders. These tax-gatherers were despised by the people and considered dishonest and collaborators of the Romans. In fact, bribery was a common practice and the "publicans" as the tax-gatherers were called, were considered "sinners" by the Jewish people.

> And behold there was a man named Zaccheus
> Which was the chief among the publicans,
> And he was rich.
>
> LUKE 19:2

The poorer people, and some in rural areas, lived in houses of perishable materials which tended to wash away during heavy rains. But in the cities, houses of the comparatively well-to-do might be built of squared stone, forty to sixty feet high, with a heavy street gate or door opening onto a courtyard planted with trees. Heating was done by large, hollow depressions in the middle of the floor or bronze or pottery braziers which burned charcoal. Some high ranking Roman officials even had a form of central heating by hot air or hot water.

It was a Roman practice to bring the water supply to their cities by means of aqueducts from reservoirs supplied by springs in the nearby hills or mountains. Running water was supplied directly to the homes of those who could afford it by clay pipes and stop-cocks to regulate its flow. Antioch is known to have had such a system in the first century. Also records mention a Jewish official in charge of the water supply to the Jerusalem Temple at the time of Christ was Nakdimon ben Gurion. Possibly the same man was the Nicodemus mentioned in the book of John. Public baths were available to the people; many of the upper classes had baths in their homes. There was a drainage and sewage disposal system for the Temple area and every city had certain sanitary rules.

Carts, carriages and wagons were to be found on the open Roman highways. These were not convenient within Jerusalem because of the steepness of the narrow streets within the city.

Marketplaces were filled with bazaars and shops offering exotic imports and services of every nature:;- Sandal-makers, tailors, scribes, weavers, dyers, carpenters, workers in brass and copper, butchers, goldsmiths, jewellers, sellers of silks, perfumes, ointments and incense. There were also restaurants and wine shops offering salted and fresh fish from Galilee, fried locusts, vegetables, soups, pastries and sweetmeats.

In Palestine, there were schools in every town and education was compulsory for all children over six. Most Jewish schools were in the synagogues or in special schoolhouses. Children were taught from the Old Testament to read and write. From ten to fifteen they were taught traditional Hebrew law. The Talmud was only taught in the Academies to those over fifteen.

The education of Gentiles was more general, including mathematics. The Greeks had educated their children outside the home for many years. Alexandria, Egypt had been a renowned center of literature, mathematics, astronomy and medicine since the third century B.C. and had the largest library in the world at that time, containing some four hundred thousand manuscripts. (Part of this library was destroyed in 390 A.D. by order of a Christian bishop and the rest of it in 640 by Moslems.)

Alexandria had a very good school of medicine. Even without anaesthetics, they were considerably more advanced in surgery than in medicine, even performing brain surgery. Some of the surgical instruments in use then have not been improved upon to this day. Hellenistic Jews of Alexandria brought this advanced medical knowledge to Palestine. Rabbinical law ordained that every town must have a surgeon or a physician qualified to practice surgery.

From the days of Moses there had always been a medical man to attend to the priesthood .

> **Is there no balm in Gilead;**
> **Is there no physician there?**
> **Why then is not the health of the**
> **Daughter of my people recovered?**
> **JEREMIAH 8:22**

At the beginning of the century the Jewish people were divided primarily into three sects: the Pharisees, the Sadducees and the Essenes. There was another group, the Zealots, who were an unorganized movement of Jewish patriots rebelling against Roman rule and united in their desire to see a Davidic kingdom established once again.

The Pharisees were known as "separatists" because of the scrupulous observance of their laws. This zeal degenerated into formalism which covered every conceivable case of public or private conduct. They were the representatives of the people, the ultimate authority on questions of faith or practice. The Pharisees opposed the aristocratic Sadducean high priesthood of the Temple, yet the Pharisees determined who were worthy of admission to the synagogues. Many were sincerely devout but they had lost sight of a spiritual relationship with God. Jesus emphasized a regenerated heart after which righteous conduct would follow. As a general rule, the Pharisees were the chief critics of Jesus. Jesus had this to say about them:

> For they bind heavy burdens
> And grievous to be borne.
> And lay them on men's shoulders;
> But they themselves will not move them
> With one of their fingers,
> But all of their works they do
> For to be seen of men.
> They make broad their phylacteries,
> And enlarge the borders of their garments.
>
> MAITHEW 23:4,5

The clothing of the Pharisees was different from other Israelites. The men wore fine, white, richly embroidered robes, purple and silver belts; the border, or hem, on their robes was indeed wider than ordinary. It was customary for them to wear gloves lest they come in contact with anything dirty. Their beards were carefully combed and perfumed, their hair-dos artistic. They also adorned themselves with neck chains and bracelets.

The Pharisee women wore veils of several styles which were decorated with precious metals and jewels. Perfume and cosmetics were customary as were painted cheeks, darkened eyebrows, dyed hair, or powdered with gold, elaborately arranged. They wore bracelets, rings on their fingers, in their hair and in their noses; necklaces, chains, earrings and ankle bracelets. They were the style setters.

The Pharisees held themselves aloof from those of lesser social rank and especially from Gentiles. They were so held in esteem by the common people that they could claim the best seats in the synagogues and were honored by being called "Rabbi," meaning "my master." At the beginning of the first century A.D., there were six thousand Pharisees in Palestine.

The Sadducees were the wealthy, aristocratic, educated segment of Jewish society. They were as political as they were religious and their beliefs were based on written law and had no Old Testament basis. Accordingly, they did not believe in resurrection, angels and spirits. Many of them were members of the Sanhedrin (the Supreme Court of the Jews; headed by the high priest) and were in good standing with the Roman government but unpopular with the common people. They numbered even fewer than the Pharisees but were to be reckoned with because of their power. Jesus warned his disciples to beware of the "leaven" in a parable referring to "teaching" by both sects.

> Then understood they how
> That he bade them not beware
> Of the leaven of bread
> But of the doctrine
> Of the Pharisees and of the Sadducees.
>
> MATTHEW 16:12

Although the Bible does not mention the Essenes, Josephus, noted first century historian, wrote about them. Other sources of information were Philo Judaeus and Pliny the Elder. The Dead Sea Scrolls and excavation of Qumran between 1951 and 1958 brought to light such a wealth of information that only a fraction of it can be covered here.

The Essenes were founded about 140 B.C. by a "teacher of righteousness", possibly a priest of the House of Zadok. Zadok was a priest in the days of king David. The Essenes were the "hasidim," the pious Jews who separated tltemselves from the worldliness of Judaism during the Maccabean dynasty and established a communal settlement near the Dead Sea at Qumran. They were ruled by a council of twelve princes, or lay leaders, three priests and a bishop. The central group practiced celibacy, although other groups living in Jerusalem and throughout Palestine were not as strict. They believed in purification by water, that they were the elect or chosen of God and designated for the exercise of authority in the last days. They did not sacrifice at the Temple as did other Jews, but put much more importance in their noon sacred banquet and in personal cleanliness before this meal. They believed in two spirits; the forces of good (The Prince of Light) and the forces of evil (Beli'al, the Angel of Darkness). They did not believe in a resurrection, but held to a belief in the immortality of the soul.

Of prime importance today is the wealth of scrolls they had hidden in nearby caves. These scrolls were of every Old Testament book except Esther. Especially important was an almost complete copy of the book of Isaiah, another less complete and both books of Samuel in a single scroll. These are almost one thousand years older than any previously found and prove today's Bible to be amazingly accurate. These precious scrolls have become the property of Israel; stored in Jerusalem in the Shrine of the Book.

CHSPTER X

PREPARE YE THE WAY OF THE LORD

Many Jews went daily to the Temple to attend services, to pray during the burning of incense, and to prostrate themselves before God when the Levites sang. Others went to hear or to teach the Torah. Daily worship began at dawn, heralded by silver trumpets. About fifty priests were on duty on a rotational basis; many had slept in the war m Chamber of the Hearth and assembled in the Hall of Hewn Polished Stones where duties were apportioned by lot. Then the lot was cast again for the duty of making the solemn offering of incense, and whoever was chosen was allowed this privilege only once in a lifetime. During the incense offering, the people gathered for prayer in the Court of the Israelites which faced the entrance to the sanctuary.

In the days of Herod, a certain priest named Zechariah and his wife, Eliza-beth, had been childless for many years.

> And it came to pass,
> That while he executed the priest's office
> Before God in the order of his course,
> According to the custom of the priest's office,
> His lot was to burn incense
> When he went into the temple of the Lord
> And the whole multitude of the people,
> Were praying without at the time of incense.
>
> LUKE 1:8-10

As he offered incense, Gabriel, an angel of the Lord, appeared before Zechariah to say his prayers were answered and that Elizabeth would have a son who would be named John. The Holy Ghost would lead him as he prepared the people for the Lord. Because Zechariah doubted, just as Abraham and Sarai had doubted that they could have a child in their old age, he was struck dumb until the baby was born. When he emerged speechless from the Temple, the people perceived he had seen a vision. When his rotation was completed he returned home and Elizabeth conceived.

Several months later Gabriel appeared again. This time to Mary, a young virgin and descendant of king David through his son Nathan. Mary was troubled and confused as he greeted her by saying she was highly favored by the Lord and blessed among women. Gabriel explained she was chosen by God.

> And behold, thou shalt conceive in thy womb,
> And bring forth a son.
> And shalt call his name Jesus.
> He shall be great and shall be called
> The Son of the Highest; and the Lord God
> Shall give unto Him the throne of His father David.
>
> LUKE 1:31- 32

JESUS. The name had utmost significance; meaning Messiah (Savior) and was the ultimate promise of God given to Adam and Eve as the "seed of the woman" which would bruise the head of the serpent. Again, the promise was given through Isaiah:

Behold, a virgin shall be with child,
And shall bring forth a son.
And they shall call his name Immanuel.
Which being interpreted is: God with us.

MATIHEW 1:23

Throughout the history of the Hebrews was the hope of each generation that they would see the coming of the Messiah. Now at last, through a young girl of poor parents, in a small, insignificant village of Galilee was that prophecy to be fulfilled. To Mary this created enormous problems; she was betrothed to Joseph, but as yet the marriage had not been consummated. How could she be with child?

And the angel answered and said unto her,
The Holy Ghost shall come upon thee,
And the power of the Highest shall overshadow thee.
Therefore also that holy thing which shall be born of thee
Shall be called the Son of God.

LUKE 1:35

Gabriel also told Mary that Elizabeth, her cousin, was six months pregnant. To Mary, knowing Elizabeth had always been childless and now too old to bare children, this was a sign that nothing is impossible with God; so she answered the angel, "Let it be according to thy word." Then, in haste and confusion, Mary departed for the home of Elizabeth, the only one who would be able to understand. Also, this would gain time and Elizabeth would be a legitimate reason for leaving as she would need help during her last months of confinement. If Mary had any doubts about her own condition, they were promptly put to rest, for as she entered the house of Zechariah, Elizabeth was filled with the Holy Ghost, her baby leaped in her womb and she prophesied.

Blessed art thou among women
And blessed is the fruit of thy womb.
LUKE 1:42

Through an insight that could only come from God, Elizabeth understood that through Mary would the Lord be born, and by His Spirit they magnified the Lord together. And Mary stayed with Elizabeth for about three months.

Unto Zechariah and Elizabeth a son was born and, overriding the protests of others who thought he should be named after his father, they named him John. Only then did Zechariah regain power of speech and it became clear to those around them that the hand of the Lord was on this child as Zechariah prophesied that he would be called a prophet of the Highest and would go before the face of the Lord to prepare his way.

Mary returned to her own house. In those days betrothal was as binding as marriage. Legally the only way Joseph could dissolve the union was by a form of divorce. Knowing his denouncement of Mary was tantamount to disgrace and possibly punishment as severe as stoning to death, he was not willing to make her a public example but sought ways of putting her away privately. While he was considering what action to take, the Lord sent an angel to him in a dream.

Fear not to take unto thee Mary thy wif e.
For that which is conceived in her
Is of the Holy Ghost.
And she shall bring forth a son,
And thou shalt call his name JESUS.
For he shall save his people from their sins.

MATTHEW 1:20, 21

Records show a Roman governor of Syria, Quirinius (Cyrenius) did conduct a census of Judaea following a decree of Caesar Augustus, although there is some controversy as to the date it was taken.

The system established for this census may seem cumbersome, but each family was required to be registered in the city of their ancestors. Joseph was also of the lineage of king David through David's son Solomon. King David had been born in Bethlehem; therefore, it was necessary that Joseph and Mary go to Bethlehem, even though the birth of her son was imminent.

As the book of Luke records it, "there went out a decree from Caesar Augustus that all the world should be taxed and the first taxing was done while Cyrenius was governor of Syria, and all went to be taxed .... and Joseph went to the city of David which was called Bethlehem."

Bethlehem, an ancient town five miles south of Jerusalem, resting on a limestone ridge of Judaean highland, poised above the Dead Sea rift, was a walled town as early as David's day. Today it reflects a character easily related to the time of Christ with its narrow streets and flat-roofed stone houses. It is traditionally the site of Rachel's burial and the birthplace of king David. Here David had tended the sheep of his father.

When Joseph and Mary arrived, because the city was overflowing with others who claimed descent from David, there was no room to be had so they were forced to accept shelter in a cave which was customarily used to house animals. The Bible does not enlarge on this point, but many homes were built over caves used as shelter for their animals. Today homes can still be found attached to or over the barn, even in rural European areas. Into such a setting was Jesus born, and Mary wrapped him in swaddling clothes and laid him in a manger.

Today an area outside Bethlehem is known as Shepherd's Field because sheep are allowed to graze here after the crops have been harvested. This has been customary for many years.

During warm weather, shepherds of Bible times customarily led their sheep into a stone-enclosed sheepfold at night and the shepherds would take turns watching for predatory animals. If there was only one shepherd, he would sleep across the only opening to the sheepfold. During the cooler months of winter, they sought the shelter of caves such as those at "Ain Fashka", near the area where the Dead Sea Scrolls were found.

And there were in the same country
Shepherds abiding in the field,
Keeping watch over their flock by night.
And, lo, the angel of the Lord came upon them,
And the glory of the Lord shone round about them.
And the angel said
For unto you is born this day
In the city of David a Savior
Which is Christ the Lord.

LUKE 2:8 - 11

To the amazement of the shepherds, the angel told them this child would be found lying in a manger. Then a multitude of angels appeared, praising God. All this time, the shepherds were bathed in a heavenly light such as they had never experienced before. As the angels and the light disappeared, the shepherds stood in fear and in awe, knowing what they had seen and heard came from God. The birth of Christ could be no less than the birth of their promised Messiah. So they hastened to Bethlehem and found Mary and Joseph with the baby Jesus who was lying in a manger. All that the shepherds had seen and heard they made known to others who wondered about these things. It seems odd that this miraculous news did not travel throughout all Palestine. Possibly, those who had not seen and heard the angels for themselves did not believe. It is also interesting to note, the shepherds were in the fields, indicating it was not yet winter. So much for the birthdate that man has assigned to Jesus.

The good news may not have spread throughout Palestine, but there were people aware of his coming.

There came wise men from the east to Jerusalem
Saying, Where is he that is born King of the
Jews?
For we have seen his star in the east
And are come to worship him.

MATTHEW 2:1, 2

The Bible does not say how many wise men or from where in the east they came. Possibly they were the Nabataeans (Arabians) who were responsible for Petra, that city of altars located sixty miles south of the Dead Sea. They were a people who worshiped many gods and being neighbors of Judea, were most likely knowledgeable of the God of Israel.

When the wise men came to king Herod for guidance, he was troubled because he sensed a threat to his throne. Nevertheless, he sent for the chief priests and scribes who said, "it is written by the prophet Micah that He will be born in Bethlehem." King Herod diligently questioned the wise men, then sent them to Bethlehem after deceitfully requesting they inform him when they found the child that he also might go to worship.

The wise men departed from king Herod, still following the star until they found the child with Mary in Bethlehem. There they fell down and wor- shipped the Christ child and presented gifts of gold, frankincense and myrrh. Tradition says the presents had special significance -gold for a king, incense for God and myrrh for mortal man.

Aware that Herod was a threat to Jesus, the wise men returned home another way.

Mosaic Law required forty days of purification after the birth of a man child before a woman could enter a sanctuary.

> And when the days of her purification
> According to the law of Moses were accomplished,
> They brought him to Jerusalem.
> To present him to the Lord.
>
> LUKE 2:22

Simeon had lived in Jerusalem many years and had faithfully served the Lord. The Holy Ghost had made known to him that he would not die until he had seen Christ. As Joseph and Mary brought Jesus to the Temple, Simeon was drawn there to recognize, to hold Him, and to prophecy:

> For mine eyes have seen thy salvation,
> Which thou hast prepared
> Before the face of all people; A light to lighten the
> Gentiles,
> And the glory of thy people Israel.
>
> LUKE 2:30 - 32

Also Anna, a prophetess, a widow of many years who served God in the Temple, recognized the Christ child and spoke of Him as the Redeemer. After this, Joseph and Mary, with Jesus, returned to Nazareth.

The Lord warned Joseph in a dream to take Mary and Jesus into Egypt; to flee from the wrath of Herod who would destroy the child.

After all that Joseph had witnessed, he did not doubt this warning, but arose and departed by night with Mary and her son. They may have joined with a caravan crossing the Sinai by the main caravan route between Ezion-geber at the head of the Gulf of Aquabah to Memphis on the Nile, but it seems more likely they would have followed one of the world's oldest highways, the Way of the Land of the Philistines which lay near the coast, a distance of approximately one hundred and fifty miles from Palestine to the Nile River. Whatever method and route they travelled, the increased traffic between Alexandria, Egypt and Palestine since the advent of Greek and Roman rule would have made it much more accessible than in the days of Moses. They remained in Egypt until the death of Herod in 4 B.C.

This trip was not in vain, for when Herod realized the wise men had no intention of informing him of the existence or whereabouts of the Christ child, he ordered all the children of Bethlehem and surrounding areas two years of age and younger killed. (This Herod was the first Herod, father of Herod Antipas, who ruled during most of the lifetime of Jesus Christ, and this action could have been expected from one who murdered his own wife and children because of jealousy.) Herod's computation of two years stemmed from his original questioning of the wise men. These wise men, knowledgeable in the ancient art of astrology, the study that assumes and professes to interpret the movement of the stars, may have been watching the constellations for two years waiting for the precise configuration to lead them to the King of the Jews.

After their exile in Egypt, Joseph returned again to Nazareth with Mary and Jesus.

> And the child grew, and waxed
> Strong in spirit, filled with wisdom;
> And the grace of God was upon him.

LUKE 2:40

Only one incident in his boyhood is mentioned. When Jesus was twelve years of age, Joseph and Mary brought hi m to the temple at Jerusalem for the feast of the Passover. As was the custom, they travelled with a group of friends and relatives. For this reason, Jesus was not missed until they had gone a day's journey toward home. It was three days before they found him in the Temple conversing with the learned scribes and teachers who were astonished at his understanding and knowledge of God's word.

Joseph was a carpenter, which was considered a lowly trade, and Jesus also learned this trade. This is all that is known of his life until he became thirty years of age.

His ministry was introduced by John the Baptist, whom God had prepared for this assignment from his conception. John spent a period of time in the desert with only the simplest of necessities and an austerity similar to that of the Old Testament prophet, Elijah. This resemblance was enhanced by his simple diet of desert fare, locusts and wild honey; and by his apparel, coarse garments of camel's hair, bound by a leather girdle. His wilderness experience drew him closer to God and prepared him for the role God intended him to play.

John's wilderness setting was near Jericho and centered around the Jordan River, the chief river of Palestine. This river flows through the great rift from the Beka'a Plain, through the Sea of Galilee, on south of Jericho to the Dead Sea. Its source is 1,200 feet above sea level and drops to 1,286 feet below sea level where it enters the Dead Sea. It looks like a twisting serpent, flowing swiftly as it leaves the Sea of Galilee, growing ever more sluggish as it nears the Sea of Sodom , reluctant to pour out its life-giving waters into an area of intense heat and desolation.

There has been speculation that John was influenced by the Essenes. Very possibly he knew them. Many Essenes lived in caves in the cliffs, just as John must have. They had more in common with John's teachings than any other religious groups of the time. Their return to a life of desert simplicity while preparing for the coming of the Messiah and the end of the age and their careful cleansing and ritual purification rites to purify body and soul, which had a distinctly spiritual aspect, resembled John's ministry. These similarities grew from the same source - a deep study of God's word, rat her than from each other.

The Lord had not sent a prophet to his Jewish children for four hundred years. They eagerly flocked to the Jordan River to see this prophet who resembled Elijah.

The voice of one crying in the wilderness,
Prepare ye the way of the Lord,
Make his paths straight.

ISAIAH 40:3

He was a fulfillment of Old Testament prophecy and preached repentance and baptism to all who came to hear him. Many confessed their sins, repented and were baptized. The Pharisees and the Sadducees were also drawn to John, but they self-righteously stood apart, observing and critical. Those John boldly denounced, calling them "a generation of vipers." They asked John who he was and why he baptized if he was not the Christ or Elijah. To them he answered he was neither, but:

I indeed baptize you with water unto repentance:
But he that cometh after me is mightier than I,
Whose shoes I am not worthy to bear;
He shall baptize you with the Holy Ghost and fire.

MATTHEW 3:11

John drew around him disciples whom he taught to pray and to fast. Some of them later became Christ's followers. Andrew , Simon Peter's brother, and John, brother of James, were originally disciples of John the Baptist.

And it came to pass that Jesus came from Nazareth in Galilee and when John saw him coming he recognized Jesus as the Lamb of God who would take away the sins of the world. John testified that for this reason he had been sent to baptize; even Jesus, whom John baptized in the Jordan River.

> And straightway coming up out of the water,
> He saw the heavens opened,
> And the Spirit like a dove
> Descending upon him.
>
> Mark 1:10

Jesus had no need to be baptized for repentance of sins, but did it to identify himself as Son of man, to f ulf ill all righteousness, and to be the perfect example in all things. This was necessary that mankind might understand the significance He placed upon baptism as a step in man's redemption. From this day baptism became a spiritual cleansing essential for salvation. God's plan for His wilderness tabernacle and one of His last instructions to Moses was:

> When they go into the tabernacle,
> They shall wash with water,
> That they die not.
>
> EXODUS 30:20

God does not change. Even then, cleanliness was a requirement before entering into the presence of the Lord.

After his baptism, Jesus was drawn by the Spirit into the wilderness where he fasted for forty days and was tempted of the devil. His weapon against Satan was the Word. The devil was, and is, powerless against God's written Word.

During this time, John the Baptist continued his ministry knowing it would diminish as that of Christ grew stronger. He witnessed to king Herod and publicly denounced him for his sinful ways. Herod had flouted biblical law when he wed Herodias, his brother's wife, while the brother yet lived. In cidentally, Herodias was also the niece of both her husbands.) The large following that John the Baptist had acquired also alarmed Herod for he could see the possibility of a revolt against himself and against Rome. This, added to the hatred Herodias had for John, resulted in John's imprisonment.

CHAPTER XI

JESUS OF NAZARETH

Jesus returned from the wilderness to Galilee in the power of the Spirit and his fame spread as he preached.

> Repent,
> For the kingdom of heaven Is at hand.
>
> MATTHEW 4:17

He came to Nazareth where he had been brought up and, as he always did, went into the synagogue on the Sabbath and stood up to read. This time he read from Isaiah:

> The Spirit of the Lord is upon me,
> Because he hath anointed me to preach
> The gospel to the poor;
> He hath sent me to heal the broken-hearted,
> To preach deliverance to the captives,
> And recovering of sight to the blind, ·
> To set at liberty them that are bruised,
> To preach the acceptable year of the Lord.
> This day is this scripture fulfilled
> in your ears.   LUKE 4:18 - 21

They in the synogogue rose up in wrath; after all this was Joseph's son.

What right had he to speak as he had just done? They rose up against him and thrust him out of the city and would have thrown him over the edge of a steep bluff, but he passed through the midst of them and went his way to Capernaum.

Capernaum, a small lake port and fishing village on the northwest shore of the Sea of Galilee became the center of his Galilean ministry. Galilee included diverse topographical features from snow-capped Mount Hermon, the mount of the transfiguration, in the north, the Plain of Esdaelor. and Megiddo, the Jordan River, the great rift area to hills and mountains as high as 4,000 feet elevation to the Sea of Galilee, 6 0 feet below sea level.

In Christ's day, this region was prosperous and densely populated, criss-crossed by Roman military roads and ancient trade routes. Most of the apostles cam e from towns on the lake shore. This area was sub-tropical, hilly, green and fertile. Palms, olives, figs and grapes grew on the hillsides and around the lake.

The heart-shaped Sea of Galilee had many names. In the Old Testament it was known as Chinneroth. In Jesus' day it was alternately called Sea of Tiberias, the Lake of Gennesaret or Sea of Galilee. By whatever name, it supported a thriving fishing industry, furnishing a livelihood for many fishermen and spawning related industries such as boat building, fish pickling and drying for export. This area was also noted for its dye works and pottery. Tiberias was a spa town famous for its hot mineral baths and healing properties.

Some Jews settled in Galilee on their return from Babylonian exile and over the years intermingled with Gentiles, adopting distinct linguistic and dialectic mannerisms which enabled the Jerusalem Jews to easily identify them. Jerusalem Jews considered the Galileans as uncultured and uncouth, looking down on them with patronizing contempt; considering themselves more strictly orthodox and of purer Hebrew blood.

As Jesus approached Capernaum he saw two brothers, Simon called Peter, and Andrew, his brother, casting a net into the sea, for they were fishers. He said to them:

> Follow me,
> And I will make you fishers of men.
>
> MATIHEW 3:19

Without hesitation, they left their nets. Andrew had been a disciple of John the Baptist before his imprisonment and now willingly followed the one John had foretold. When they had gone a little further, they saw James and John, sons of Zebedee, in a boat mending their nets. They too forsook

everything to follow Jesus. As they entered Capernaum, they went directly to the synagogue, it being the Sabbath. He taught as one with authority. The first to recognize where this authority originated was an unclean spirit who cried out:

> I know thee, who thou art,
> The Holy One of God.
> And Jesus rebuked him, saying
> Hold thy peace, and come out of him.
>
> MARK 1 : 24 - 25

The people were amazed at Jesus' doctrine and his power to command the spirits of Satan. Nevertheless, the people lacked the understanding and insight of the unclean spirits who knew that he was the Christ.

On leaving the synagogue, they entered the home of Peter and Andrew, where they found Peter's mother-in-law ill wit h fever. When Jesus touched her she was immediately healed. That evening the people of Capernaum brought those who were diseased and he laid hands on them and they were healed. Also he cast out many devils; suffering the devils not to speak, because they knew him. The next day he departed for other towns.

> Let us go into the next towns,
> That I may preach there also;
> For therefore came I forth.
>
> MARK 1:38

> And the fame of him went out
> Into every place in the country round about.
>
> LUKE 4:31

The day that Jesus went forth from Capernaum he found, Philip of Bethsaida and Philip found Nathaniel and said unto hi m:

> We have found him, of whom Moses in the law
> And the prophets did write.
> Jesus of Nazareth, the son of Joseph.
>
> JOHN 1 : 45

On the third day there was a marriage in Cana of Galilee. Jesus, his disciples, and his mother were invited to the wedding.

Jewish weddings began with a betrothal in which the couple were as much bound to one another as if they were already married. The marriage itself took place later. There was no set period of time. The marriage began with the wedding procession in which the husband brought his bride to her future home. This precession was accompanied wit h shouting, singing and dancing. The marriage supper took place in the house of the husband's family and was a tremendous affair. The meal was lavish, as extravagant as the means of the family allowed. It w as a serious breach of hospitalit y to run short of anything like wine. That was what happened at this wedding. Mary turned to Jesus, knowing he was able to wor k miracles. Jesus said:

> Woman, what have I to do with thee?
> Mine hour is not yet come.
>
> JOHN 2:4

Undaunted, Mary was not to be deterred. With complete trust in Jesus, she instructed the servants to do whatever he told them. Following his instructions the servants filled six stone waterpots with water and when it was served to the guests it had turned to wine; not just any wine, but the best.

> This beginning of miracles
> Did Jesus in Cana of Galilee
> And manifested forth his glory;
> And his disciples believed on him.
>
> JOHN 2:11

Casting out devils and healing the sick were wonders, but the people could explain them to their own satisf action and still see Jesus as just a man. (Af ter all, they could reason, the man was not really as sick as it had seemed. He would have recovered his health anyhow.) Turning water to wine was a miracle no man could do; this was a supernatural act, not to be explained.

As the days grew closer to Passover, Jesus went up to Jerusalem as did tens of thousands of other Jews from Galilee, Judaea and the whole Diaspora (that is other countries, wherever the Jews were dispersed.) This pilgrimage might be every year for those close by. Possibly only once in a lifetime for

those far away. Others might journey to Jerusalem for the feasts of Pentecost or Tabernacles. A few fortunate, dedicated ones would make all three sacred feasts. The pilgrims would overflow Jerusalem during the sacred feast days, filling the outlying villages and pitching tents outside the walls of Jerusalem; but on the day they brought the sacrificial lamb and offered it at the temple, they had to remain in Jerusalem through the night. Townspeople generously opened their doors to strangers during the feast days. During those days laws regarding uncleanliness were relaxed to accommodate the large influx of visitors.

The Temple was undoubtedly the biggest business entity in Jerusalem. Besides purchasing immeasurable quantities of livestock for the public sacrifices, it supported approximately seven thousand priests and Levites, a staff of scribes, physicians, incense manufacturers, weavers and bakers of shewbread. The area swarmed with traders selling animals.

No images were allowed in the sacred precincts of the Temple. This precluded the exchange of foreign coins because the majority of them featured images of their kings and emperors. But the money changers were exceedingly busy in the Tyropean Street close to the Temple Mount, and in the lower precincts beneath it, where local currency could buy the animals for sacrifice. Jesus was filled with righteous indignation as he surveyed these transactions:

> **And he found in the temple those that sold**
> **Oxen and sheep and doves and the changers of money**
> **sitting.**
> **And when he had made a scourge of small cords,**
> **He drove them all out of the temple,**
> **And the sheep and the oxen;**
> **And poured out the changers' money**
> **And overthrew the tables,**
> **And said unto them that sold doves,**
> **Take these things hence;**
> **Make not my Father's house a house of merchandise.**
> **JOHN 2:14 - 16**

Thus did Jesus clash with the ecclesiastical rulers of Jerusalem. The corruption of the priestly house of Annas was notorious. It has been suggested that the high priest Caiaphas allowed merchants to set up animal stalls in the Temple confines; in the lower halls or subterranean structures of the Temple Mount. The subterranean domed halls under the Hanuyot served as temple storerooms and the gathering center of the cattle, sheep and doves. This was controlled by the high-priestly administration, allied with the Sadducean aristocracy of Jerusalem.

King Herod had had the Temple platform extended over the south, east and west slopes of Mount Moriah. The slopes beneath were filled with stone vaults and halls which lie hidden today by the Islamic Dome of the Rock and adjoining buildings. One complex of honeycomb halls and vaults was known as Solomon Stables (a misnomer because they were built by Herod). Subterranean passages and ramps linked Solomon Stables to the upper public buildings known as Herod's Royal Portico, or the Hanuyot. About 30 A.D. the Hanuyot became the new location of the Sanhedrin (previously located in the Chamber of Hewn Stone). This reorganization allowed moneychangers and other dealers to operate in the lower sections of the Hanuyot which was regarded as only semi-sacred. The upper levels of the Hanuyot are now part of the El Aqsa Mosque complex. Recent archeological evidence supports

Christ's encounter with the merchants and moneychangers. An unsuspected passage abutting the inner side of the southern wall of the Temple Mount was discovered due to extensive repairs made at the lowest foundation levels of the El Aqsa Mosque after a fire in 1969. This passage apparently linked various underground vestibules, halls and stables with the sacred Temple precinct itself.

When the Jews questioned Jesus' angry attack upon the merchants, he answered them:

Destroy this temple, and in three days
I will raise it up.

JOHN 2:19

No one, not even his disciples, understood Jesus was referring to God's spirit that was housed in his earthly body. The only temple they could comprehend was the solidly built ediface built by Herod., Nevertheless, they were to recall his statement at a later date.

One man among the Pharisees named Nicodemus had contemplated the miracles wrought by Jesus. Although he did not want to disclose his interest in Jesus to the other Pharisees, his desire to know more led him to secretly come by night to Jesus. In his heart he knew Jesus had been sent by God. Nicodemus sensed that for all their outward appearance of holiness, he and his fellow Pharisees lacked the spiritual communion with God that was so evident in the life of Jesus. Because this lack was known to Jesus, he tried to penetrate Nicodemus' ingrained habits of conformity, respectability and tradition by lifting their conversation to a spiritual plane.

Verily, verily, I say unto thee,
Except a man be born of water and of the Spirit,
He cannot enter into the kingdom of God.
That which is born of the flesh is flesh;
And that which is born of the Spirit, is spirit.

JOHN 3:5 - 6

Jesus tried to open his understanding by exampling the wind which blows but cannot itself be seen; neither does anyone know where it comes from or where it goes, nor where it starts or stops. So it is with God's Spirit which cannot be seen but must be received through faith in its existence. Just as the wind has power to turn windmills which pump water or generate electricity, so God's Spirit has power to regenerate the lives of men.

For the first time in his ministry, Jesus was revealing his plan of salvation which was misunderstood and rejected by Nicodemus who could only perceive what he already knew of the laws of nature. He was unable to open his mind to a broader concept or to reach the spiritual plane Jesus was presenting to him. Sadly, Jesus went on to tell him no man had reached heaven; only the heaven-sent Son of man could attest to its reality and that only by believing in Him was eternal life possible.

For God so loved the world,
That he gave his only begotten Son,
That whosoever believeth in him should not perish,
But have everlasting life.
JOHN 3:16

Leaving Judea, Jesus again departed for Galilee. This time he travelled through Samaria, the shortest route from Jerusalem to Galilee, although this route was normally avoided because of the long-standing enmity between the Jews and Samaritans. It is probable that his journey took him from Bethany, about twenty miles over a rough, steep road, to Jacob's Well which was just south of Sychar and at the junction of several ancient roads. (Today Jacob's Well remains the most certified ancient landmark in Palestine.) Jesus stopped to rest at the well while his disciples went into Sychar to buy food. While he rested, a Samaritan woman approached the well and Jesus asked her for a drink. The woman was most surprised, first, because of the traditional enmity between their people and secondly, because it was not lawful for a Jewish Rabbi to speak to a woman publicly. When Jesus told her that if she only knew who he was she would ask him for living water, the woman was filled with disbelief until he further revealed that he knew all about her past sinful life. Perceiving him to be a prophet, she answered that she knew the Messiah, called Christ, would come. Jesus answered her:

> **I that speak unto thee am He.**
>
> **God is a spirit; and they that worship him**
> **Must worship him in spirit and truth.**
> **JOHN 4:26, 24**

As the disciples approached the well, the woman returned to the city to tell everyone about Jesus and how he had told her everything she had ever done. The Samaritans were so impressed, they came out to hi m requesting he tarry with them. For two days he remained and many believed that he was indeed Christ, the Savior of the world. By the simple testimony of a sinful woman many were brought to believe that this Jesus was the long sought Messiah.

Word of the miracles performed by Jesus in Jerusalem preceded him as he again entered Galilee. People gathered wherever he went. Those spiritually hungry sought him out, and multitudes of afflicted and diseased pressed forward to touch him and be healed.

After a night spent in prayer, Jesus gathered together his disciples and from them chose twelve apostles in whom he would instill faith, knowledge, power and authority to carry on his mission. These twelve, chosen to be his closest associates, would become the repository of his teaching and miracles. The apostles were primarily simple Galileans. Several were fishermen, one a publican and one a Zealot. Judas, the traitor, was the only one from Judea.

Peter's name heads every list of apostles. Jesus saw through the impetuous nature of Peter to the rock-like strength, dependability and loyalty that would endure in the end, and because of this potential named him "Cephas." He and his brother, Andrew, were fishermen, as were James and John. Peter was married; his mother-in-law and Andrew lived with him, yet he opened his home to Jesus during their Galilean ministry. Peter was the chief spokesman of the apostles and one of the three apostles closest to Jesus.

Little is recorded of Andrew but it is known he was a disciple of John the Baptist and first brought Peter to the Lord. He appears to have been sensitive to the Lord in that it was he who told Jesus of the lad's five loaves and two fishes.

James, son of Zebedee, was one of Christ's inner circle along with Peter and John. James and John were kindred in spirit and faithfully served as "fishers of men." Because of their ardent championship of Jesus, he called them "Boanerges" (sons of thunder). Their mother Salome, was also a follower of Jesus and believed to be related to Mary, the mother of Jesus.

John, the "beloved disciple" alone was faithful to Jesus during his trial and crucifixion and was entrusted with the care of Mary, mother of Jesus. His love and trust in the Lord was evident in all his actions and his spiritual recognition of Christ is portrayed in every word in the Book of St John.

Philip was of Bethsaida. From the first, his faith in Jesus was strong.

He it was who sought out Nathanael to tell him:

We have found him,
Of whom Moses in the law,
And the prophets, did write.
Jesus of Nazareth,
The son of Joseph.

JOHN 1 : 45

He was of a practical disposition, insisting on facts. It is possible, judging from his Greek name, that he was a Hellenistic Jew.

Nathanael (Bartholomew) lived in Cana and little is known of him. He was one of those who witnessed the water turned to wine at the wedding feast. Jesus said he was an Israelite without guile.

Nathanael understood from the beginning that Jesus was the Son of God, the King of Israel.

Thomas, also identified as Didymus (twin), showed little imagination, but he was loyal in the face of danger. He followed Jesus to Jerusalem even when he believed it might mean his death also. Because of his insistence on truth, the world knows him as "doubting Thomas" but profited by his doubt as proof was given to all of the nail scarred hands of Jesus.

Matthew, also known as Levi, was one of the hated publicans, a tax collector of Capernaum who gladly left his job and security to follow Jesus.

> And Levi made him a great feast
> In h s own house
> And there was a great company
> Of publicans and others
> That sat down with them.
>
> Luke 5:29

Even the disciples of Jesus must have been shaken when he called out a publican to follow him, and it was a test of their faith to sit at supper with such a gathering. By befriending these people, the worst of sinners, Jesus "made Himself of no reputation" to the scribes and Pharisees.

Nevertheless, Matthew was one of the disciples chosen to become an apostle and from this time forth would cast off the name of Levi and become Matthew (the Gift of God). His training and education would enable him to set down the most complete outline of the sermons and teachings of Christ.

James, son of Alpheus, was also called James the Less. His mother, Mary, was present with Mary Magdalene and Salome as they waited at the cross and when they went to Jesus' tomb. These were women who followed and ministered to Jesus when he was in Galilee. He was brother to Joses for Mark declares Mary was the mother of James the Less (the younger) and of Joses.

Little is known of Thaddeus (Lebbeus) who is listed in Matthew and Mark, but not in Luke or in Acts. Perhaps Thaddeus was replaced by Judas (not the one who betrayed him) in the latter part of Jesus' ministry.

> Is not this the carpenter's son?
> Is not his mother called Mary?
> And his brethren James, and Joses (the Greek form of
> Joseph) And
> Simon and Judas?
>
> MATTHEW 13:55

In all likelihood James the Less and Judas were brothers of our Lord Jesus. Some people hesitate to believe that Mary was ever anything but immaculate and remained a virgin, but the Bible reads otherwise:

> **Then Joseph did as the angel of the Lord had**
> **bidden him**
> **And took unto him his wife;**
> **And knew her not till**

She had brought forth her firstborn son.
MATTHEW 1:24, 25

Simon, the Canaanite, was also called Zelotes or Zealot indicating he belonged to that radical group of Jewish patriots who opposed the Roman government. Accepting Simon as one of the apostles linked Jesus with the revolutionary movement directed against the Romans. Herod and Pilate would not overlook this charge when Jesus came before them.

Judas Iscariot, believed to be from Kerioth in the south of Judea, was the only apostle not a Galilean. Jesus entrusted their finances to him. Un- questionably, Jesus was aware of the shortcomings of this man; yet he was chosen as one of the twelve. Seemingly the eleven did not mistrust him because he was not singled out by them as the "betrayer of Jesus" during the last supper. Judas Iscariot remained loyal as long as he thought that Jesus would usher in an earthly kingdom. Possibly he didn't realize his betrayal of Jesus would result in death. Ironically, Judas filled a position foreordained to precipitate the death of Jesus. If Judas' soul had been right with God, he would never have betrayed the Lord; in which case, someone else would have been available, for without the betrayal there would have been no cross; and without the cross, no resurrection.

The Sermon on the Mount was given especially for the Apostles who had just been chosen but was shared by a multitude of others who crowded close to hear what the Master had to say. These teachings have continued to influence mankind throughout the ages. This sermon taught moral principles far beyond human standards and outlined the righteousness of His heavenly kingdom. These ideals exceeded the laws of Moses, particularly as they were depicted by the Scribes and Pharisees. He taught a strange, new doctrine: Blessed are the poor in spirit, the meek, the merciful, the pure in heart, and those that sorrow, those persecuted for righteousness sake for their reward is in heaven. Jesus did not promise them a better life on this earth but gave them a hope of a blessed heavenly kingdom. He didn't expect men to attain this by themselves, but through a power that would come from Him.

He made it clear it was not his intention to break the laws of Moses, but to fulfill them. The laws themselves had become so cluttered with restrictions imposed upon them by the scribes and Pharisees that it was impossible for any man to obey them all. Yet, Jesus confounded them by quoting a law "Thou shalt not kill" and adding "it is just as dangerous to be angry." Also, their soul would be in as much jeopardy lusting in their heart as committing adultery.

Jesus taught: If you be struck on one cheek, turn the other; love your enemies; give to those who ask of you; if someone steal your coat, give him your cloak also. Do these things that you be the children of your heavenly father, for he sends the sun to shine on good and evil and the rain to fall on the just and the unjust.

Jesus gave the classic example of prayer with the Lord's Prayer which he meant to be just that -- an example; for the Lord desires prayers from the heart, not by rote.

Jesus cautioned against trusting earthly treasure; for your heart will be where your treasure is and it is far better to have treasure laid up in heaven.

> **No man can serve two masters;**
> **For either he will hate the one,**
> **And love the other;**
> **Or else he will hold to the one,**
> **And despise the other.**
> **Ye cannot serve God and mammon (the world).**
> **MATTHEW 6:24**

His advice was to seek first the kingdom of God and his righteousness, and all things shall be added -- every daily necessity.

Jesus taught: Judge not, that ye be not judged. Ask and it shall be given you; seek, and ye shall find; knock, and it shall be opened unto you. Beware of false prophets - ye shall know them by their fruits. Wide is the gate and broad is the way that leads to destruction, but narrow is the way which leads to life and few find it. For not everyone shall enter into the kingdom of heaven.

Jesus concluded with a warning: Everyone who hears these sayings and does them is like a wise man who builds his house on a rock for when the winds and rain come, the house will stand. But those that hear and do them not are like foolish men who build on sand and cannot withstand the storm.

When Jesus ended his sermon, the people were astonished at his doctrine for he taught as one having authority, and not as the scribes.

Jesus honored faith and worked miracles through the faith of others. A centurion's servant was healed in the self-same hour that he asked, even though the servant was some distance away. Another was healed of palsy because the men who brought him to Jesus had faith. A woman with an issue of blood for twelve years knew she could be healed if she could only touch the robe of Jesus, and through her faith was made whole. Through faith, blind men received their sight and lepers were cleansed.

Frequently the Pharisees were enraged by Jesus disregard for the Sabbath which began at sunset on Friday and ended at sunset on Saturday. There were restrictions laid down in the Mosaic law, but these did not compare with the prohibitions added by the Rabbis. Moses law said no work was to be done on the Sabbath; but the Rabbis listed thirty-nine works; to do any of these could result in being stoned to death. From "reaping" evolved "plucking a head of wheat." Even writing two letters of the alphabet together was forbidden. The observance of the numerous rules laid down by the Rabbis had become impossible, even for themselves. Thus, "intention" was made a method of evasion. It was unlawful to eat an egg on the Sabbath, but if the hen that laid the egg was "intended to be eaten, then it became lawful to eat the egg. Even though the Pharisees used subterfuge to evade their own laws, they were uncompromising toward others.

The Pharisees saw the disciples of Jesus plucking heads of wheat as they walked through a field on a Sabbath and accused them. Jesus defense of his disciples was that if the Pharisees understood mercy and sacrifice, they would not condemn the guiltless; after which he entered their synagogue. Seeking to trap Jesus, they asked if it was lawful to heal on the Sabbath. Jesus answered that it was lawful to do well on the Sabbath and promptly healed a man's withered hand. While the Pharisees sought to destroy him, Jesus withdrew. A multitude followed him and he healed them all.

Jesus returned to Jerusalem for a feast, possibly the Passover, and on the Sabbath he went to the pool of Bethesda, located in the northeast corner of Jerusalem, just inside the east wall. This was a spring-fed rectangular pool having "five porches." This is thought to be the pool found during repairs in 1888, deep below the present level of Jerusalem with remnants of a five-arched portico. This pool periodically bubbled, fed by an intermittent spring. It is believed that this water contained curative mineral powers. Possibly imagination and superstition had created a legend of the angel who stirred the waters and healed the first one who stepped in.

Undoubtedly, Jesus knew he would find a large number of sick and also that the Pharisees would be watching him. Jesus chose to heal a man who had waited thirty-eight years for help.

And therefore did the Jews persecute Jesus,
And sought to slay him,
Because he had done these things
On the Sabbath day.

JOHN 5:16

Jesus defense was:

My Father worketh hitherto, and I work
For the works which the Father Hath
given me to finish,
The same works that I do, bear witness of me,
That the Father hath sent me.

JOHN 5:17 & 36

Again Jesus found it necessary to leave Jerusalem. The Jews were more determined than ever to kill this Sabbath-breaker who called God his own Father; claiming divinity, the right to judge, and that eternal life was through Himself. They considered His claims blasphemy of the highest order.

On his return to Galilee, Jesus was continually besieged by innumerable multitudes, so much so that they trod upon each other. Often Jesus would be forced to enter a ship to put a safe distance between himself and the crowds. But he continued to teach. More and more of ten it would be in simple parables about things they were familiar with, such as the parable of the sower and the seeds that fell by the wayside, upon stony places, among thorns, and some into good ground. Then Jesus explained to his disciples that the seed was the word of the kingdom and the seed planted in good ground is he that hears and understands.

Again, he taught of a man who planted good seed only to have an enemy plant tares with the wheat and to advise that they should both grow together until the harvest, when the tares would be gathered and burnt and the good preserved.

After the multitude was sent away, his disciples asked for an explanation. Jesus explained "He that planted good seed is the Son of man, the field is the world, the good seed are the children of the kingdom; but the tares are the wicked ones of the devil, the harvest is the end of the world and the reapers are angels who shall cast the tares into the fire. A similar parable compared the kingdom of heaven to a net cast into the sea and every kind of fish gathered into it. The good fish were saved, the bad cast away. So shall it be at the end of the world. There shall be wailing and gnashing of teeth.

Jesus' purpose in teaching parables was so those who were honest-hearted and loved God would hear and understand. Others would not.

Another time, Jesus taught a parable of a rich man whose barns were full and he thought to himself to build greater barns to store even more, giving no thought to anything but the enjoyment and ease he would have from them. But that very night God demanded his soul.

So it is with anyone who lays up treasure for himself, yet is not generous with God. Jesus told his disciples to take no thought for themselves, but to seek first the kingdom of God.

Another time Jesus taught "Blessed are those servants whom the Lord, when he comes, finds watching. Or if he comes in the second or third watch, if he finds them so; for if the good man had known what hour the thief would come, he would have watched and not let his house be robbed."

> Be ye **therefore ready also;**
> **For the Son of man cometh at an hour**
> **When ye think not.**
>
> **LUKE 12:40**

Another parable was of a certain man who made a great supper and invited many. They all made excuses. So the master sent his servants into the streets and lanes of the city to bring in the poor, the maimed, the halt and the blind. Still the table was not full. Again, the servants went out into the highways and byways to compel them to come, "For none who were first invited to my supper, " saith the master, shall come."

At other times he told of the prodigal son, about the dishonest steward, the lost coin, the hidden treasure, the pearl of great price and many more. Each parable had a superficial meaning for those who just came for healing and miracles, and a deeper meaning for the more perceptive who wanted to understand his teachings.

When John the Baptist had heard, while he was in prison, of the works of Christ; he sent two of his disciples to inquire if he was the Messiah. Jesus sent the disciples back to tell John:

The blind receive their sight,
And the lame walk,
The lepers are cleansed,
And the deaf hear,
The dead are raised up,
And the poor have the gospel preached to them
And blessed is he
Whosoever shall not be offended in me.
MAITHEW 11:5, 6

John's disciples continued to baptize and to witness in his stead for a time, but as he himself had said, he must diminish. Herod Antipas had imprisoned him in his summer palace, the Castle of Machaerus, on the east shore of the Dead Sea. This was not far enough away from Galilee for Herodias, who wanted him permanently stilled. John remained in this prison for approximately a year during which time Herod saw him occasionally and was greatly influenced by John in spite of John's denunciation of his incestuous marriage. He knew John was an honest and holy man and was reluctant to have him killed as Herodias desired. But the day came during a birthday celebration that Herod held a great feast for his lords, captains and chief men of Galilee in his summer palace. After the guests had dined and drank their fill, Salome, teenage daughter of Herodias, came to dance before them. The dance was so exotic and pleasing to Herod that he promised her anything she asked of him. At her mother's instruction, she asked for the head of John the Baptist. Much as Herod regretted his rash promise and understood he had been tricked, his pride and fear of criticism by his drunken guests kept him from refusing her outrageous request. He had John beheaded in the prison and his head brought to Salome, who took it to her mother.

And his disciples came and took up the body and buried it and went and told Jesus who had had the highest regard for John, at one time saying:

> He was a burning and a shining light;
> And ye were willing for a season
> To rejoice in his light.
>
> JOHN 5:35

And, again:

> Verily I say unto you
> Among them that are born of women
> There hath not risen a greater
> Than John the Baptist.
> Not withstanding he that is least
> In the kingdom of heaven, is greater than he.
>
> MATTHEW 11: :11

Jesus withdrew into a desert place, but even here the crowds followed. From time to time Jesus would seek solitude and a respite from the demands of the people, but they went to any length to find and follow him. Jesus' com- passion for them led him again to heal the sick. Since they were in a desert place there was nothing to eat and when evening came the disciples would have sent everyone home. But not Jesus. He took the only food available - five loaves and two fishes; broke it and as the disciples passed it out to five thousand men, plus women and children, it multiplied so much that after everyone had eaten their fill there remained twelve baskets full. No man had seen miracles such as this and Jesus' fame spread even more extensively than before. Jesus had no trouble sending them home now; they were eager to be the first to tell someone of this latest miracle.

Then he sent his disciples across the sea while he went into the mountain alone to pray. As the disciples approached the middle of the sea, a sudden storm arose, threatening to capsize the ship. In the midst of the storm, Jesus came to them, walking on the water. The distraught disciples believed they were seeing a spirit (ghost) until Jesus spoke. Then Peter said:

> Lord, if it be thou,
> Bid me come unto thee on the water.
> And he said, Come.
> And when Peter was come down out of the
> ship,
> He walked on the water to go to Jesus.
> MATTHEW 14:28, 29

Peter did walk on water until his faith failed him. When he took his eyes off Jesus and saw the angry sea his feet rested upon, he began to sink. Imme- diately Jesus stretched forth his hand and saved him. As they came into the ship, the wind ceased, the waves were calm and the disciples worshipped him. Could there be any doubt in their minds as to His true identity? Who else but the one who created the earth and all that is within it could command the wind and the sea?

> And to make all men
> See what is the fellowship
> Of the mystery,
> Which from the beginning of the world
> Hath been hid in God,
> Who created all things by Jesus Christ.
>
> EPHESIANS 3:9

The apostles had seen Jesus perform many strange miracles that could only have been accomplished by supernatural powers, yet they did not fully understand Him. Once He asked them whom the people thought that He was and they answered John the Baptist, Elijah, or another of the old prophets is risen again. But when He asked them whom they thought he was, Peter answered:

> Thou art the Christ,
> The Son of the living God.
>
> MATTHEW 16:16

> Jesus blessed him for his spiritual understanding and
> said: Upon this rock I will build my church
> And the gates of hell shall not prevail against it.
> And I will give unto thee
> The keys of the kingdom of heaven.
>
> MATTHEW 16:18, 19

This prophetic pronouncement would shortly be fulfilled. As yet, their understanding was not complete; but the day was coming when God's true church would be founded upon the revelation given to Peter that Jesus was the foundation and the cornerstone of the church and that He was truly Jesus the Christ.

CHAPTER XII

MORE THAN A SON

From this time forth, Jesus began to prepare his disciples for his last trip into Jerusalem. They could not comprehend when he told them he would be killed and raised again the third day; even though they were perfectly willing to accept a resurrection of prophets of old!

Jesus took Peter, James and John into a high mountain, believed to be Mount Hermon which is over 9,0 00 f eet above sea level. From its peak can be seen Lebanon, Damascus, Tyre and Car mel, the mountains of Upper Galilee and the Gordan Rift to the Dead Sea. It is covered with snow the year around and its shining whiteness is reflected in the Sea of Galilee. But that day, this shining snow-covered peak was rivalled by the transfiguration of Jesus, for his f ace shone as the sun and his garments white as the light. As the disciples beheld Jesus, there appeared Moses and Elijah talking to Him. As Peter spontaneously off ered to make shelters for them, unconsciously hoping they would stay, a cloud overshadowed them and a voice said "This is my beloved son..." The disciples f ell to their faces and when they again looked up Jesus was alone. The vision they had seen would be a great comfort and reassurance in the days ahead, even though Jesus commanded them not to speak of what they had seen until the Son of man was risen from the dead.

The last three months of Jesus' ministry was concentrated in Judea and Perea. He had gone again to Jerusalem and aroused such hostility that his enemies had tried to stone him. Aware his time was short, Jesus chose seventy disciples and dispatched them by twos throughout Judea into every city and place that he would come to. He sent them forth without money or extra clothing, but they were not empty-handed, for to the m He gave power.

> And the seventy returned again, saying,
> Lord, even the devils are subject to us
> Through thy name.
>
> LUKE 10:17

Bethany was a small, out-of-the-way village less than two miles from Jerusalem. A footpath over the Mount of Olives led to this village. Jesus spent many nights here during the final months of his ministry at the hospitable home of Martha, Mary and their brother, Lazarus. This was the scene of his greatest miracle. Mary, Martha and Lazarus had come to know Jesus intimately and to have much faith in him. At a time when he was several days from Bethany, Lazarus became mortally ill and the sisters sent word to Jesus. His disciples were puzzled when for two days he made no move to return to Bethany. They knew he loved Lazarus and his sisters, but concluded he was afraid to go so close to Jerusalem after the recent stoning attempt. How little they understood Christ, even when he said that Lazarus slept and now he would go awaken him. When

Jesus spoke of the death of Lazarus, they still persisted in believing he only slept. Yet, believing Jesus was in danger by returning, the disciples still followed when Thomas said "Let us also go, that we may die with him."

When Jesus returned, Lazarus had already lain in the grave four days. Martha went to meet him, knowing if he had come in time Lazarus would not have died. Jesus told her:

> Thy brother shall rise again.
> I am the resurrection, and the life:
> He that believeth in me,
> Though he were dead, yet shall he live.
>
> JOHN 11:23, 25

Martha assured him she believed him to be the Christ, the Son of God, which should come into the world. Having said this, she went to call Mary.

When Mary arose hastily, many Jews who had come to mourn and to comfort the sisters, followed her. As she fell weeping at the feet of Jesus, the Jews wept with her. Jesus groaned in the spirit, and as he asked where Lazarus lay, Jesus also wept. When the Jews observed his grief they wondered among themselves why Lazarus had not been healed as had so many others.

Lazarus had been placed in a cave with a stone rolled against the opening as was the custom. When Jesus commanded, the stone was reluctantly removed; for all knew how terribly decomposed a body became in four days and, as Martha had commented, "by this time he stinketh." Nevertheless, Jesus spoke in a loud voice,

Lazarus, come forth.

JOHN 11:43

And he that was dead came forth. Shrouded in grave clothes and his face bound about with a napkin. It was usual to place a cloth around the face; that is, under the chin to keep the mouth closed as rigor mortis set in. He may even have been loosely bound, at least sufficiently to allow for some movement. Lazarus, miraculously alive, firm of flesh and sound of limb came forth that the glory of God might be revealed in these last days. Seeing, many believed Jesus could be none other than the Messiah, prophesied of old, but others returned to the Pharisees and told them what Jesus had done.

The chief priests and the Pharisees met together to decide what measures they could take to rid themselves of this man Jesus. Not all of the Sanhedrin or the Pharisees plotted against him for Nicodemus and Joseph of Arimathea, who belonged to the Sanhedrin, and certain others of the Pharisees who warned Jesus against Herod, had no desire to see him harmed.

The chief priests hastily called together certain of the Sanhedrin, who banded together with some Pharisees, all of whom were much concerned for their own positions. They could not allow Jesus to continue performing miracles; all the people would soon be proclaiming him the Messiah. The chief priests were concerned about losing their authority, while the Pharisees could foresee the inevitable, bloody clash between the Romans and Jews for the Messiah could have no other role than king of the Jews. As there was no easy solution, they turned to Caiaphus, high priest for twelve years and son-in-law of Ananus who was of a powerful, priestly family and also a high priest at one time. Caiaphus had held the position of high priest for much longer than others before him because he ruled through craft and compromise, first under Gratus and then under Pontius Pilate. Privately, each one of this council knew they were seeking the death of Jesus, yet none wanted to be the first to express this thought. Not so Caiaphus, as he cunningly gave them a reason.

Ye know nothing at all,
Nor consider that it is expedient for us,
That one man should die for the people,
And that the whole nation perish not.
JOHN 11:50

Caiaphas did not realize that he had prophesied a deeper truth than he knew and that it was the will of God that His Son should die, not just for a nation, but for all of the children of God for all time.

Jesus, aware they were plotting his death, withdrew until the week of the Passover. In an effort to prepare his disciples, he told them he would be betrayed, condemned to death, mocked by Gentiles, scourged and crucified, then raised from the grave on the third day. They were uncomprehending and bewildered.

Many people came to Jerusalem before the Passover to purify themselves and they spoke quietly among themselves, speculating whether Jesus would come for they knew the chief priests and the pharisees had commanded that anyone knowing of his whereabouts should report it.

Then, six days before the Passover, Jesus came to Bethany. Many Jews knew he was there and came to see him and also to see Lazarus whom he had raised from the dead. This caused the chief priests to consider putting Lazarus to death too.

The next day many people came out from Jerusalem to meet Jesus as he walked toward the city. They surrounded him, waving palm branches and crying

Hosanna;
Blessed is the King of Israel
That cometh in the name of the Lord.
JOHN 12:13

As they neared a small settlement, Jesus sent two of his disciples into the village to bring him a colt, the offspring of a donkey, that they would find tied there. He assured them the owner would consent to its use by the Lord. Never before had Jesus been seen riding, but his hour had come to proclaim his Messiahship to the world. Riding upon a donkey, a colt which had never been ridden, fulfilled prophecies by Isaiah and Zachariah. The donkey was a symbol of peace and of humility, which proclaimed his mission as Prince of Peace. A "colt which no man had ever ridden" showed respect for Jewish religious belief that an animal which had served a profane purpose was not fit for sacred use, again underlining his divinity. Also, what ordinary man could mount a colt for the first time and have such perfect control over that animal that he could sedately ride in the midst of a tumultuous, cheering crowd? In every way, Jesus was proclaiming his Messiahship as the meek and humble Savior. The crowd, which continued to grow, spread branches of figs, almonds and olive trees, as well as their garments, before him as a special mark of honor, as they continued to believe he was coming to be their political king, with power from on high, as they shouted "Blessed is the Kingdom of our father David: and He that cometh now in the name of the Lord!" and "Blessed is He that cometh, the King of Israel, in the name of Jehovah."

By now they had reached a height on the Mount of Olives that looked across at Jerusalem in all its splendor. The beautiful temple built by Herod of gleaming white stone, capped by its golden facade; the square tower of Antonio, the barracks of the Roman soldiers, and everywhere extravagant palaces of the priests and the wealthy. In the lower part of the city stood the Tower of David, built upon the same terraces where he had once dwelt. As Jesus looked upon this holy city, he paused and wept over it, saying:

> I(thou hadst known, even thou,
> At least in this thy day,
> The things which belong unto thy peace!

But now they are hid from your eyes.
For the days shall come upon thee,
That thine enemies shall cast a trench about thee,
And compass thee round,
And keep thee on every side.
And shall lay thee even with the ground
And thy children with thee;
And they shall not leave in thee
One stone upon another,
Because thou knowest not
The time of thy visitation.

LUKE 19:42 - 44

Jesus foresaw the time when the Roman army, led by Titus, would besiege and destroy Jerusalem. The crowds, densely packed around Jesus, began to grow still as they sensed he would not accept a material kingdom which would set them free of Roman bondage. They had never understood the Spiritual kingdom he offered them, so they grew uneasy and one by one drew away. These would become a part of the crowd soon to shout "crucify him." As the remainder entered Jerusalem through the Golden Gate, those within the city asked who Jesus was and instead of shouting as before that he was King of Israel, they said "This is Jesus the prophet of Nazareth of Galilee."

Jesus went directly to the temple and observed that corruption and greed were profaning his Father's house as they had before his first visit. Once again the porticos were filled with money-changers, the courtyards and lower hallways had become cattle markets. Again, his indignation rose and he began to cast out those who sold and bought in the temple, and overthrow the tables of the money-changers and the seats of those who sold doves. And he told them:

My house shall be called the house of prayer;
And ye have made it a den of thieves.

MATTHEW 21:13

Certain Greeks had come to worship at the Passover, so it was to Jews and Gentiles that Jesus preached in the last week. His enemies had tried in vain to lay hands upon him, but they feared the populace, many of whom still worshipped Him. He returned to Bethany for the night, but the next day went again to the temple. The council sent delegations to trap him but on every occasion Jesus answered in such a way that they could not fault him. With each attempt, they grew more determined he must die; but still the crowds around him prevented them. Ordinarily at odds with each other, Sadducees, Pharisees and Herodians were of one mind in their desire to trap Jesus. There were a few from each group who wished him no harm, but fear of loss of respect from their peers kept them silent. The rejection of Israel to the spiritual truths he had offered them deeply affected Jesus, even though he understood them. They would gladly have proclaimed Him king over an earthly empire but wanted no part of a spiritual kingdom that held forth a hint of deprivation and sacrifice before attainment.

Again Jesus tried to prepare his disciples:

Ye know that after two days
Is the feast of the passover.
And the Son of man is betrayed
To be crucified.

MATTHEW 26:2

At this same time the chief priests, scribes and elders of the people were gathered together at the palace of the high priest, Caiaphas, to devise a means of killing Jesus. They had decided against acting on the Passover as the people might rebel at his death on that holy day. As the priests sought how they might kill him, Judas Iscariot sought them out to betray Jesus. They willingly agreed to pay him thirty pieces of silver to lead them to Jesus. Thirty pieces of silver was a ridiculously small price to pay; it was only as much as their law required as compensation f or killing a slave and was an undeniable insult to Jesus.

One can only speculate on why Judas had turned against Jesus, or whet her he realized this betrayal would actually culminate in death. At any rate, Satan found his way into the heart of Judas and from that moment he looked for a way to betray Jesus. Ironically, through this betrayal, Judas played a part in the master plan for man's salvation; but he could be used for this purpose only because his heart was not right with God. Plainly, the treachery of Judas was a part of the divine plan; a prophecy in scripture that had to be fulfilled.

Now the first day of the feast of unleavened bread
The disciples came to Jesus, saying to him,
Where will thou that we
Prepare for thee to eat the passover?

MATTHEW 26:17

Jesus delegated this assignment to Peter and John, advising them to go into Jerusalem where they would find a man bearing a pitcher of water and to follow him home. This man would have a large chamber furnished and prepared for the Passover. Tradition has it that he was father to John Mark, who is known to have resided in Jerusalem. Even if the man was unknown to the apostles, he would have been easily identifiable, as it was most unusual for a man to carry water - that was a task for women.

When the Passover was prepared, Jesus assembled with his twelve disciples to partake of the Passover. Even today, some Jewish homes have a large upper room reserved for guests. The furnishings would have included a large table open on one side to facilitate serving, and surrounded on three sides by couches on which the guests reclined. This was a popular custom introduced by the Romans.

The Passover, then, as it does today, followed a standard pattern or ritual. (First, an opening prayer, then the blessing of the wine. The first of four cups of wine was passed around the table.)

As Jesus sat with his disciples, he told them how much he had desired to eat the Passover with them before he suffered.

For I say unto you, I will not anymore eat thereof
Until it be fulfilled in the kingdom of God.
And he took the cup, and gave thanks,
And said, "Take this and divide it among yourselves."

LUKE 22:15-17

(Then each person took herbs, possibly parsley, and dipped in salt water. The head of the family takes one of three loaves of unleavened bread and puts the others aside. At this point, the story of the passover is recounted and Psalms 113 and 114 are sung. Psalms which so beautif ully sing praises to the Lord our God who dwelleth on high and before whom the earth trembles at his presence. The second cup of wine is filled and passed around, then before the meal begins, all wash their hands.)

Everyone had entered the upper room and gone directly to the table. Possibly Peter and John were remiss, for it was customary to offer guests a basin of water to wash their feet when they entered a room and before reclining on couches. For whatever reason this omission occurred, Jesus chose this time to pour water into a basin, wrap a towel about himself and begin to wash the feet of his disciples. When he came to Peter, Peter, in his impetuous manner, protested until the Lord said to hi m:

What I do thou knowest not now;
But thou shall know hereafter.
If I wash thee not, thou has no part of me.

JOHN 13:7, 8

This was comparable to the Tabernacle Plan the Lord had given Moses when he said "For Aaron and his sons shall wash their hands and feet when they go into the tabernacle; they shall wash wit h water that they die not." Jesus presented more than one critical lesson at this point, for he demonstrated that the servant is not greater than his Lord. Jesus had com e as a servant and the mission of his disciples would remain the same. Glory would not be theirs in this world.

(Grace was said and bread broken. Bitter herbs were dipped in sauce and distributed.)

> And as they were eating,
> Jesus took bread, and blessed it,
> And brake it, and gave it to the disciples,
> And said, Take, eat, this is my body.
> > MATTHEW 26:26

> Verily, I say unto you
> One of you which eateth with me
> Shall betray me.
> > MARK 14:18

The center place on the couch at one end of the table was the seat of honor, undoubtedly reserved for Jesus; that to the right of it was called "the bosom of the Father." Since the guests reclined on their left elbow and John, the beloved disciple, was to the right of Jesus, the least movement brought him toward the breast of the Lord. Peter, who sat on Jesus' left, beckoned to John to ask who was the betrayer.

> He then, lying on Jesus breast
> Sayeth unto him, Lord, who is it ?
> Jesus answered. He it is, to whom I give the sop,
> When I have dipped it.
> And when he had dipped the sop,
> He gave it to Judas Iscariot, the son of Simon.
>
> JOHN 13:26

The disciples heard Jesus tell Judas, "That thou do, doest quickly," but they assumed he had been sent on an errand. Judas left immediately and it was night; it was not only actual but symbolic that Judas departed from the light into darkness.

(The Passover La m b was served at this time.)

After Judas' departure the passover lamb was eaten. This was a leisurely process for it all must be consumed. Jesus spoke to his disciples of the short time he would be with them until God would be glorified in the Son of man. At this point he instituted the Lord's Supper. Breaking the bread laid aside earlier and passing round the third cup of wine, he said:

> Take, eat; this is my body.
> And he took the cup and gave thanks
> And gave it to them saying
> Drink ye all of it
> For this is my blood of the new testament,
> Which is shed for many
> For the remission of sins.
>
> MATTHEW 26:26, 27

This was only one more of the mystifying things Jesus had told them recently. Only later would they truly understand the events of this night. Jesus continued to pour all he could into them on this last evening. Later they would understand. He told them not to be troubled, but to believe in God and in himself. He told them:

> I am the way, the truth and the life;
> No man cometh unto the Father but by me.
> If ye had known me,
> Ye should have known my Father also;
> And from henceforth ye know him
> And have seen him.
>
> JOHN 14: 6, 7

Still Philip asked to see the Father; he could not conceive that Jesus and the Father were one and the same. All he could see was a mortal body like his own. Jesus told them it was expedient that he go away, that he might send them the Comforter who would abide with them forever.

> Even the Spirit of truth;
> Whom the world cannot receive
> Because it seeth him not, neither knoweth him.
> But ye know him;
> For he dwelleth with you,
> And shall be in you.
>
> JOHN 14:17

> The Comforter which is the Holy Ghost
> Whom the Father will send in my name.
> He shall teach you all things,
> And bring all things to your remembrance,
> Whatsoever I have said unto you.
>
> JOHN 14:26

The supper was concluded with the fourth cup of wine. And when they had sung the last hymn (the Jewish Passover would include Psalms 115 through 118 and conclude with Psalm 136) they went into the Mount of Olives where they would spend the night.

> When Jesus had spoken these words,
> He went forth with his disciples over the brook Cedron.
> JOHN 18:1

The most convenient road crossed the bridge which led over the Tyropean, a deep valley through which ran the brook Cedron, to the temple and from there through the Golden Gate to the Mount of Olives. Only the priests could go into the temple by night, so Jesus and his disciples were forced to descend into the lower part of town and around the temple. Perhaps they took a graduated pathway which has been uncovered recently. It is a roadway with steps wide enough to allow donkeys and camels to go up and down without undue strain.

As they walked, Jesus warned them they would all be offended because of himself before the night was over. Peter hastily said the others might, but never would he deny the Lord. In his heart he meant it, but Jesus knew before the cock had crowed twice, Peter would have denied hi m three times.

Gethsemane was a garden on the Mount of Olives where Jesus and his disciples had come before. Today this beautiful spot is marked by ancient olive trees. That night it witnessed the most fervent prayers ever uttered. Taking Peter, James and John, Jesus went a short distance from the others. He was exceedingly sorrowful and asked them to pray not to be drawn into temptation and to watch as, drawing apart from them, he began to pray.

> Father if thou be willing,
> Remove this cup from me.
> Nevertheless, not my will
> But thine be done.
>
> LUKE 22:42

As he prayed more earnestly, his sweat, like great drops of blood, fell to the ground. Although it rarely occurs, medical science recognizes that under extreme stress and anguish, small capillaries burst and bleed through the skin. No man had ever been put to a greater test, for he was faced with a choice - he could die for remission of sins and fulfill the mission which had ordained his presence on earth or save himself, for he had the power to do so. God's plan of salvation had always called for shedding of blood for redemption of mankind and only one free from sin could pay that price. More likely what caused the greatest stress was concern that his mortal body could not stand the punishment it would receive in the next few hours and that it might die before his commission was fulfilled. Added to all of this was acceptance of every sin of man; taking them all upon hi mself - drinking that bitter cup of corruption, licentiousness, murder, hate, revenge, greed and every evil thought and deed of mankind.

Twice he checked on his disciples and they were sleeping. He awoke them to pray that they would not f all into temptation;

but after all they had recently seen and heard, they were too emotionally drained to heed him.

Jesus went apart again and prayed for the Lord's will to be done, after which he returned a third time to awaken his disciples to tell them his time had come to be betrayed. As he was speaking, Judas approached with a great multitude of people sent by the chief priests, Pharisees and elders of the people. A multitude that consisted of Captains and troops from the temple guard armed with swords and rabble armed with staves and clubs

Judas went directly to Jesus and identified him with a kiss. Then, as they began to lay hold on him, Peter, always quick to react, drew a sword and cut off the ear of Malchus, servant of the high priest, but Jesus' touch healed it. Then he turned to the multitude, and the high priests, reminding them he had sat daily teaching in the temple and they had not laid hold on him.

> **Thinkest thou that I cannot pray to my Father,**
> **And he shall presently give me**
> **More than twelve legions of angels?**
> **But how then shall the scriptures be fulfilled?**
> **MATTHEW 26:53-54**

Then all of the disciples forsook him and fled. The captains, possibly of the Roman troops, and officers of the Jews took Jesus and bound him and led him away to Annas.

Excavations have led to the belief that the palaces of Annas and Caiaphas shared a common courtyard. Annas, who had been high priest from 6 to 15 A.D. and had secured this position successively for his sons and for Caiaphas, his son-in-law, had allied himself politically to the Roman officials. He owned the famous Bazaars of Annas, which provided a monopoly on the sale of sacrificial animals and controlled the stalls of the money-changers. He had every reason to hate Jesus, who threatened the priesthood and his lucrative business. From the first time Jesus had cleansed the temple, he had sought to trap him. At last, Jesus stood before Annas for a preliminary hearing. Annas questioned Jesus about his disciples and his doctrine. Privately he wanted to ascertain how large a following Jesus had. When he received no satisfactory answer, he sent him bound to Caiaphas who had assembled all the chief priests and elders and scribes who sought for witnesses against Jesus to put hi m to death and found none for no witnesses could agree. At last Caiaphas asked him "Art thou the Christ, the Son of God?" When Jesus answered "Thou hast said," it was an admission that he was truly the Christ. At this, the high priest rent his clothes and pronounced it blasphemy and the rest agreed it warranted the death penalty. But they were powerless to act. Blasphemy would not be recognized by Pilate and only the Roman government had authority to pass a death sentence.

Then did they spit in his face and buffeted him;
And others smote him with the palms of their hands,
Saying, Prophecy unto us, thou Christ,
Who is he that smote thee?

MATTHEW 26:67, 68

Peter and John followed Jesus at a distance and anxiously waited in the courtyard. One of the maids of the high priest saw Peter warming himself before a fire and asked if he wasn't with Jesus of Nazareth; but he denied it and as he went to the porch, the cock crew. The maid saw him again and began to say "This is one of them," and Peter denied it again. About an hour later another affirmed "Of a truth this fellow also was with him, for he is a Galilean." (For their manner of speech and Galilean accent set them apart from other Jews.)

And Peter said, Man,
I know not what thou sayest.
And immediately, while he yet spoke,
The cock crew.
And the Lord turned and looked upon Peter.
And Peter remembered the word of the Lord
"Before the cock crow, thou shalt deny me thrice."
LUKE 22:59-61

Early the next morning, at the first break of day, the whole Sanhedrin Council was convened to give a semblance of formality to the mock trial that had been perpetrated in the home of Caiaphas. Jesus had been brought from Caiaphas to the Sanhedrin Council Chamber, the Hall of Hewn Stone in the temple. This hall was partially within the sacred temple area and part on profane ground. The judges entered from the temple side; the accused from the other side. Then, with undue haste they questioned him: "Art thou the Son of God?" "Ye say that I am," he replied. That was all the Sanhedrin needed to pass sentence of blasphemy. From the Hall of Hewn Stone, Jesus was bound and delivered to Pilate.

Pontius Pilate was the Roman Procurator from 26 to 36 A.D. Usually he dwelt in Caesarea, but during the feasts he made it a practice to be present in Jerusalem, at which time he resided in the Antonio Fortress, adjacent to the temple. It was normally garrisoned by a contingent of six hundred men. The fortress was built on the highest point of the city; 300' x 150' with square towers rising some 90 feet at each of the four corners. From it, stairs descended to the temple courts. It too was honeycombed with subterranean passages and contained a large, open, paved court which was uncovered around 1930. Remains of this fortress, which was destroyed in 70 A.D., have yielded sufficient evidence to confirm its identity.

Pilate had experienced the fanaticism and stubborn inflexibility of the Jews whenever he violated one of their religious restrictions. Pilate had marched his unit of Roman soldiers into Jerusalem displaying a metal standard bearing the image of the emperor. Infuriated Jews thronged to Caesarea demanding its removal and Pilate had been forced to yield to their demands. Another time, Pilate had placed shields of gold in the Antonio Fortress. Jews, and even Herod Antipas and king Agrippa, protested this act but Pilate refused to remove them.

Pilate had made a serious mistake in planning when he arranged for a system of aqueducts to supply the city with water and cover the cost from the temple treasury. Only with the greatest cruelty and the most stringent measures was he able to suppress the resulting revolt.

The Jews posed a serious threat to Pilate wit h their knowledge that the Roman emperor supported his appointed governors only as long as they raised sufficient revenue and kept peace within their provinces. Pilate could afford no more blunders.

The Jews believed they could obtain the desired death sentence, but they were aware that the accusation of blasphemy would not suffice with the Roman government. Pilate would have no part in anything involving their religion; therefore, they accused him of sedition and forbidding tribute to Caesar and claiming to be Christ the King.

Jesus was brought into the Judgement Hall for questioning by Pilate, who asked "Art thou the King of the Jews?" Jesus answered:

> Thou sayest that I am a king.
> To this end was I born.
> And for this cause came I into the world,
> That I should bear witness unto the truth.
> Everyone that is of the truth heareth my voice.
>
> JOHN 18:37

Pilate asked "What is truth?" but without waiting for an answer returned outside to the waiting crowd, convinced that Jesus was harmless and told them he could find no fault with him. At this, the people became more vehement; accusing Jesus of stirring up the people from Galilee to Jerusalem. As soon as Pilate heard that Jesus belonged under Herod's jurisdiction, he sent him to Herod, who was also in Jerusalem at this time.

Herod was especially glad to receive Jesus, for he had desired to see him for a long time and hoped to witness miracles. Jesus was a great disappointment to Herod, for Jesus would not so much as speak to the man who had beheaded John the Baptist. Frustrated, Herod and his men of war mocked hi m and arrayed him in a gorgeous robe, demeaning the idea he could possibly be Christ the King. They sent him again to Pilate.

Upon being confronted by Jesus for a second time, Pilate tried to reason with the people. Herod had found nothing worthy of death in Jesus and Pilate still found no fault in him, so in hopes of appeasing the people, he had him scourged.

Although the Romans used this means of punishment upon the Jews and upon slaves, they considered it too degrading for Roman citizens.

Scourging had been practiced by the Jews since ancient times for certain offenses. Their laws proscribed no more than forty stripes. In practice, only thirty-nine were given; thirteen on the chest and thirteen on each shoulder. The Romans used a flagella, a whip with several leather thongs, each ending in irregularly shaped leaden balls or sharp pieces of bone or spikes which cut deeply into the flesh, exposing bones and veins.

It was customary to scourge victims before crucifixion. The victim was stripped of his clothes and his hands tied to a low column or stake with his back bent and exposed to the merciless whipping that stripped flesh from bones and almost always ended in fainting, or even death.

In Jesus case, this was made even worse by the cruel mockery which followed,

> And the soldiers plaited a crown of thorns,
> And put it on his head,
> And they put on him a purple robe,
> And said, Hail, King of the Jews!
> And they smote him with their hands.
>
> JOHN 19:2, 3

Pilate then brought Jesus before the people again in hopes they would relent when they saw the horrible suff ering he had already endured. But it was not to be. They were merciless. Neither would they hear of releasing Jesus instead of Barabbas, for it was the custom to release one Jewish prisoner at the Passover. Instead, they cried out "Crucify him, crucify him!" When Pilate sought one last time to release Jesus, the Jews threatened him:

> If thou let this man go,
> Thou art not Caesar's friend:
> Whatsoever maketh himself a king
> Speaketh against Caesar.
>
> JOHN 19:12

Pilate knew if this accusation reached Caesar, his political appointment would be speedily withdrawn, he would be stripped of all property and banished to some undesirable outpost of the Roman empire.

When Pilate saw he could not prevail against the mob who was clambering for the crucifixion of Jesus, he called for water and washed his hands before them, demonstrating he was not guilty of the death of this innocent man whom he was beginning to suspect was more than a man.

**Then answered all the people, and said,
His blood be on** us, and **on our children.**
MATTHEW 27:25

Jesus own garments were again put upon him. The cross he would soon be nailed to was placed upon his bloody, lacerated shoulders and they led him away to crucify him. This foul deed would not be committed within the walls of Jerusalem, as if that would exonerate the people! Their destination was called Golgotha in Aramaic and Calvary in Greek; the place of the skull, a high place or hill adjacent to the tombs and burial place of the city.

A great multitude of people followed as a Centurion and four of Pilate's soldiers led Jesus from the Antonio fortress, down narrow cobblestone streets to the Ephraim gate on the northern side of Jerusalem. Although the distance was not far, Jesus was so weakened and exhausted he was physically unable to carry the heavy burden placed upon him. As he fell under the grievous load, the soldiers realized it was utterly impossible for Jesus to go another step without help. Seeing Simon, a Cyrenian, passing by, they ordered him to carry the cross.

Cyrene was a city of North Africa which had a large colony of Jews. Simon was the father of Alexander and Rufus, converts of Jesus. Undoubtedly, the crucifixion of Jesus had a profound effect upon Simon and his family.

It was a mixed crowd that followed Jesus: priests, there to witness the execution of the death sentence passed upon Jesus; throngs of the idle and morbid curiosity seekers (ever ready to witness violence and bloodshed);

Jesus' mother and a few of the women followers; John, the only disciple; and other women who also wailed and lamented as they saw his suffering. For these women Jesus stopped; and lifting his weary, battered, blood streaked head, he turned to them and said:

> Daughters of Jerusalem, weep not for me,
> But weep for yourselves, and for your children.
> For behold, the days are coming,
> In which they shall say
> Blessed are the barren,
> And the wombs that never bare.
> Then shall they begin to say to the mountains,
> Fall on us; and to the hills, cover us.
> For if they do these things in a green tree,
> What shall be done in the dry?

LUKE 23:28-31

Within a generation, the people of Jerusalem would experience extreme suffering and death. Not only at that time, but throughout history the Jewish people have continued to suffer persecution and wholesale slaughter by the nations they have resided in. It is only because of God's desire to preserve a remnant of the people, that a Jewish nation survives today.

He was also referring to the people's rejection of himself when he came to earth as their Saviour. If they would kill him at this time, what rejection was yet to come from future generations who would refuse him or corrupt Christianity, and what retribution and judgement awaits them ?

It was 9:00 A.M. when Jesus was placed on the cross between two criminals. No other means of execution provided the extreme physical anguish and torture afforded by crucifixion. The muscles of the body, under severe torture, alternately grow rigid and are seized by violent spasms, accompanied by immeasurable pain. The lungs, heart, and head become congested as they fill with fluid and the resulting chest pain becomes atrocious. This condition is also accompanied by extreme thirst. Breathing can only occur when, by excruciating effort, the weight of the body is lifted by the very arms and legs nailed to the cross. Death is gradual and may take hours, or even days.

Initially, Jesus was offered a drink of wine mingled with myrrh (a drugged drink to deaden the senses) but he refused it. He would not shirk any part of the price to be paid for man's redemption, but preferred to remain in full possession of all his powers throughout his ordeal.

He was stripped of his clothes and nailed naked to the cross, adding final humiliation to all that he had previously suffered. Four soldiers each took an article of his clothing and then they cast lots for his outer garment, which was woven without a seam. Again, scripture was fulfilled:

> **They parted my raiment among them,**
> **And for my vesture they did cast lots.**
> **PSALMS 22:18**

It was customary to publicize the crime that had been committed. This afforded Pilate an opportunity for revenge as he ordered a superscription of Jesus' accusation be set over his head, reading:

> **JESUS OF NAZARETH,**
> **THE KING OF THE JEWS.**
> **JOHN 20:19**

This title was written in Hebrew, Greek and Latin so all who passed by could read it. The chief priests of the Jews, displeased with this, protested to Pilate that the sign should not read "Jesus, the King of the Jews" but should show only that Jesus claimed to be king of the Jews. Pilate adamantly refused to let the sign be changed.

Many people unfeelingly reviled and mocked Jesus as they observed him on the cross. Shaking their heads, they observed he was the one who claimed he would rebuild the temple in three days if it were destroyed and they wondered that he had no power to save himself. One of the malefactors hanging by Jesus also insolently remarked "If thou be the Christ, save thyself and us." But the other one reproached him for his unbelief and asked Jesus to remember him when he came into his kingdom. Here was a man, a criminal, who was able to perceive of and believe in a spiritual kingdom. Faced with death, he believed in a future life and in Christ. Despised and outcast on earth, he received the greatest of promises because of his trust and faith:

> And Jesus said unto him,
> Verily I say unto thee,
> Today thou shalt be with me
> In paradise.
>
> LUKE 23:43

At noon, a great darkness descended upon the land. For three hours an unearthly stillness and oppressive nightfall bound the earth. No sunlight penetrated the heavy shadow of doom. Just as the people walked in spiritual darkness, so was darkness physically imposed upon them this day. Uneasiness, foreboding and doubt assailed the people.

In the heavy gloom, Jesus observed John, the only disciple who had not left him, and a small group of women, Mary (his mother), Salome (John's mother), Mary the wife of Clophas and Mary Magdalene standing by the cross. Jesus committed his mother into John's charge and from that hour John took her into his own home to care for her.

After this, Jesus knowing all things were now accomplished,
That the scripture might be fulfilled, said:
I THIRST.

JOHN 19:28

The soldiers filled a sponge with vinegar, put it upon hyssop and lifted it to his mouth. (Hyssop was a reed-like four to five feet tall sorghum plant used to sprinkle the blood of the sacrificial lambs on the doorposts at the Passover in Egypt. It was also used during purification rites for lepers and plagues.) What could have been more fitting to serve the Lord with as he completed his worldly ministry of salvation as the sacrificial lamb who shed his blood for us and took on the sins of mankind, requiring purification and cleansing?

At the ninth hour (3:00 P.M.), Jesus cried out with a loud voice, saying:

Eloi, Eloi, lama sabachthani?
Which is, being interpreted,
My God, my God, why hast thou forsaken me?
MARK 15:34

As Jesus' spirit departed from him and he gave up the ghost, there was a great earthquake, the veil of the temple was torn from top to bottom, and graves burst open disgorging the dead who walked the streets of Jerusalem as the city was shaken to its very foundations.

Pandemonium reigned, chaos and panic were everywhere and there was no place to hide from destruction or from the fact they had killed the King of the Jews, for Jesus last words were:

It **is finished.**

JOHN 19:30

As the centurion witnessed his death, he said "Truly, this man was the Son of God."

CHAPTER XIII

A DOOR WILL OPEN

Only later would the significance of the supernaturally torn veil become apparent. This veil, a palm-breadth thick was sixty feet long and thirty feet wide. It hung in Herod's Temple, separating the Holy from the Most Holy places. It was woven in such a fashion that even an earthquake could not have torn it. Only the hand of God could account for its being torn apart "from top to bottom." Previously, once a year the High Priest entered the Holy of Holies. Nobody else was ever allowed in this hallowed place.

But now, the way had been opened to all who desired to enter God's presence.

> **Having therefore, brethren,**
> **Boldness to enter into the holiest**
> **By the blood of Jesus.**
> **By a new and living way,**
> **Which he hath consecrated for us.**
> **Through the veil.**
> **That is to say, his flesh.**
>
> **HEBREWS 10:19, 20**

Ever hidebound and ruled by the laws they had imposed upon themselves, the Pharisees could not override these restrictions. Not even the supernatural events that had just transpired. Because the Sabbath would begin at sunset, and the Passover Sabbath was of greater than average importance, it was imperative to remove the bodies from the crosses. First, they must die. To this end, the soldiers broke the legs of those on either side of Jesus. Without the use of their legs, the victims were powerless to raise themselves enough to breathe, and so they suffocated. When they came to Jesus, they saw he was already dead, so they did not break his legs, but pierced his side, and there came out blood and water. Again, scripture had been fulfilled for it prophesied "A bone of him shall not be broken."

Mosaic law required the body of an executed man must not be left to hang on the cross, but must be buried the same day. But, according to the Talmud, bodies of condemned criminals were put in pits to remain until the flesh rotted away. Only then could their bones be returned to their families. There was only one recourse. Roman law could override the Talmud.

> **Joseph of Arimathea, an honorable counselor,**
> **Which also waited for the kingdom of God, came**
> **and went in boldly unto Pilate,**
> **And craved the body of Jesus.**
>
> **MARK 15:43**

After confirmation of his death by the Centurion, Pilate released the body to Joseph. Nicodemus, who first came to Jesus by night, accompanied him as he attended the body. They bought fine linen, removed the body of Jesus from the cross, wrapped him in the linen and laid him in a new sepulcher, belonging to Joseph of Arimathea, which was hewn out of rock. All of this was done in haste. The body was not washed or anointed as was customary, although Nicodemus had brought 100 pounds of myrrh and aloes. (Possibly in atonement for not having accepted Jesus' teaching while he was yet alive.) The women who had come with Jesus from Galilee followed as far as the grave and observed the sepulcher and how his body was laid. They watched as the men rolled a huge stone against the entrance. Stones similar to millstones were customarily used to close the cave openings and fitted into a grooved slot before the entrance. Sepulchers were carved from rock, with a rock shelf on one side for the body.

The women then returned home and prepared spices and ointments for the time they could attend the body after the Sabbath. During the trial and crucifixion all the disciples except John, had gone into hiding. Some to Bethany, some back to the Upper Room or to John's house and to the home of Joanna. It remained for the women to attend to Jesus. They anxiously awaited the first opportunity to return to finish the burial preparation for Jesus. This could not be done until after the Sabbath, and then not until the first hint of dawn to lighten their way. Jewish custom also required a visitation to grave sites on the third day. Experience had proved some were only in a coma and had returned to life. In this case, there was no hope of life. They had witnessed his gruesome and final death throes.

Unknown to the women, the Chief Priests and Pharisees had come to Pilate requesting he set a guard at the sepulchre to prevent Jesus' disciples from removing the body and then claiming his resurrection. Pilate refused to accede to any further demands regarding

Jesus, but reminded them they had temple troops of their own. These were subsequently assigned to watch closely, on penalty of death if the body should disappear.

Mary, the mother of Jesus; Salome, Joanna, Mary Magdalene, and other women, hastened to the sepulchre at first dawn. They brought sweet spices that they might anoint him and as they walked they wondered who would help them roll the stone from the doorway.

> And behold, there was a great earthquake;
> For the angel of the Lord descended from heaven,
> And came and rolled back the stone from the door,
> And sat upon it.
> His countenance was like lightening,
> And his raimant white as snow:
> And for fear of him the keepers did shake
> And became as dead men.
> And the angel answered and said unto the women,
> Fear ye not: For I   know that ye seek Jesus
> Which was crucified.
> He is not here: for he is risen, as he said.
> Come, see the place where the Lord lay.
>
> MATTHEW 28:2 - 6

With fear and trembling the women glanced into the tomb and saw it was empty. In great haste they ran to tell the disciples. They were much perplexed even after the angel reminded them that this was what Jesus had foretold. The disciples received the women's account of their visit to the tomb with disbelief. Only Peter and John felt a need to verify their story and ran to see for themselves. John arrived first, stooped, and looking in, saw the linen cloths lying empty. Simon Peter was the first to enter the sepulchre and noticed:

The napkin, that was about his head,
Not lying with the linen clothes,
But wrapped together in a place by itself.
JOHN 20:7

Only then did John enter, and as he looked closely and observed the neatness of the linen cloths, he realized this was no work of thieves; yet even now they did not understand what had transpired.

Mary Magdelene had followed Peter and John and after they returned to the other disciples, she remained at the sepulchre, weeping. As she stooped and looked in again, she saw there were two angels within the sepulchre, sitting one at the head and the other at the foot of where the body of Jesus had lain. As she was asking where his body had been taken, Jesus appeared and spoke to her. Mary Magdelene, for whom Jesus had cast out seven devils, was the first to see and touch Jesus.

Later he appeared to Cleopas, and another, as they walked in the country to Emmaus and they knew him not until he went into their home and broke bread with them. At this time he vanished from their sight and they hastened back to Jerusalem and found the eleven disciples gathered together. The disciples were quick to say that Jesus had also appeared to Peter.

That same evening Jesus appeared to all of his disciples, except Thomas. He had suddenly appeared in the midst of them, saying "Peace be unto you." They were terrified, supposing they had seen a ghost. To reassure them, Jesus said:

Behold my hands and feet;
That it is I myself:
Handle me, and see;
For a spirit hath not flesh and bones,
As ye see me have.

LUKE 24:39

Then he ate fish and honeycomb before them just as mortal man might do. Or, as the Lord had done many years before when he appeared to Abraham and ate butter, milk and veal that was set before him.

When Thomas heard from the other disciples that they had seen the Lord, he could not believe - only a personal experience would suffice. Ever compassionate, Jesus appeared again eight days later in their midst, inviting Thomas to touch his pierced side and nail scarred hands.

And Thomas answered and said unto him,
My Lord and my God.

JOHN 20:28

The disciples returned to Galilee at a loss to know how to conduct their lives. They now believed that Jesus had died and rose again, but their lives. were purposeless without his leadership. They had resumed their former occupations and were fishing the Sea of Galilee when they next saw Jesus. Peter, James, John, Andrew, Nathaniel and two other of his disciples had fished all night and caught nothing. From the shore Jesus called out to them.

> **Cast the net**
> **On the right side of the ship,**
> **And ye shall find.**
>
> **JOHN 21:6**

When they did as the Lord bid them, they drew in a net laden with fish, and Jesus served them a meal of fish and bread. At this meeting Jesus absolved Peter's guilt for the three times he had denied the Lord and committed him to lead the other disciples in spreading the Lord's gospel to all people, even though there was the implication of his own eventual crucifixion.

For forty days Jesus appeared at diverse places, showing himself alive and speaking of things pertaining to the kingdom of God. For the last time, Jesus led his disciples to Bethany and gave them final instructions:

> Go ye therefore, and teach all nations,
> Baptizing them in the name of the Father,
> And of the Son, and of the Holy Ghost.
>
> MATTHEW 28:19

> And behold, I send the promise of my Father upon you:
> But tarry ye in the city of Jerusalem,
> Until ye be endued with power from on high.
>
> LUKE 24:49

They saw him rise and disappear from their sight as he was carried up into heaven. Two angels appeared before them with the promise Jesus would return in the same manner in which he departed. But this time Jesus had left them with a peace of mind they had not had before.

They obediently returned to Jerusalem and to the upper room where, for about seven days, they praised and blessed the Lord. During this time Peter felt a necessity to elect another disciple to replace Judas Iscariot; so after careful consideration and much prayer, Matthias was duly appointed. They were unaware that in the near future Jesus would call out his own disciple, Saul of Tarsus, whom he would use mightily.

The Passover was significant because it celebrated deliverance through the sacrificial lamb, but at the same time a wave offering or sheaf of the first fruits of the harvest was presented to the priest. Fifty days later, on Pentecost, came the harvest festival. On this Pentecost morning they were all with one accord in the upper room; about one hundred twenty men and women, including Mary, the mother of Jesus.

> And suddenly there came a sound from heaven
> As of a rushing, mighty wind.
> And it filled all of the house
> Where they were sitting.
> And there appeared unto them
> Cloven tongues like as of fire,

> And it sat upon each of them.
> And they were all filled with the Holy Ghost
> And began to speak with other tongues,
> As the Spirit gave them utterance.
>
> ACTS 2:5

Wind and fire are God's symbols for spirit and cleansing. What better means could have been employed by God for the initial ushering in of the Holy Ghost into the hearts of men and what better method than control of the tongue, which is the last part of man to surrender to God's will?

Jerusalem was filled with devout Jews out of every nation who were drawn to this strange, exciting event. They were amazed to hear these unlettered Galileans speak to them of God in familiar languages of Egypt, Libya, Italy, Africa, Arabia and of every nation. Some marvelled, but others mocked; accusing them of drunkeness.

Peter stood in the midst of the disciples and with a boldness born of the Holy Ghost responded to the multitude. This is that of which Joel did prophecy:

> And it shall come to pass
> In the last days, saith God.
> I will pour out my Spirit upon all flesh:
> And your sons and your daughters shall prophecy.
> And your young men shall see visions,
> And your old men shall dream dreams:
> And on my servants and on my handmaidens
> I will pour out in those days of my Spirit
> And they shall prophecy.
>
> ACTS 2:17 - 18

Peter spoke of Jesus of Nazareth, by whom God performed miracles and signs, who had been slain and crucified with their consent, but that God could not allow him to remain in the grip of death and had raised him up. This Jesus was the one whom God had promised would sit on the throne of David. King David himself had prophesied of the resurrection of Christ, that his soul would not be left in hell, nor his flesh see corruption.

> Therefore, let all the house of Israel know assuredly,
> That God hath made that same Jesus
> Whom ye have crucified, both Lord and Christ.
>
> ACTS 2:36

Those who heard this were filled with guilt and fear. They anxiously inquired what they could do now to be saved. Through enlightenment that accompanied the infilling of the Holy Ghost, Peter, and all of the disciples now understood that Jesus was God manifest in the flesh and that his instructions to baptize in the name of the Father, and of the Son, and of the Holy Ghost meant:

> **Repent, and be baptized every one of you**
> **In the name of Jesus Christ**
> **For the remission of sins.**
> **And ye shall receive the gift of the Holy Ghost.**
> **For the promise is unto you, and to your children,**
> **And to all that are afar off,**
> **Even as many as the Lord our God shall call.**
>
> **ACTS 2:38, 39**

That very day about three thousand people received the Holy Ghost. This began God's new testament church which originated in his holy city, Jerusalem, and which was only possible through the shedding of his precious blood and through his resurrection. Signs and wonders were done by the apostles. Miracle healings were wrought in his name and the Lord added to the church daily such as should be saved.

Their strongest opposition came from the Sadducees who had never accepted the concept of resurrection. As they saw these apostles turning many to Jesus through preaching his resurrection from the dead, they turned to the high priests, Annas and Caiaphas, who accosted the apostles, asking by what power, or by what name, they worked these miracles.

Peter, filled with the Holy Ghost, was undaunted by the high priests. (What a change from a few short weeks before.) He replied, "by the name of Jesus Christ of Nazareth, whom ye crucified and whom God raised from the dead. This is the stone which was counted for nothing of you builders, but has become the chief cornerstone."

> **Neither is there salvation in any other;**
> **For there is none other name**
> **Under heaven given among men,**
> **Whereby we must be saved.**
>
> **ACTS 4:12**

When the stone had been rolled from Jesus' tomb and the angel appeared before the temple guards who were stationed there to ensure this very thing did not happen, they had returned to the high priests in extreme trepidation. Upon consultation, the high priests and council members gave money to the soldiers to spread the rumor that the disciples of Jesus had stolen his body. Even today many people prefer this version to the truth.

God's truth cannot be hidden. In his perfect time it will always be revealed. Proof of Jesus' resurrection was recently given to the world by a group of scientists, many of whom believed the Shroud of Turin was fraudulent and whose chief desires were to discover how the image had been imprinted upon this old linen cloth.

The first documented appearance of the shroud was about 1357 A.D. during its exhibition in France by the widow of Geoffrey de Charney. Local authorities ordered the exhibition stopped, doubting it was the true burial cloth of Jesus. Only after the shroud was given to the House of Savoy was it accepted as the true Shroud of Christ. The Roman Catholic Church has never possessed it nor claimed it to be genuine.

An interesting fact that warrants consideration is a look at early paintings of Christ. The oldest existing paintings are of a young, beardless, emaciated man. Not until around the Sixth Century A.D. did the art works of Jesus show him as bearded, long-haired and with Semitic features; a picture we are familiar with and also the image appearing on the Shroud of Turin. The image that changed artists' concepts of Christ was probably a cloth found in 525 A.D. in a niche above the west gate of Edessa in Turkey during repairs. It was called the "Holy Mandylion" or "Image of Edessa."

It was taken to Constantinople, the capital of the Eastern Empire, in 944

A.D. Here it was regarded as holy and the true likeness of Jesus. Emperor Justinian built a shrine and cathedral for the Mandylion (Arabic for veil or handerchief).

In 1204 A.D. it disappeared. No historical record exists to prove who possessed it until 1357 A.D., but during 1204 A.D. the Fourth Crusade captured Constantinople. Chronicles mention a Frenchman, Otto de la Roche took the linen cloth measuring 1.10 meters by 4.36 meters back to France. It bore marks of blood and a faint outline of a human body. Geoffrey de la Charnay was also on the roster of crusaders.

The shroud is fourteen feet by three and one-half feet wide, yet the Mandylion displayed only a head. Its true nature may have been hidden for centuries by placing the folded shroud within a framework so that only the head was visible. This may have been deliberate because burial garments were considered unclean and many would have viewed it with abhorrence if they had seen it in its entirety. Sensitive photographs of the shroud reveal an eight-fold pattern of folds, which would substantiate this theory.

Only rarely has the shroud been exhibited; but in 1898 Secondo Pia, an Italian photographer, was allowed to photograph it and then, for the first time, the image was discovered to be a negative.

Reverse imaging was unknown until the invention of photography in the nineteenth century. This discovery excited scientific interest which culminated in the Shroud of Turin Research Project in 1978. Physicians and pathologists noted the remarkable, anatomical details of the image which surpassed medical knowledge of the fourteen century. The image is of a man, nearly six feet tall, thirty to thirty-five years old and approximately one hundred seventy-five pounds; a healthy, well-built man, showing every indication of scourging, beating, slashes, cuts, bruises, crucifixion and side wound in accord with the sufferings of Christ. Every wound is scientifically correct.

In 1976, a team of United States Air Force scientists made a computer analysis of the photographs taken by Secondo Pia and made the startling discovery that it was three-dimensional. This was in no way normal. As scientists probed deeper into the little evidence available to them, they became more intrigued with its mysteries, until in 1978, it was finally arranged for forty scientists, with the most advanced and sophisticated equipment known to man, to do a detailed examination of the shroud.

They discovered the image is superficial, that only the topmost fibers are discolored. In no instance does the image penetrate through the material, or even through the individual threads. Yet there is greater density in some areas than others. The image is brightest, or densest, in areas where the body touched the cloth and lighter where the body was some distance from it. It was deter mined this produced the three-dimensional eff ect.

An important area of examination was the apparent bloodstains which were anatomically correct, although there was no evidence they had been smeared or dislodged as would happen if the cloth was removed from the body. All the tests, from electromagnetic spectrum tests, ultraviolet floures cence photographs (which indicated blood serum separation) and tests for protein and iron gave positive results.

Every test they could devise ruled out all pigmentation, vegetable or mineral. They tested for chemical reactions of ammonia, body sweat, urea and oil. Every substance would have penetrated the linen, and, furthermore, a fire which had burnt portions of the linen in 1532 A.D. would have affected any chemically produced image.

Next, they tested for scorch, which logically could produce the image on the Shroud. Although the scientists agree it is probable that the image was produced by scorching, it is slightly different from that resulting from the known fire in 1532.

Even though unwilling to speculate on the man's identity, the scientists agreed evidence warranted a belief that the image was formed by a real corpse; that it could not have been produced by a forger, and that it dates back to the First Century A.D.. The presence of pollen from the Middle East points to the right geographical area; an impression of coins covering the eyes appears to be the size and likeness of the lepton of Pontius Pilate which was coined between 14 and 37 A.D. Furthermore, the weave of the linen was typical of the Middle East in the First Century A.D.

Evidence pointing to the likelihood that this is the Shroud of Jesus Christ is astronomical. Facial features are Semitic, the beard and long hair parted in the middle are Jewish. The image shows evidence that the back hair formed a pigtail. This was a common hair style of Jewish men in the First Century.

In 1968 a Jewish burial site was uncovered in Jerusalem. One skeleton was of a crucified man. A seven inch nail was still imbedded through his heel bones. The bones showed evidence nails had been driven just above the hands between the radius and ulna bones and the leg bones were broken. This would be normal for a crucified body. A common misconception is that people were smaller two thousand years ago than today, but burial sites of that period contain evidence their size was similar to today's. One tomb contained a skull with coins dating during the reign of Herod Agrippa (41 - 44 A.D.). Although evidence of crucifixion was discovered during archeological explorations, such as the above examples, none corresponded to the Biblical details of Jesus' crucifixion. Only the Shroud of Turin matches detail for detail.

Body wounds were determined to be of a multi-thonged whip with dumbbell shaped metal or bone on the ends. Numerous puncture wounds on the head differ from those on the body, perhaps a crown of thorns was responsible. Facial bruises and swellings and a possible broken nose attest to repeated slaps and blows to the face. There is evidence of bruising and scraping across the upper back indicating a heay object was carried after the scourging. This is apparent because the scourge wounds in this area have been altered from those on the rest of the body. There is evidence of cuts and bruises on the knees as would be the case during a fall. Logically this occurred when Simon was recruited to carry the cross. The wrists have been pierced at the base of the palms and through the feet. (Nails through the palms would have ripped out; anatomically the nails would have to be in the wrists to support body weight. Also, the Greek word for hand used in the Bible included the wrist.) The legs were not broken, but a stab wound in the side is evident. The scientists identified a mixture of blood and water which flowed vertically down the right side of the chest to the waist and then across the back. Medical evidence indicates both the pleural cavity and the heart were pierced and the pattern of blood flow on the shroud is that of a man already dead. Bloody fluid resulting from a severe whipping would settle in two layers, heavier blood cells at the bottom and lighter serum at the top. If pierced, the blood would flow out first, then the lighter serum. A crucified man's abdomen would swell; this was especially evident in the three dimensional image constructed by the scientists.

Evidence of hasty burial is also consistent with Biblical accounts of Jesus' burial. The body was placed on the cloth and then it was folded over the front of the body which had not been washed or prepared for burial.

It appears the beard is covering some unseen object when viewed as three dimensional and the beard is divided. A chin band might be responsible for this and could be the napkin that was about the head of Jesus. It was natural to bind the chin to keep the mouth closed just as it was to place coins on dead men's eyes to keep them shut.

The Shroud of Turin presents a wealth of evidence that it belongs to Christ and that he rose from the dead. It is understandable that scientists could not account for the method of scorch or how the body could be removed without disturbing blood clots. Man can witness the supernatural, but not explain it.

> **Behold my servant, whom I have chosen;**
> **My beloved, in whom my soul is well pleased;**
> **I will put my Spirit upon him,**
> **And he shall show judgment to the Gentiles.**
> **He shall not strive, nor cry;**
> **Neither shall any man hear his voice in the streets.**
> **A bruised reed shall he not break,**
> **And SMOKING FLAX shall he not quench,**
> **Till he send forth judgment unto victory.**
> **And in his name shall the Gentiles trust.**
> **MATTHEW 12:18 - 21**

Jerusalem continued to witness the miracles wrought through the disciples of Jesus as they assembled in Solomon's porch of the temple. Each day new believers were added. Faith was so strong that even being in Peter's shadow brought healing. Multitudes came from the cities around Jerusalem, bringing their sick and those filled with unclean spirits. They were all healed.

Once more the high priest and Sadducees moved against the disciples and put them in the common prison. Even prison bars could not hold them. When the apostles were upbraided by the Sanhedrin Court for teaching in the name of Jesus, they answered:

We ought to obey God rather than men.

ACTS 5:29

As the believers increased, the apostles appointed others to assist them. Steven, a man full of faith and of the Holy Ghost, was one of these. When he preached in a certain synagogue, the Jews became extremely angry at his words; knowing he spoke truth, but unwilling to accept it. They brought him before the Sanhedrin Court and testified falsely against him. As Steven presented his own defense, they noted his face appeared as the face of an angel. He spoke of Moses and of the God of their fathers who brought them out of Egypt; of their fathers' rejection of God and of the golden calf they made in his stead and to whom they offered sacrifices; how God then gave them up to the worship of idols until David found favor before God, after which they again backslid; of the prophets they had persecuted and slain. Then Steven addressed the court directly:

Ye stiffnecked and uncircumcised in heart and ears,
Ye do always resist the Holy Ghost,
As your fathers did, so do ye.

ACTS 7:51

This was too much for them. As Steven looked toward heaven and beheld Jesus, they ran upon him with one accord; cast him out of the city and stoned him to death. Saul of Tarsus, a young man of the Sanhedrin, did not join in the stoning but stood by and watched Steven die as he guarded the cloaks of those who stoned him. From that moment Saul was greatly tor mented in spirit and expended every moment in persecuting the Jesus-name people, going from house to house to search them out and imprison them. From this time the persecution grew more intense from every quarter, but this did not stop them. Great persecution only scattered them into Galilee and into Samaria - which was God's intent from the beginning.

Armed with letters from the Sanhedrin Court giving hi m authority to arrest any Christians he discovered, Paul journeyed toward Damascus, Syria where a church had been established. Somewhere on his week's journey, after crossing the Jordan River and travelling northeast toward Damascus, a great light, brighter than the noonday sun shone upon him and he f ell to the ground as he heard a voice saying:

> Saul, Saul, why persecutest thou me?
> And he said, Who art thou, Lord?
> And the Lord said,
> I am Jesus whom thou persecutest;
> It is hard for thee to kick against the pricks.

ACTS 9:4 - 5

Trembling and astonished, he inquired what he should do and was instructed to go on to Damascus; there he would be told more.

Blinded and helpless, he was led to his destination. For three days he was without sight and neither ate nor drank until Ananias, sent by the Lord, came to pray for him.

> Brother Saul, the Lord, even Jesus,
> That appeared unto thee in the way as thou camest,
> Hath sent me,
> That thou might receive sight
> And be filled with the Holy Ghost.
>
> ACTS 9:17

Immediately receiving his sight, he arose and was baptized. With this came insight and total conviction that Jesus was Lord. Straightway he preached Christ in the synagogues, confounding those who heard him and knew he had been their deadly enemy only days before. Saul preached with such ardor that Orthodox Jews sought to kill him; now he was one of the persecuted! The disciples smuggled him out of Damascus and sent him to Jerusalem. He was again met with distrust until Barnabas took him to the apostles and vouched for his conversion. Soon his preaching had so angered the people that they threatened to kill him   This prompted the disciples to take Saul to Caesarea and put him on board ship for Tarsus. He had become a fire brand too hot for the apostles who were keeping a low profile in Jersusalem. Only a nucleus of the church remained at Jerusalem which still served as the titular church headquarters.

From Jerusalem Peter would travel to outlying areas, supervising and guiding as necessary. When Phillip had gone to Samaria and preached the kingdom of God some had believed and been baptized in the name of the Lord Jesus. Then Peter and John came, prayed and laid hands on them and they received the Holy Ghost.

Another time, Peter travelled through the old Philistine coastal area, through Lydda to Joppa, in the vicinity of modern Tel Aviv. Here he lodged with Simon, a tanner, which was evidence of the tolerance he had learned from Jesus. Simon's trade was considered unclean and before his conversion Peter would never have associated with him, let alone lodged in his home. Most likely as Peter rested on the roof to catch the cool sea breeze, he was shaded by a leather awning.

In this setting, he fell into a trance and in a vision saw a great sheet, let down from heaven, containing all manner of unclean fourfooted animals, creeping things and birds. He heard a voice say: "Rise Peter, kill, and eat." Too much Orthodox Jew remained in Peter for this and true to his nature he protested. Three times this was repeated, after which there was a knock on the street gate and the Lord commanded Peter to go with the men who had been sent by Cornelius, a devout, God-fearing Roman centurion.

Taking several Christian Jewish brothers from Joppa with him, they journeyed two days to Caesarea, a Roman port and garrison town north of Joppa. Herod had presented Caesarea to his Roman protectors and had equipped it with the best of facilities. Cornelius was a respected officer of a detachment stationed at Caesarea. He was to become the first Gentile Christian convert.

Cornelius had assembled his family and friends in anticipation of Peter's coming. Although by Jewish law it was unlawful to associate with one of another nation, Peter had come in obedience to the Lord. When Cornelius requested Peter tell them of God, he began with Jesus Christ, Lord of all; of his ministry, crucifixion, resurrection, and that through his name whosoever believes shall receive remission of sins.

> **While Peter yet spoke these words,**
> **The Holy Ghost fell on all of them**
> **Which heard the word.**
> **(And the Jews) were astonished**
> **Because that on the Gentiles also**
> **Was poured out the gift of the Holy Ghost.**
> **For they heard them speak with tongues,**
> **And magnify God.**
>
> **ACTS 10:44 - 46**

Peter realized they had received the same experience he had in the Upper Room on the day of Pentecost, with the same evidence - speaking in an unknown heavenly language as the Spirit gave them utterance. He knew to fulfill Jesus' commandment they must also be baptized in Jesus' name.

Acceptance of Gentiles into their religious fold brought great opposition and protest from the apostles at Jerusalem. They could not understand Peter fellowshipping and eating with Gentiles. He explained it was by God's will, that the Spirit had commanded it and showed him

What God hath cleansed,
Call not thou common.

ACTS 11:9

Step by step, he told them of his visit to Cornelius, that as he spoke the Holy Ghost fell on them the same as on Jews and that since God had given them the gift of his Spirit, he, Peter, had no right to refuse to baptize them. At this, they held their peace. Previously, there had been small numbers of Gentiles converted to Judaism by their belief in one God and they had been welcomed into the synagogues and expected to conform to their laws. The apostles could not foresee the spread of Christianity throughout the Gentile world and would always be uneasy with it.

Inevitably, the seat of Christian power changed from Jerusalem to Antioch as the Christian doctrine spread. Antioch, third largest city in the world (after Rome and Alexandria), was a thriving seaport city and capitol of the Roman province of Syria. Earlier Roman emperors often visited it and enhanced its appearance with new colonnaded, lamp-lighted streets and buildings. It was noted both for its culture and for its corrupt moral reputation. Its status as a free city drew people from all nations. This Galatian city was a center of Hellenistic influence and was colonized by liberal-minded Jews. The martyrdom of Stephen was responsible for an influx of Jewish Christian refugees.

> Now they which were scattered abroad,
> Upon the persecution that arose about Stephen
> Traveled as far as Phoenicia and Cyprus and Antioch
> Preaching the word to none but unto the Jews only.
> And some of them were men of Cyprus and Cyrene,
> Which, when they were come to Antioch,
> Spoke unto the Grecians,
> Preaching the Lord Jesus.
>
> ACTS 11:19 &: 20

The church at Antioch grew as great numbers believed and turned to the Lord. Jerusalem, seeing a need for capable ministers, sent Barnabas to Antioch. He was a good man, full of the Holy Ghost and of faith and the church continued to grow. Barnabas, recognizing a need for another Spirit-filled minister, went to Tarsus in search of Saul. Finding him, they returned to Antioch where, for about a year, they ministered to many people. Other prophets and teachers such as Simeon, Lucius of Cyrene, and Manaen, foster brother of Herod, were added to the church. Here the believers of Jesus Christ were first called Christians.

> As they ministered to the Lord, and fasted.
> The Holy Ghost said,
> Separate me Barnabas and Saul
> For the work whereunto I have called them.
>
> ACTS 13:2

Saul, soon to be known as Paul (his Gentile name), was ideally suited to the mission ahead. He was a Jew, of the tribe of Benjamin, born in Tarsus, a cosmopolitan city containing a university equal to those of Athens and Alexandria. Tarsus was located in Cilicia (now Turkey), an important meeting place of East and West. A member of a privileged group, Paul held Roman citizenship. He was highly intelligent and his education was the finest available. He was conversant with Greek philosophy and the multiple cultures of Tarsus. Proficient in Aramaic, Hebrew, Greek and Roman, he was uniquely fitted to carry the gospel unto all nations.

Paul learned the trade of tent-maker, working in goat-hair felts which were indigenous to this region. Today Tersoos is a little town of 20,000 inhabitants at the foot of the Tarsus mountains whose chief industry is tent-making. The goat hair still comes from Taurus mountain goats.

Raised a Pharisee, Saul was dedicated to the priesthood and sent to Jerusalem to study under the best Hebrew teacher of his time, Gamaliel. His extensive knowledge of the Old Testament would become an invaluable asset to his Christian ministry.

Paul and Barnabas, sent forth by the Holy Ghost, departed to Seleucia and from there sailed to the isle of Cyprus, a proconsular province where Barnabas was born. Their first stop was indicative of success for they converted Sergius Paulus, proconsul of Cyprus, the most powerful man on the island. Leaving Cyprus, they sailed back to the mainland and inland to Antioch of Pisidia (not to be confused with the church center). Following the example of Jesus, they went into the synagogue on the Sabbath day. When asked to speak, Paul rose and spoke of the God of Israel, covering the period from Abraham to John the Baptist to Jesus Christ and how those at Jerusalem knew him not and put him to death; how Jesus rose again and through him is salvation. When the Jews had departed, the Gentiles (religious proselytes) requested he preach again. The following Sabbath, most of the city came to hear the word of God, which the Jews contradicted and blasphemed because they were envious.

> **Then Paul and Barnabas waxed bold and said,**
> **It was necessary that the word of God**
> **Should first have been spoken to you;**
> **But seeing you put it from you,**
> **And judge yourselves unworthy of everlasting life,**
> **Lo, we turn to the Gentiles.**
> **For so hath the Lord commanded us, saying,**
> **I have set thee to be a light of the Gentiles,**
> **That thou shouldest be for salvation**
> **Unto the ends of the earth.**
>
> **ACTS 13:46 - 47**

This was to become a pattern of their missionary journeys. It was first presented to the Jews, some of whom were receptive; the Gentiles gladly heard the word of the Lord but resentful Jews would stir up opposition and expel them from their midst. Continuing on to the neighboring town of Iconium, they found many Jews and Greeks who believed; therefore, they remained for a considerable time, until the opposition had mustered sufficient strength to be a dangerous threat. Then they fled to the neighboring cities of Lystra and Derbe.

At Lystra, Paul healed a man who had been crippled from birth. This miracle convinced the people Paul and Barnabas were gods. Traditionally, they worshipped many gods, among them Jupiter and Mercurias who they believed had now come to them as men. Paul and Barnabas vehemently denied they were anything but men; that there was only one God, Jesus Christ. This upset the people and left them in a receptive frame of mind to listen to all the accusations of Jews who came from Antioch and Iconium with the intent of killing Paul. Joining forces, they took him outside the city and stoned him, presumably to death. But Paul rose up and the next day departed with Barnabas to Derbe. Paul would later write in a letter to the church at Corinth:

> I knew a man in Christ above fourteen years ago,
> (Whether in the body, I cannot tell,
> Or whether out of the body, I cannot tell:
> God knoweth:)
> Such a one caught up to the third heaven
> How that he was caught up into paradise, And
> heard unspeakable words,
> Which it is not lawful for a man to utter.
>   II CORINTIDANS 12:2 - 4

After Paul and Barnabas established a church in Derbe, they returned to Lystra, Iconium and Antioch, ordaining elders in every church, and commending them to Jesus Christ on whom they believed.

At that time, Antioch of Pisidia was the central Roman army post in Asia Minor. In the center of this city, archeologists have discovered a broad flight of stairs leading to three triumphal arches with reliefs depicting the victories of Emperor Augustus. In the Roman quarters they found gaming tables. Sixty miles south and east of Antioch, Iconium was uncovered in 1885 by Professor Sterrett. Twenty-five miles further south was Lystra. Here a thick stone slab bears an inscription relating to a Roman colony "Lustra." Professor Sterrett also identified Derbe. These four cities were located in the province of Galatia, the home of the Galatians. Paul began his letter to them:

> Paul, an apostle, (not of men, neither by man,
> But by Jesus Christ and God the Father,
> Who raised him from the dead.)
>   GALATIANS 1:1

This sums up an important part of Paul's ministry - salvation through the resurrection of Jesus Christ. It might also appear to be an allusion to his stoning at Lystra. It is indicative of his testimony of Jesus Christ because many Biblical phrases are only understood through the knowledge that Jewish dialect customarily bracketed two words together, both of them nouns, instead of using an adjective and a noun. For example: "fire and brimstone" could be "volcanic fire;" "a mouth and wisdom" mean "wise speech;" and "of Christ and of God" mean "Divine Messiah."

About fifteen years ago Peter had baptized Cornelius' Gentile household in the name of Jesus. The church, still young and unformed, had no conception of the Gentile conversion that was ahead. Now, reports of Paul's successful ministry among the Gentiles filtered back to Jerusalem. A party of Judean Christians, independently travelled to Galatia expressly to teach the Gentiles that Moses' circumcision and the keeping of his laws were necessary to be saved. Recognizing the harmful effects upon newborn Christians, and the challenge posed against their doctrine, Paul and Barnabas returned to Jerusalem to resolve this dissention sown among the Christians. After much discussion and argument, Peter declared with the authority that was rightfully his that God had made the choice to call Gentiles to salvation.

> **And God, which knoweth the hearts,**
> **Bare them witness,**
> **Giving them the Holy Ghost,**
> **Even as he did unto us.**
> **And put no difference between us and them.**
> **Purifying their hearts by faith.**
> **Now therefore why tempt ye God,**
> **To put a yoke upon the neck of the disciples,**
> **Which neither our fathers nor we**
> **Were able to bear.**
>
> **ACTS 15:8 - 10**

James, brother of Jesus and head of the church at Jerusalem, agreed to this and so it was decided the only stipulations to be imposed on the Gentiles should be abstaining from meats offered to idols, from blood, from things strangled and from fornication. Judas and

Silas returned to Antioch with Paul and Barnabas to deliver this decision. All but Judas remained at Antioch, teaching and preaching until, accompanied by Silas, Paul set out to revisit the churches at Galatia.

Here he first met Timothy, son of a devout Jewess and a Greek father. When it was decided Timothy should accompany him, Paul had him circumcised because of the Jews. This was still a very sensitive issue and Paul realized he had sufficient opposition from his Pharisitical brothers without adding to it. A weakness of the Jews who accepted Christianity was their inability to separate the legalism of Judaism from Christ's plan of salvation. They could not conceive of a new plan embracing a spiritual redemption through faith and the power of the Holy Ghost rather than justification by the works of the law.

> For in Christ Jesus neither circumcision availeth anything.
> Nor uncircumcision, but a new creature.
> GALATIANS 6:15

Later, Paul would further clarify this controversy in a letter to Colosse.

> For in him dwelleth all the fullness of the Godhead bodily.
> Ye are complete in him, which is the head of all
> Principality and power;
> In whom also ye are circumcised
> With the circumcision made without hands,
> In putting off the body of the sins of the flesh
> By the circumcision of Christ.

Buried with him in baptism,
Wherein also ye are risen with him
Through the faith of the operation of God,
Who hath raised him from the dead.

COLOSSIANS 2:9 - 12

Under the new dispensation of grace, spiritual circumcision of the heart stripped away the old nature and gave a new beginning to each freshly baptized Christian.

After travelling throughout Galatia, Paul sought to go into Asia but was forbidden by the Holy Ghost. Seeking the will of God, they came down to Troas where Luke was added to Paul's party. Luke was a Greek physician, born in Antioch and probably converted there. He became the travelling companion of Paul and the author of the Gospel of Luke and The Acts. Upon joining Paul's group, they were prompted by Paul's vision, to go into Macedonia. No longer opposed by the Spirit, but abetted, they went straight to Philippi. Embarking at Troas (Troy) they set sail for Europe where they straightway took the Via Egnatia (the main east-west highway between Rome and Asia), up the wild mountains of Macedonia to Philippi. When Macedonia was taken by the Romans in 168 B.C., Philippi was included in the first of the territories four divisions. In 42 B.C. the forces of Octavian and Anthony defeated those of the Roman republic, ushering in Empirical rule. To commemorate this victory, Philippi was given Roman citizenship privileges and status. Because of this preferential treatment, the citizens were extremely loyal to Rome.

Philippi had a medical school which Luke most likely attended. It would account for his familiarity with the city and his desire to remain after Paul's departure.

On the Sabbath, Paul sought the synagogue and finding none, turned to the river where Lydia and others were praying. Paul was familiar with this practice which originated during Babylonian exile where the Jews gathered at the river to worship.

Philippi was the first European city to receive the gospel and Lydia, a seller of purple in the city of Thyatira, was the first to be baptized. A colony of Macedonians had settled in Thyatira, 600 miles away, in the Third

Century B.C. The town was famous for its textile craftsmanship and for its purple dye. Lydia was a cloth merchant who did business in Philippi. During this period of history it was not unusual for women to be prominent in business affairs. What was unusual was the prominence they attained in the church world, particularly at Philippi.

Guided by the Bible, French archeologists excavated Philippi. They found the old forum, temples and public buildings, pillared arcades, paved streets and squares complete with rain gutters. A great colonial archway extended across the Via Egnatia which soon afterward crossed the Gangites River; the river that served Lydia and Paul as a place of worship.

Because Paul cast a spirit of divination out of a young girl, her masters were angered and brought Paul and Silas before the magistrates. When the multitude turned against Paul and Silas, they were beaten and cast into prison. An earthquake served to loose their bonds. That very night the jailer believed on the Lord Jesus Christ and was saved.

Leaving Luke at Philippi, Paul departed with Silas and Timothy. They followed the Egnatian Way to Thessalonica, a busy seaport and the capital city of Macdonia. Land and sea connections made it a stategic and prosperous commercial center. It too was a free city, which entitled it to autonomy in internal affairs. Luke's reference to politarchs as the rulers of the city (long thought to be a mistake) was vindicated by the discovery of an inscription on a triple carved Arch of Galerius which spans the Via Egnatia.

A large number of wealthy Jews, involved in the commerce of the city, had attracted a number of Greeks to their synagogues. After three weeks of teaching, a few Jews had become Christians but a great multitude of Greeks and influencial women had been won over by the gospel of Jesus Christ. This aroused the envy of the dissenting Jews, who gathered together a mob of "lewd fellows of the baser sort" and turned the city against Paul and his party.

Jason, Paul's host, was brought before the rulers of the city and he was required to post bond as security Paul would leave Thessalonica.

> **And when they had taken security of Jason.**
> **And of the others, they let them go.**
> **And the brethren immediately sent away**

Paul and Silas by night unto Berea.
Who coming thither,
Went into the synagogue of the Jews.

ACTS 17:9 - 10

The citizens of Berea were of higher standards than the mixed crowd typical of seaports and they readily received the word. But the Jews of Thessalonica had such extreme resentment for Paul and his teaching that they followed him to Berea. Leaving Silas and Timothy to nurture a young church, Paul went on to Athens, a city totally influenced by idolatry.

Athens was noted as a center of learning. Prominent Roman families, desirous of culture, sent their sons to the famous Athenian schools. It was a religious center for every known pagan god. Among pagan temples still standing are the Temple of Zeus, Wingless Victory and the Parthenon. To assure no god was overlooked there were even altars to "unknown gods."

Paul witnessed in the synagogues and market place until he attracted the attention of certain Epicureans and Stoics who took him to the Arcopagus to speak to a learned gathering of philosophers. Paul knew the Epicureans who belittled deity, believed in chance and the pursuit of pleasure, would have little sympathy for Christian doctrine. Therefore, he addressed the Stoics, who practiced dogged endurance and self-restraint, accepted a god as the all-pervasive Force in the universe and believed that the supreme goal of hu man lif e was virtue.

Paul appealed to their religious nature, as witnessed by their altars to many gods including ones to unknown gods. He proved he too was well versed in Greek literature as he quoted their own poet and philosophers.

> **And when they heard of the resurrection of the dead,**
> **Some mocked; and others said,**
> **We will hear thee again on this matter.**
>
> **ACTS 17:32**

Although a few believed, chief among them Dionysius, Paul left no church at Athens.

Paul next stopped in Corinth, another cosmopolitan seaport; a Mediterranean gateway between east and west. The worship of their chief idol, Aphrodite, encouraged carnality and moral corruption. Rising above the city, eight columns still stand, remnants of a temple to Apollo. Diogenes, a noted Stoic philosopher who was buried in Corinth, greatly influenced the city by teaching that heaven was watching their great virtue. In their inflated arrogance, the Stoics believed they needed nothing Paul had to offer.

> Paul found a certain Jew named Aquila,
> Born in Pontus, lately come from Italy
>
> With his wife, Priscilla;
> (Because that Claudius had commanded
> All Jews to depart from Rome.)
> And came unto them.
>
> ACTS 18:2

About 49-50 A.D., Claudius issued an edict against the Jews in Rome for "constant rioting at the instigation of Chrestus." Apparently the Emperor was irritated by the altercations and accusations of the Jews against Christians in his city.

Sharing common bonds of tentmaking and Christianity, Paul dwelt with Aquila and Priscilla. Silas and Timothy came to join them and for a year and one half they remained teaching the word of God and baptizing many.

> And when Gallio was the deputy of Achaia,
> The Jews made insurrection
> With one accord against Paul,
> And brought him to the judgement seat,
> Saying, This fellow persuadeth men
> To worship God contrary to the law.
>
> ACTS 18:13

Remains of the old city indicate a broad road of limestone blocks lined with colonnades and shops. Drinking vessels uncovered here indicated the presence of taverns. Inscriptions identified shops as "meat market" and "fish market". An ingenious system of water mains under the shops provided fresh, cool spring water for refrigeration. In the midst of the agora (market) stood the bema (a high, broad platform built of white and blue marble) with a Latin inscription indicating it was the rostra, or judgement seat.

Historical records indicate Lucius Junius Annaeus Novatus Gallia was proconsul of Achaia at Corinth from 51 - 52 A.D. His brother was Lucius Annaeus Seneca, a great Roman philosopher and tutor of Nero.

For once judgement was against the Jews instead of Paul. Gallio would have no part in their accusations that Paul had violated their laws. At this, the Greeks beat the chief ruler of the synagogue. Apparently the Jews were in the minority and the magistrate could afford to disregard them. Also, Claudius' recent edict at Rome would influence his decision.

Concern for the church at Thessalonica prompted Paul to write twice to them while at Corinth. At first the Christians had expected Jesus to return any day. But what of those who died before his coming? Paul assured them that Jesus' resurrection guaranteed the resurrection of the saints.

> For, the Lord himself
> Shall descend from heaven with a shout,
> With the voice of the archangel,
> And with the trump of God.
> And the dead in Christ shall rise first
> Then we which are alive and remain
> Shall be caught up together
> With them in the clouds
> To meet the Lord in the air.
> And so shall we ever be with the Lord.
>   I THESSALONIANS 4:16, 17

Paul warned the Thessalonians to be ready to meet the Lord, but to understand his coming would be like a thief in the night; no man knew the day. Yet there would be signs:

> Let no man deceive you by any means;
> For that day shall not come,
> Except there come a falling away first.
> And that man of sin be revealed.
> The son of perdition,
> Who opposeth and exalteth himself
> Above all that is called God,
> Or that is worshipped;
> So that he as God sitteth in the temple of God,
> Showing himself that he is God.
>
> II Thessalonians 2:3, 4

This was the first clear warning against the Anti-Christ who is to come, the tool of Satan, with all the powers of Satan. One who will be able to deceive those who have not believed the truth of God's word preached to the churches. (Many such men have had their place in history, but before the end, the world will be deceived by the ultimate master of them all.)

Paul's time with the church at Thessalonica had been so short there was much he had not been able to teach them, but he knew in spite of the wickedness surrounding them, they had a love for the truth which could keep them separated from it. He exhorted them to stand fast and not to follow those who had walked disorderly and not after the teachings received from Paul and Timothy, for there were those in the church who were weak and inclined to sinfulness.

Paul tarried for some time at Corinth, until he again f elt compelled to move on. Priscilla and Aquila went with him as far as Ephesus, but Paul continued on to Syria. Landing at Caesarea, he first went up to Antioch and from there visited the churches established in Galatia. Continuing on, he came to Ephesus. This time he felt disposed to linger. Finding certain disciples he asked:

> **Have ye received the Holy Ghost since ye believed?**
> **And they said unto him,**
> **We have not so much as heard**
> **Whether there be any Holy Ghost.**
>
> **ACTS 19:2**

These disciples only understood John the Baptist's baptism of repentance.

Paul explained that John had only been the messenger for Jesus Christ.

> **When they heard this,**
> **They were baptized in the name**
> **Of the Lord Jesus.**
> **And when Paul had laid his hands upon them,**
> **The Holy Ghost came on them.**
> **And they spoke in tongues, and prophesied.**
>
> **ACTS 19:5, 6**

For three months Paul preached in the synagogue, but when many opposed his teaching, he separated the Jews who did believe and taught them in the school of Tyrannus, a hired hall, for two years. His ministry prospered among both Jews and Greeks as God wrought miracles by the hands of Paul and the name of the Lord Jesus Christ was magnified.

Although the once fine harbor at Ephesus was filling with silt from erosion and was no longer on the main shipping lines, it was still reckoned as one of the great cities of the eastern Mediterranean. Ephesus was a racial melting pot of Asiatic peoples, Ionian Greeks, Romans and Jews.

For hundreds of years a Lydian fertility goddess, similar to the Phoenician Astarte, Artemis to the Greeks and Diana to the Romans, a many-breasted mother-goddess figure, dominated the city and encouraged prostitution. A great statue of Diana, as well as a "sacred stone from the sky" (which was most likely a meteorite) were enthroned in a magnificent temple at Ephesus. A profitable trade flourished in the sale of miniature silver statues of Diana, a lewd, many-breasted goddess wearing a crown decorated with signs of the zodiac. When the temple of Artemis was uncovered, under the sponsorship of the British Museum, a large collection of bronze, gold, silver and ivory statues of the goddess were located near the altar.

The Romans showed favor to Paul and his Christian religion because it made inroads on the worship of Diana; something they had not been able to do. During this period of relative calm, Paul's ministry spread throughout the area into the inland valley towns of Thyatira, Pergamum, Laodicea, Sardis, Philadelphia, Colossae and Hieropolis, as well as the port city of Smyrna.

Paul's zeal won many converts, so many in fact that it inf ringed upon the sale of statues to pilgrims come to worship Diana. Therefore, Demetrius called together the silversmiths who made their living from crafting images of Diana and exhorted them in the following fashion:

> Moreover ye see and hear, that not alone at Ephesus,
> But almost throughout all Asia,
> This Paul hath persuaded and turned away much people,
> Saying that they be no gods,
> Which are made with hands.
>
> ACTS 19:26

Understanding their livelihood was threatened, they stirred up the whole city against Paul for endangering the worship of Diana. Filled with wrath and crying "Great is Diana of the Ephesians" they caught two companions of Paul, men of Macedonia, and rushed them into the theater, an amphitheater whose ruins still exist. When Alexander, a Jew, would have offered a defense, the people shouted "Great is Diana of the Ephesians" for two hours while the disciples prevented Paul's entering the theater. At last the town clerk, answerable to the Romans for such a riotous assembly, quieted the people, assuring them the men they were holding were neither robbers of churchs nor yet blasphemers of Diana. They were only innocent by-standers. After the uproar had ceased, Paul deemed it necessary to take leave of Ephesus.

He remained in Greece for only three mont hs before winding his way toward Jerusalem; from Philippi to Troas, from port to port until his ship docked at Miletus where Paul sent word to Ephesus to the elders of the church. (Because of the silted harbor at Ephesus, at certain seasons it was safer for larger vessels to use the nearby port of Miletus.) When the elders came to meet him, Paul advised them he would see them no more for he was bound for Jerusalem despite the warnings he received in every city.

> **And now, behold, I go**
> **Bound in the spirit unto Jerusalem,**
> **Not knowing the things that**
> **Shall befall me there;**
> **Save that the Holy Ghost witnesseth**
> **In every city**
> **Saying that bonds and afflictions abide me.**
>
> **ACTS 20:22-23**

Aware of his own danger, as Paul took leave of the Ephesian disciples, he forewarned them of dangers ahead for the church; of grievous wolves entering among the flock, of false doctrine and witnessing that would draw church members from Christ. Nevertheless, because of the three years Paul ministered to the Ephesians and the sound doctrine he had instilled in them, they remained a solidly planted church, thriving in the midst of corruption.

Sailing on toward Phoenicia, past Cyprus to Syria, Paul and his party landed at Tyre. While the ship unloaded, they tarried with Christian disciples who, through the Spirit, tried to dissuade Paul from going on to Jerusalem, to no avail.

At Caesarea, they again tarried, accepting the hospitality of Philip, the evangelist. While they lingered at Caesarea, a prophet, named Agabus, came to Paul and binding his own hands and feet with Paul's girdle as an example, warned:

> So shall the Jews at Jerusalem
> Bind the man that owneth this girdle,
> And shall deliver him into the hands
> Of the Gentiles.

ACTS 21:11

Paul had been aware for years of the antagonism that many Jews held for him throughout all of the Mediterranean area. They held extreme resentment and hatred for Paul because he used his Roman citizenship to advantage. This was compounded by his ministry to the Gentiles. Attempts on his life had been made before and could be expected again.

In addition to this, the atmosphere in Jerusalem had intensified against Roman rule, and against anyone who associated with them. Paul would be especially vulnerable since he was known to many as a Roman citizen. His desire to continue to Jerusalem appeared unreasonable to his friends, who were plainly aware of the danger to him and filled with anxiety, yet they could not stop him. Luke was among those who accompanied Paul to the Holy City where they were received by James and all the elders.

The Christian Jews who had remained in Jerusalem were disturbed by Paul's ministry. They had heard distorted rumors that Paul was teaching Jews to abandon circumcision and the law. They said unto Paul:

Thou seest brother, how many thousands of Jews
There are which believe;
And they are all zealous of the law
And they are informed of thee,
That thou teachest all the Jews
Which are among the Gentiles
To forsake Moses
Saying that they ought not To circumcise their children
Neither to walk after customs.

ACTS 21:20 - 21

When James suggested Paul purify himself at the temple, he agreed for he had no desire to antagonize his fellow ministers who were hide-bound by tradition and mistrust of his Gentile ministry.

Asian Jews, seeing Paul in the temple and recognizing him, stirred up the people by accusing him of bringing a Greek into the inner court which was forbidden to Gentiles. They had previously seen him with Trophimus, an Ephesian, whom they supposed Paul had brought into the temple. A large crowd gathered around Paul in the outer court and would have killed him, but the chief captain of the troops stationed in the tower of Antonio, which overlooked the court, immediately descended the stairway with soldiers and centurions. Only their intervention stopped the angry, violent mob. Unable to discover why Paul was being beaten, the chief captain had him bound and carried up the stairs to the fortress. Paul, ever mindful of winning converts for the Lord, requested permission of the chief captain to speak to the mob. Standing on the stairs, bound in chains, surrounded by Roman troops, he spoke to them in Hebrew. As they listened he recounted his history of being as zealous a Jew as they were; of how he had persecuted the Christians until God's light shone on him on the road to Damascus and how the Lord had chosen him to be his witness unto the

Gentiles. The crowd had listened quietly until he said "Gentiles" which incited them anew. In haste, the chief captain commanded Paul to be brought inside the fortress and would have had him scourged. Discovering Paul was a Roman stopped them. the chief captain, Claudius Lysias, was a Greek as his last name indicated and he had acquired his Roman first name when he purchased his Roman citizenship, which he prized.

In order to resolve the guilt and innocence of Paul, Lysias called the San- hedrin Council together and brought Paul before them. Ananias, the high priest, was so unreasonable that Paul, observing both Sadducees and Pharisees on the council, appealed to the Pharisees.

Men and brethren, I am a Pharisee,
The son of a Pharisee
Of the hope and resurrection of the dead
I am called in question.
ACTS 23:6

This created such dissention among the council, that Lysias feared Paul would be torn to pieces and again sent his men to the rescue. That night the Lord appeared to Paul and said:

Be of good cheer, Paul;
For as thou hast testified of me in Jerusalem,
So must thou bear witness also in Rome.

ACTS 23:11

The next day a conspiracy was formed to kill Paul. The Sanhedrin planned to call for Paul and as he was brought forth from the Tower of Antonio, to slay him. Paul's nephew heard of this plot and informed Lysias who arranged to take Paul to Caesarea. It is indicative of the tense atmosphere between Jews and Romans at this time, that Lysias believed it necessary to form a guard of two hundred soldiers, seventy horsemen and two hundred spearmen and send them forth in the middle of the night.

Caesarea was headquarters of the Roman province of Judea. Felix, Pilate's successor and governor of Judea, received Paul and sent for Ananias to hear his accusations, which could not be substantiated, so Felix commanded a centurion to keep Paul, allowing him the liberty of visitors. For two years Paul remained at Caesarea, probably from 58 - 60 A.D.

Felix visited Paul from time to time, bringing Druscilla, a daughter of king Agrippa I. She was married and only about sixteen when Felix seduced her and made her his third wife. They could not reconcile themselves to Paul's teaching.

And as he reasoned of righteousness,
Temperance and judgement to come,
Felix trembled, and answered,

> Go thy way for this time;
> When I have a convenient season,
> I will call for thee.

ACTS 24:25

After two years Felix was recalled for mishandling riots in Caesarea and was replaced by Porcius Festus. Festus had inherited a tense political situation that would erupt into open rebellion within a few short years. Aware of the situation, and being an able administrator, he sought to appease the Jews by suggesting Paul go to Jerusalem to be judged. Knowing the dangers of that course, Paul took advantage of his Roman citizenship and requested trial by Caesar, who at that time was Nero.

Before Paul could be sent to Rome, king Agrippa and Bernice came to Caesarea to meet Festus. Hearing about Paul, Agrippa sent for him and listened to his testimony.

> Having therefore obtained help of God,
> I continue unto this day,
> Witnessing both to small and great.
> Saying none other things than those
> Which the prophets and Moses di say should come:
> That Christ should suffer
> And that he should be the first
> That should rise from the dead,
> And should show light unto the people,
> And to the Gentiles.

ACTS 26:22, 23

When Festus protested, Paul turned to king Agrippa, asking if he did not believe in the prophets. At which Agrippa replied:

Almost thou persuadeth me
To be a Christian.

ACTS 26:28

Later king Agrippa told Festus Paul might have been set free if he had not already appealed to Caesar.

Again Luke accompanied Paul as he was placed in the custody of Julius, a Roman centurion in charge of other prisoners. They set sail for Rome, passed Cyprus to Lycia where they were transferred to a ship of Alexandria bound for Italy. They encountered off-shore winds which caused much delay and forced the ship off course so that they sought refuge under the lee of Crete. They waited out the storm at Fair Havens, midway on the island. Each day added to the danger of continuing as winter was fast approaching. Mediterranean navigation was increasingly dangerous at this season. Paul suggested remaining at Fair Haven until spring and safer passage, but the Centurion trusted the advice of the captain and owner of the ship more than Paul's, so at the first slacking of the violent winds, they sailed for Phenice, fifty miles west, a port whose harbor was considered safer than Fair Havens and where they would be more comfortable.

Hardly had they attained open sea when there arose a tempestuous wind, a violent northeaster called Euroclydon (or Euraquilo) which drove the ship south toward the distant African coast where lay a graveyard of ships. To prevent a similar end, every effort was made to maintain a westerly course. Cables were drawn around the hull to strengthen the battered vessel. All dispensable tackle and gear were thrown overboard. For many days they tossed and rolled uncontrollably until all hope was gone. Neither sun nor stars had appeared for many days; navigation was impossible and their destination unknown. But God took a hand in their situation; it was his intention for Paul to go to Rome and Paul was so informed:

> For there stood by me this night
> The angel of God, whose I am,
> And whom I   serve.
> Saying, fear not, Paul;
> Thou must be brought before Caesar:
> And lo, God hath given thee
> All of them that sail with thee.
>
> ACTS 27:23, 24

The ship was driven near Melita (Malta) but was unable to attain the shore because of a sandbar and cross currents that grounded the bow of the ship and violent waves beat the ship apart. Nevertheless, because God's Word does not fail, they all swam safely to shore. Here they wintered, gladly accepting the hospitality of the "barbarous" people, which simply means a people unable to speak Greek, the civilized language of the Mediterranean nations.

Malta had been colonized by Phoenicians a thousand years before. Their language was Semitic, similar to Hebrew and Aramaic, so it was possible that Paul could converse with them. If the shipwreck had not occurred, these out-of-the-way people would have had little chance to hear of Jesus Christ.

After three months, when it was again safe to travel, they were given passage to Rome on another ship which had wintered at Malta.

At Rome, Julius delivered Paul to the captain of the Praetorian guard. Because of his Roman citizenship and his good conduct, he was placed under military guard but given private quarters and liberal visitation rights. Possibly because his papers had been lost in the shipwreck, Paul was held for two years without a trial.

Paul's first act was to contact the synagogues and call the Jewish leaders together. When they came, he explained w hy he was a prisoner in Rome. They had heard nothing from Jerusalem; neither did they understand Christianity.

> **But we desire to hear of thee**
> **What thou thinkest;**
> **For as concerning this sect,**
> **We know that everywhere**
> It is **spoken against.**
>
> ACTS 28:22

Appointing a day, many came to hear Paul; some believed, some did not. At which Paul retorted "The Gentiles will hear." From that day, he received all who came to him.

Apparently Emperor Nero had rescinded the Jewish exile imposed by Claudius, but it is reasonable to assume they lived quietly, as did the Christians, so as not to draw attention to themselves. For that reason, they dared not hinder Paul's ministry. During the first five years of Nero's reign, he left the governing of his empire primarily to

Burrus, his commander, and Seneca, his former tutor; which accounted for the tolerance and good government of that period.

A Christian community at Rome had been established before Paul arrived at the city. During Paul's imprisonment there, Gentiles predominated in the church. By 64 A.D., Tacitus described the church as an "immense multitude." How much of this was due to Paul's influence is unknown, but in his letter to the Philippians he mentioned :

> **But I would ye should understand brethren,**
> **That the things which happened unto me,**
> **Have fallen out rather unto**
> **The furtherance of the gospel,**
> **So that my bonds in Christ**
> **Are manifest in all the palace,**
> **And in all other places.**
>
> **PHILIPPIANS 2:12, 13**

Surely he had a ready-made access to many of the troops of Caesar's household who were assigned over the years to guard him.

During his confinement, Paul wrote not only to Philippi, but to Colossae and another letter, presumably to Ephesus. To the Philippians he showed his gratitude for their concern, their faithfulness and for the gifts and necessities they had sent to hi m. He wrote to them of Jesus Christ who:

> Made himself of no reputation,
> And took upon him the form of a servant,
> And was made in the likeness of men.

And <u>being</u> <u>found in fashion as a</u> man,
He humbled himself, and became obedient unto death.
<u>Even the death of the cross.</u>

PHILIPPIANS 2:7, 8

Aware of Jewish and Hellenistic influence in the young Christian community at Colossae, which threatened to undermine the solid teaching they had initially received, Paul wrote to dispel erroneous doctrine. According to records of early councils and church fathers, this section of Asia was receptive to every exorbitant theological whim. Eastern cults and Greek philosophy influenced the church and encouraged moral laxity. Here were the first hints of Gnosticism which would become a strong threat to Christianity in the next century. Paul wrote to open their understanding:

to the acknowledgment of the mystery of God, And of
the Father, and of Christ; In whom are hid all the
treasures Of wisdom and knowledge.

COLOSSIANS 2:2, 3

He cautioned them:

Beware lest any man spoil you
Through philosophy and vain deceit,
After the tradition of men,
After the rudiments of the world,
And not after Christ.
For in him dwelleth all
The fullness of the Godhead bodily.

COLOSSIANS 2:8, 9

Paul's letter to the Colossians mentioned they should share their letter with Laodicea and also read the letter written to the Laodiceans. It seems likely that Ephesians was this letter. Possibly it was sent to Ephesus, as the chief city of the province, to be delivered to Laodicea. This epistle is particularly applicable to today's church, just as Laodicea depicts the end-time church. It speaks of a foreordained church and of a chosen people, chosen before the foundation of the world. A people redeemed through the blood of Jesus Christ and the forgiveness of sin through his grace.

> **That in the dispensation of the fullness of times**
> **He might gather together in one**
> **All things in Christ,**
> **Both which are in heaven,**
> **And which are in earth, even in him.**
> **EPHESIANS 1:11**

He wrote of the dispensation of grace of God and of how Jews and Gentiles both have access by one spirit (the Holy Ghost) to the Father and to the Lord Jesus Christ, of whom the whole family in heaven and earth are named. For:

> **There is one body, and one Spirit,**
> **Even as ye are called in one hope of your calling;**
> **One Lord, one faith, one baptism,**
> **One God and Father of all,**
> **Who is above all, and through all, and in you all.**
> **EPHESIANS 4:4 - 6**

He wrote them of putting off "the old man" who was steeped in things of the world because of spiritual blindness and taking on "the new man" and becoming followers of God, filled with the Spirit; and clothed in the whole armor of God for only then can man withstand the wiles of the devil. During his confinement, Paul had much time to seek the wisdom and guidance of the Lord in solving problems faced by the early churches. These letters are as applicable today as they were nearly two thousand years ago.

Nero was a forerunner of the anti-Christ prophecied for the end time. Nero was the nephew of Caligula and adopted son of the Emperor Claudius. His mother was Agrippina, of Herodian lineage. Nero attempted to drown her and later had her assassinated. He also ordered the death of Seneca, noted Roman philosopher and his tutor and advisor. King Agrippa II administered his Palestinian territory and Nero experienced the first tentative Jewish revolts against the Roman Empire. But he is best known for his corrupt administration, for his incontinent behavior, depraved character and sensual appetites.

In 64 A.D., much of Rome burnt in a great fire. It has been suggested that Nero himself was responsible. Be that as it may, while the city was aflame he went up to the tower of Masaenas, played his harp, exulted in the flaming ruins and sang of the burning of Troy. Why Troy? The answer may be found in Homer's famous poem, Aeneid, a national poem of Rome and of the removal of the gods of Troy into Italy. The poem sings of a man who traversed the seas to found a city and transport his gods to Latium (Italy). These were also the gods of Nero. Did Paul gain audience with Nero? Could it be possible Christianity and Jesus Christ had gripped his heart and his soul was torn between his gods and the one true God?

Much of the Imperial city was destroyed, thousands perished in the flames. For days the fire raged uncontrollably. When Nero found himself condemned for the conflagration, he laid the blame on the Christians. This was the first wholesale persecution, concentrated mainly in Rome. Nero led the persecutions with the most vile and atrocious refinements of cruelty ever devised. Possibly because he sensed the inroads Christianity had made in his own household (it has been claimed even his wife was a Christian), he inflicted inhuman torture upon the Christians as he gloated. For example, he had their clothing saturated with oil and wax, then had them affixed to stakes and they became human torches lighting his courtyard. Did Nero, like Paul, kick against the pricks?

It is not known if Paul died at this time or within the next few years, for Nero continued to sporadically persecute Christians. As Paul himself said, "I have finished my course, I have kept the faith." He had suffered much in the years he served the Lord,

> Are they ministers of Christ?
> (I speak as a fool.) I am more;
> In labors more abundant,
> In stripes above measure,
> In prisons more frequent, in deaths oft.

Of the Jews five times received I forty stripes, save one.
Thrice was I beaten with rods.
Once was I stoned, thrice I suffered shipwreck.
A night and a day I have been in the deep,
In journeyings often, in perils of waters,
In perils of robbers, in perils of my own countrymen.
In perils by the heathen, in perils in the city.
In perils in the wilderness, in perils in the sea.
In perils among false brethren.

II CORINTHIANS 11 : 23 - 26

Paul did more than any one man to spread the glorious gospel of Christ throughout the world. He faithfully taught repentance, baptism in Jesus' name and the infilling of the Holy Ghost as he established and taught fledgling churches throughout the cradle of civilization. Never faltering from the commission levied upon him by Christ, he opened the door of salvation to all people. Paul told the Romans:

I say the truth in Christ,
I lie not, my conscience
also bearing me witness
In the Holy Ghost.

ROMANS 9:1

CHAPTER XIV

SEPARATION

Jerusalem, Antioch, and Ephesus were the centers of Christian faith.

The apostles had established other Christian communities which thrived on adversity, for nowhere was this new Christian movement received without opposition. There had been martyrs in the past and there would be more.

In 62 A.D., James, brother of Jesus and titular head of the church at Jerusalem, was arrested by the Sanhedrin Court. Asked to explain "the door of Jesus" he replied "Jesus is the door of salvation" at which they cast him from the roof . Found to be still alive, he was clubbed to death. (Years previously, James the Apostle had been beheaded at Herod Agrippa's orders.) According to prophets of the Old Testament, to Jewish tradition and to the teachings of Jesus, Christ's second coming, which Christians looked for momentarily, would occur at Jerusalem.

Here Christ had been crucified and after his resurrection had left his apostles with the promise he would return again. The Jewish Christians placed great importance on maintaining roots in Jerusalem but after the death of James, ties binding the faith to Jerusalem were loosened.

Hatred for Roman rule intensified under the despotic rule of Roman procurators and Herodian appointees. This hatred was fanned by Jewish patriots, a group of "Zealots" who spasmodically encouraged uprisings against Roman authority. The climax came in 66 A.D.. Led by John of Gischala, open revolt broke out in May of that year when the procurator, Florus, increased his demands upon the temple treasury. The Roman garrison was captured. Jerusalem was in the hands of the rebels and war was declared openly against the Roman Empire. From Jerusalem, rebellion spread throughout Palestine. Florus lost all authority and control. The governor of the Syrian province, C. Cestius Gallus, hastily sent a legion heavily reinforced with auxiliary troops which the rebels overcame. Realizing their time would be short before Rome retaliated, they hastened to reinforce city walls and organize a military force. Josephus, later a renowned historian, was appointed commander-in-chief of Galilee. Rome sent General Titus Flavius Vespasianus to quell the open revolt of the Jews.

In command of three of the best Roman legions, he attacked Galilee from the north. In October 67 A.D., the Galileans revolt was stamped out. Josephus was among the Jewish prisoners interred for the remainder of the Jewish War. Six thousand Jews went as slave labor to build the Corinthian canal across the Isthmus; a project undertaken by Nero.

The following spring, during fighting in Judea, the campaign was halted at the news Nero had committed suicide. Civil war broke out in Rome and Vespasian awaited developments.

While the war was abated, the Jewish Christians abandoned Jerusalem and settled in Pella on the other side of the Jordan River. Eusebius wrote "they were commanded to go to Pella through an oracle." In reality, knowledgeable Jews understood Jesus' prophecy.

> **As for these things which ye behold,**
> **The days will come**
> **In the which there shall not be left**
> **One stone upon another**
> **That shall not be thrown down.**
> **And when ye shall see Jerusalem,**
> **Compassed with armies,**
> **Then know that the desolation thereof is nigh.**
> **Let them which are in Judea**
> **Flee to the mountains;**
> **Let them which are in the midst of it, depart out.**
> **LUKE 21:6, 20, 21**

Vespasian was proclaimed the latest Roman Emperor. Leaving immediately for Rome, he left his son Titus to finish the war. Titus positioned an enormous army around Jerusalem; four legions, additional cavalry, engineers and auxiliary troops, totalling about 80,000 men. He positioned siege engines, stone throwers capable of catupulting huge stones as far as 600 feet to batter the walls of the city. The beleagued city, filled to capacity with people, unable to replenish food supplies, died of starvation. Every animal was long ago consumed;

crazed, half-starved people ate their own babies. Still the people would not surrender. Titus sent Josephus, their former commander, to entreat them to save their city and their temple. To no avail.

Daughter of Jerusalem,
Weep not for me,
But weep for yourselves,
And for your children.

LUKE 23:28

As the outer wall was broken down, the battle surged against the castle of Antonio and the temple was threatened. Still the Jews fought back, erecting wooden barriers in place of their crumbled walls. At night, half-starved Jews would creep out to attack the Roman camp. Titus ordered that anyone caught outside the walls be crucified. As many as five hundred a day were nailed to crosses just outside Jerusalem. Tree after tree had been sacrificed; for crosses, for siege ramps, battering rams and ladders. A once beautiful countryside be- came a barren waste. As the famine increased within the city, bodies were thrown over the walls, creating an unbearable stench. Nobody had strength left for burials.

Day and night the battering rams hammered at the city's defenses. Titus was in a hurry. He was appalled at the suffering of a city who would not surrender. As his soldiers finally entered the city, Titus attempted to save the temple from destruction, but the Jews continued to fight within its holy precincts, until at last Titus was forced to set fire to its wooden gates. During the night the fire reached the inner court and the battle continued in the sanctuary. One Roman soldier, in spite of Titus's order to spare the temple, threw a lit torch into the inner sanctuary where wood paneling, draperies, and jars of holy oil supplied such a quantity of inflammable materials that the fire could not be contained.

John of Gischala, leading the last of the patriots, took a final stand at the strong towers of Herod's palace. In September 70, the last defense crumbled. Roman soldiers took possession of the city, plundering, murdering and burning as they went. Stone by stone, the city was destroyed. Only three towers of Herod's palace (Phasael, Hippicus and Mariamne) were left standing to provide quarters for the legion left behind. A legion remained for sixty years which bore the symbol "Leg XF."

> 0 Jerusalem, Jerusalem, thou that killest the prophets,
> And stoneth them which are sent unto thee.
> How often would I have gathered thy children together.
> Even as a hen gathereth her chickens under her wings,
> And ye would not!
>
> MA'ITHEW 23:37

All that remained of a once glorious temple were the seven branched candle- stick and the golden table of the shewbread which were taken to Rome and placed in the Temple of Peace in that city. The great arch of Titus, built to commemorate his victory, includes images of these Jewish relics.

One outpost, Masada, held out until 73 A.D. King Herod the Great had taken over an old fortress between 36 and 30 B.C. He enlarged it, added defense towers, large cisterns, storerooms and strengthened its walls. Jewish zealots had captured Masada from the Romans in 66 A.D. and held it throughout the war. From this lofty fortress which loomed over the Dead Sea, they continued to harass the Romans after the destruction of Jerusalem.

In 73 A.D., Flavius Silva, Roman governor of the province, determined to end this revolt. He assigned the Tenth Legion to Masada, together with auxilliary troops and prisoners of war to carry water and provisions to the troops in this isolated area. Masada, set strategically atop an almost inaccessible mount, 1,300 feet above the Dead Sea, was not easily captured.

The Romans erected a great ramp to gain access to the walls and then employed siege works against them. As fast as the wall was penetrated, the Zealots replaced it with an ingenious wooden barrier stronger than the original walls. The siege had been long and at last the wooden barrier was set afire. The Romans withdrew until the next day, allowing the fire to consume it. During the night, rather than allow the abuse and slavery the Romans would inflict upon their wives and children, each slew their own families and were in turn killed, until the last man took his own life. When the Romans entered the fortress, they found only one old woman and another woman with five children who had hidden in an underground cavern. Nine hundred and sixty people had died of their own volition rather than surrender. Today Masada stands as a mighty symbol to Israel of their determination to defend their nation and keep it free.

Archeological explorations were conducted by Yigael Yadin, the Hebrew University, Israel Exploration Society and the government of Israel between 1963 - 1965. They found remnants of a system of collecting rainwater in nearby wadis that was channeled to cisterns at Masada. Within the ruins of the palace, they found wall paintings. Of special interest was a Roman bath with a hot room whose walls were imbedded with clay pipes leading from a nearby oven. Fragments of scrolls were uncovered along with coins dating from 66 A.D. to 70 A.D., proving the scrolls could be older, but not later, than those dates. Portions of Psalms, Leviticus and Ecclesiasticus were identified and found to be identical to today's Bible. Scroll fragments were also found that indicated the Essenes had joined the Zealot's in their last stand.

Little is known of the Jerusalem Christians who lived quietly in exile near Scythopolis, waiting patiently for the coming of the Lord.

> This same Jesus
> Which is taken up from you into heaven,
> Shall so come in like manner
> As ye have seen him go into heaven.
>
> ACTS 1:11

They elected Symeon, Bishop of the church. Thirteen more bishops "of the circumcision" were elected, but Symeon was the last with family ties to Jesus. Unable to relinquish their bonds with tradition and the influence of Mosaic law, these Christians could not accept a Christianity that included people of all nations. For too many years, the Jews had known a God who was exclusively their God. They became impotent as they clung to the past and they became just another Jewish sect while evangelization among the Gentiles continued to grow.

With the fall of Jerusalem, Christianity was faced with new problems and persecution. From 81 - 96 A.D., Vespasians' younger son, Domitian, persecuted the Christians with an intense hatred. Naturally cruel and vengeful, he first killed his own brother, Titus. Venting his rage on his own countrymen, he even had some of the Roman Senators put to death. Then turning his animosity on the Christians, he demanded all the lineage of David be put to death. The only ones to be found were a few peasants, grandsons of Jude. They were brought before Emperor Domitian who inquired into their beliefs. When they responded that Jesus would return on the last day to judge the living and the dead, he dismissed them as har mless lunatics.

> And I saw another angel
> Fly in the midst of heaven
> Having the everlasting gospel
> To preach unto them that dwell on the earth,
> And to every nation and kindred,
> And tongue, and people.
> Saying with a loud voice,
> Fear God, and give glory to Him,

For the hour of his judgement is come:
And worship Him that made heaven,
And earth, and the sea,
And the fountains of water.

REVELATION 14:6 & 7

Among the numerous martyrs of Domitian's persecution was Symeon, Bishop of Jerusalem, who was crucified; and John, of whom it was said he was boiled in oil but could not be killed. Therefore, John was banished to the Isle of Patmos, an Aegean island near Miletus; a desolate, rocky, penal islet.

John had outlived all the other apostles. James was the first to be martyred; beheaded by king Agrippa. Traditionally, Peter was crucified in Rome with his head at the bottom of the cross, not considering himself worthy to be cruci- fied like Christ. Andrew had been crucified at Petrae in Achaia (hanging upon the cross for two days and testifying of Jesus until his last breath.) Philip was said to have been hanged against a pillar in Phrygia. Thomas had carried the gospel to India and been martyred there. Matthew died by the sword in Ethiopia. Nathaniel (Bartholomew) had been flayed alive.

Then shall they deliver you up to be afflicted.
And shall kill you.
And ye shall be hated of all nations,
For my name's sake.

MATTHEW 24:9

John is believed to have spent his last years in Ephesus, and returned there after his imprisonment on Patmos. Of all the apostles,

John was spiritually closer to Jesus than the others and is known as "the apostle of love."

> Herein is love, not that we loved God,
> But that he loved us,
> And sent his Son to be
> The propitiation for our sins
> If we love one another, God dwelleth in us,
> And his love is perfected in us.
> Hereby know we that we dwell in him,
> And he in us,
> Because he hath given us of his Spirit.
>
> I   JOHN 4:10-13

John never lost the original in-f illing of the Holy Ghost he received on that memorable day of Pentecost in an upper room in Jerusalem. Even imprisoned on that desolate, forbidding Isle of Patmos, John could say:

> I was in the Spirit on the Lord's day.
>
> REVELATION 1:10

In his latter years, John's concerns were for the seven Asian churches, Ephesus, and the other six mentioned in Revelations. Paul had built a strong church at Ephesus during his third missionary journey. Later the church was blessed with John's presence. Nevertheless, the Lord had a word of caution for this upstanding church.

> Unto the angel of the church at Ephesus write
> Nevertheless I have somewhat against thee,
> Because thou hast left thy first love

But this thou hast, that thou hatest the deeds
Of the Nicolaitans, which I also hate.
                    REVELATIONS 2:1, 4, 6

The Ephesian church was not fooled by f alse doctrine; it was f aithful, patient and labored hard for the Lord, but they were taking their salvation for granted, treating their love of God as a matter of course and not as their most precious possession.

The Nicolaitans were a little-known sect of ungodly men, turning the grace of God into lasciviousness; thereby denying the Lord. This sect was closely related to a type of Gnosticism which taught that only the spirit was good, that the flesh was evil and therefore what was done in the flesh was of no consequence.

And unto the angel of the church in Smyrna, write I
know thy works, and tribulation, and poverty.
{But thou art rich.)
Fear none of these things which thou shalt suffer.
Be thou faithful unto death,
And I will give thee a crown of life.
                    REVELATIONS 2:8, 10

Today Smyrna is the modern Izmir, an important Aegean port of West Anatolian Turkey. Even in Biblical times it appeared to be a prosperous city whose public buildings rivalled those of Ephesus and Pergamum. It's first Christians were converts of Jewish proselytes. Possibly persecution had affected their livelihood. There was pressure at this time from Domitian who, near the end of his reign in 96 A.D., had become a mortal adversary, demanding he be worshipped as "Lord" and "God." A Christian's f aith was often tested by a demand for a public choice between Christ and Caesar. This practice did not stop with Domitian. In 155 A.D., Polycarp, aged Bishop of Smyrna, who had at one time sat at the feet of John, was martyred. In order to stem the growing influence of the church, Roman authorities called for the martyrdom of eleven Christians. When it came Polycarp's turn to recant, he answered: "I have served Him for eighty-six years and He has done me no wrong. How can I speak evil of my King, who saved me?" He was burnt at the stake, refusing to be tied, and was untouched by flames which roared above him until he had been killed by a sword.

Smyrna was the last city in Asia Minor to yield to Moslem conquest. Greek and Ar menian Christians continued to be numerous.

> And to the angel of the church in Pergamos write:
> I know thy works, and where thou dwellest,
> Even where Satan's seat is:
> And thou holdest fast my name.
> And hast not denied my faith.
>   REVELATIONS 2:12, 13

Pergamum was the principal center of emperor worship in the region. The first temple of the imperial cult was placed in Pergamum; a temple to Rome

& Augustus. Temples were also built to honor Tragan and Hadrian; temples to men, not God. It was the location of a great altar of Zeus, decorated with sculptured scenes of struggling gods and giants with snake-like tails, worthy of being called "Satan's Throne." The sanctuary of Asclepius, the god of healing whose symbol was the serpent, drew many people to the city. Asclepius sat upon a throne, with a staff in his hand, and his other hand upon the head of the serpent. The Christians must have found this pagan symbolism extremely diabolical.

> But I have a few things against thee
> Because thou hast there
> Them that hold the doctrine
> Of the Nicolaitanes, which thing I hate.
>
> REVELATIONS 2:15

Clement of Alexandria complained that some members of the early church, following an injunction to treat the flesh with contempt, were even sharing each others wives, living in absolute promiscuity. Nicolaus, one of seven deacons, went as far as to of fer his wife to the apostles. The term Nicolaitanes may have been derived from this ungodly deacon.

> And unto the angel of the church in Thyatira
> I have a few things against thee,
> Because thou sufferest that woman Jezebel
> which calleth herself a prophetess,
> To teach and seduce my servants To commit fornication.
> And to eat things sacrificed unto idols.
>
> REVALATIONS 2:18, 20

Thyatira was on a key highway of commerce. The town was famed for its guilds of weavers, dyers of wool and linen textiles, leather-workers, metal craftsmen and potters. It would seem that the Nicolaitanes also practiced liberal and wider measures of participation in the pagan lif e of the Greek and Roman world. Obviously they taught that the banquets of the world of guilds and pagan- ism were not stumbling blocks to Christianity.

Lydia, Paul's first convert in Europe, had been a cloth merchant from Thyatira. Ironically, John mentions another woman - Jezebel. Jezebel was a part of a trade alliance between Tyre and Israel. The Phoenician wealth, which built king Ahab's ivory palace, was in return for Israel's produce. Jezebel was the daughter of king Ethbaal, a Phoenician. She brought Baal worship to Israel and led the country into the gross immoralities of this religion. John's Jezebel belonged to another trade alliance and also lured God's people into ungodly, pagan practices.

> And unto the angel of the church in Sardis
> I know thy works, that thou has a name that livest
> And art dead.
> Be watchful, and strengthen the things which remain
> That are ready to die,
> For I have not found thy works perfect before God.
> REVELATIONS 3:1, 2

Sardis was a highland city of West Asia Minor, capital of the powerful kingdom of Lydia, home of the fabulously rich Croesus. It has been credited as the first to mint coins of gold and silver. It was once a city arrogant and proud, but twice had been captured by guile and stealth in spite of its nearly impregnable fortifications strategically located atop a ridge.

Its rich citizens had adopted mystery cults, including that of Cybelle, which claimed power to restore life to the dead. Her Christianity degenerated until the majority reverted to paganism and witchcraft.

Howard Butler, excavating the ruins of Sardis for Princeton in 1910, was surprised to find remnants of a synagogue adjacent to the temple of Artemis. Today the church, as well as the city, are dead; with no hope of resurrection.

> And to the angel of the church in Philadelphia
> Him that overcometh will I make a pillar
> In the temple of my God, And he shall go no more out.
> And I will write upon him the name of my God. And
> the name of the city of my God.
> Which is New Jerusalem.
> Which cometh down out of heaven from my God. And
> I will write upon him my new name.
> REVELATIONS 3: 7,12

There was no condemnation for the little church at Philadelphia located in a small farming town near Sardis, whose name meant "Brotherly Love." In 17 A.D. it was almost destroyed by an earthquake. After being rebuilt by emperor Tiberius, the city adopted the name "New Caesarea" in his honor, but later assumed their old name. Another time, they attempted to rename their city in honor of Vespasian, but were not successful. It was not meant for these godly people to give honor to men. They belonged to the Lord and he would supply their name. Today, it remains a small town, and its present name is Alasehir, meaning "city of God."

> And unto the angel of the church of the Laodiceans
> So then because thou art lukewarm, And neither cold nor hot,
> I will spew thee out of my mouth,
> Because thou sayest, I am rich and increased with goods, And have need of nothing.
> And knowest not that thou art wretched,
> And miserable, and poor, and blind, and naked. Behold,
> I stand at the door and knock.
> REVELATIONS 3:14, 16, 17 &: 20

This is an accurate portrayal of many of today's churches in America. Notice this is the only one of the churches in which God is on the outside! In 60 A.D. much of Laodicea was destroyed by an earthquake, but this city was so wealthy it financed its own rebuilding without help from Rome. The prosperity of the people, and a need for nothing, had reduced their zeal for God. They were unaware of their spiritual poverty. Laodiceans could easily relate to the distasteful qualities of "lukewarm." Their city water supply came from hot springs which arrived lukewarm -neither hot nor cold.

John was aware of the insidious encroachment of Gnosticism which was sowing confusion in the Christian communities. John's efforts to combat this was evident in his writing.

> Hereby know ye the Spirit of God:
> Every spirit that confesseth that Jesus Christ
> Is come in the flesh, is of God:

> And every spirit that confesseth not That Jesus Christ
> is come in the flesh Is not of God.
>
> I JOHN 4:2, 3

To the end, John's life remained spiritually close to God. Only Paul's under- standing of Jesus Christ equalled that of John. They clearly understood and taught the "oneness of God." The revelation, or mystery of God, had been imbedded in their ministry as they preached of God: omnipotent, all-powerful; omni-present, simultaneously everywhere; eternal, having no beginning or end of existence, everlasting; spiritually invisible; man's saviour, the sacrificial lamb; and the Holy Ghost, God's Spirit sent to comfort, to give power, and to indwell those born again of the water and of the Spirit. They preached of the sacrificial lamb; God who became the Son of man through Mary and simultaneously the Son of God, manifest in the flesh, that his blood might be shed to redeem man; God Almighty, who suffered for the sins of man through crucifixion; One who rose again that there might be eternal life for those who believed on His name - Jesus Christ; for believers, who through faith, understood the necessity of baptism in Jesus' name and the infilling of the Holy Ghost.

> **For all have sinned, and come short**
> **Of the glory of God;**
> **Being justified freely by his grace**
> **Through the redemption that is in Christ Jesus.**
> **ROMANS 3:23, 24**

For it pleased God to give credit to Jesus Christ, whom he revealed as his Son, a role He chose to play as man's redemptor.

CHAPTER XV

INFILTRATION

Gnosticism began in Alexandria, Egypt. The first concrete evidence of this was uncovered in 1945 near Nag Hammadi in the upper Egyptian desert when a peasant discovered an ancient earthenware jar containing fifty-two papyrus texts, including gospels and other secret writings dating from the early Christian era. They were originally sold on the black market to antique dealers in Cairo, until the government became aware of them. Today ten and one-half of thirteen leather-bound books or codices have been recovered and placed in the Coptic Museu m of Cairo.

Translations reveal distorted gospels; some familiar sayings in unfamiliar context. Others are entirely different; such as "These are the secret words which the living Jesus spoke, and which the twin, Judas Thomas, wrote down." These "secret" words have a ring of ancient Babylonian religions - shades of Ni mrod. The Gospel of Thomas was only one of fif ty-t wo texts.

The "secret" book of John, The Testimony of Truth, tells the story of the garden of Eden from the serpent's view point; a serpent who appears as "divine wisdom", who persuades Adam and Eve to partake of knowledge while a jealous god looks on.

But I fear, lest by any means,
As the serpent beguiled Eve
Through his subtilty.
So your minds shall be corrupted
From the simplicity that is in Christ.

II CORINTHIANS 11:3

Further evidence of Satanic influence in these books deny the divinity and the resurrection of Jesus. God is referred to as both father and mother, the virgin birth is profaned and denied by the reference to Christ's twin. These tests also contain myths, magic and instructions for occult practices.

Gnostic means "knowing" or "knowledge", but gnosis is not rational know- ledge. Abetted by philosophers of schools of learning at Alexandria, their beliefs spread. They taught "look within yourself for God, the self and the divine are identical." Their Jesus speaks of illusion and enlightenment, not of sin and repentance as Jesus taught when he walked the hills of Galilee and the streets of Jerusalem. Gnosticism taught when a disciple attained enlightenment, Jesus was no longer his master - the two became equal - or identical. This teaching parallels Buddhaism and ancient Babylonish and Persian religions. Repeatedly, heathen religions have worshipped goddesses. The original gnostic codices credit Eve with giving life to Adam; claiming Mary Magdelene's insight was f ar greater than that of the apostles, and even oblique references to God being a woman.

The gnostic's greatest inroads upon Christianity were through their teachings that matter was evil and their denial that Christ had a natural, corporeal existence; thereby denying the reality of the Incarnation and nullifying all of Christianity.

> Now if Christ be preached
> That he rose from the dead,
> How say some among you
> That there is no resurrection of the dead?
> But if there be no resurrection of the dead,
> Then is Christ not risen.
> And if Christ be not risen.
> Then is our preaching vain,
> And your faith is also vain.
> I CORINTHIANS 15:12 - 14

In practice, the gnostic's teaching that matter was evil was interpreted in either of two ways. Either extreme asceticism and denial of the flesh; or total experience -- leading to extremes in sensuality and moral excesses.

The extreme importance of gnosticism is in its influence on religious move- ments. Usually it is not recognized by its true name, but its essence is incor- porated into that of others.

Greek philosophy also intruded on Christian beliefs. Plato, in particular, had a direct bearing on the direction the church would take. In the post-Apostolic period, Neoplatonism influenced Justin Martyr, who called Plato "a Christian before Christ." Plato's philosophy was not Christian, but was easily assimilated into it. Plato identified Good with

God, but not god as a personal being, and he believed in a visionary or mystical union with God in which virtue must be sought for the health and harmony of the soul, for goodness is harmony with the Good which is the Real. Such a hypothetical religion lef t no room for reality and denied the existence of sin and evil. Further more, it denied a need for salvation or for the incarnation of Christ.

> Beware lest any man spoil you
> Through philosophy and vain deceit,
> After the tradition of men,
> After the rudiments of the world,
> And not after Christ.
>
> COLOSSIANS 2:8

The early post-Apostolic f athers (90 - 140 A.D.) emphasized Old Testament monotheism, the diety and the humanity of Christ. The Greek Apologists (130 180 A.D.) also emphasized the oneness of God. Polycarp of Smyrna (69 - 156 A.D.) was John's disciple and a pastor of the church at Smyrna who espoused the belief in one God. Poly-carp and Ignatius were acquainted as correspondence between them proves. John appointed Ignatius as pastor of the church at Antioch. His writings prove him to be a Christian "oneness" or "Monarchian" leader who believed in one God who was Jesus Christ our Lord. Ignatius was also termed "Theophorus" (God-bearer), referring to the Spirit within him, or his having received the baptism of the Holy Ghost. When, old in years, Ignatius was summoned to Rome and sentenced to die a martyr, Emperor Trojan asked him "And who is Theoporus?" Ignatius replied, "He who has Christ within his breast."

> But ye are not in the flesh.
> But in the Spirit.
> If so be that the Spirit of God dwell in you.
> Now if any man have not the Spirit of Christ,
> He is none of His.
>
> ROMANS 8:9

Ignatius and Polycarp taught only one God. A trinity of three persons was not a part of the Apostolic doctrine, nor of theirs. They taught God was the Father in creation, became the Son in redemption and is the Holy Ghost in regenera- tion. They were called "Modalists" because their ministry was modeled upon that of the Apostles.

During the second and third centuries, forms of binitarianism and trini- tarianism began to infiltrate the churches and corrupt the tenets of Christianity. But as a whole, Modalist doctrine was upheld. Some of the more noteworthy Modalists were Clement of Alexandria, Noetus, Praxeas and Sabellius. Two Roman bishops (later classified as Roman popes) Callistus and Zephrenus were accused of being Modalists by their opponents. Although each of these Modalists differed in their theologies, each upheld one person in the Godhead.

Originally, it was clearly understood by those converted to Christianity that God created man in spite of foreknowledge that man would fall into sin. God would never have created man without knowing exactly how he would redeem fallen mankind. The Son was conceived in the mind of God before the beginning of the world. God saw man's redemption through the atoning death of Christ, and His manifestation in the flesh as Son of God and Son of man, was conceived before He made man in His image. His plan - the Word - existed from the beginning in the mind of God.

> In **the beginning was the Word,**
> **And the Word was with God,**
> **And the Word was God.**
> **And the Word was made flesh,**
> **And dwelt among us.**
>
> **JOHN 1:1 & 14**

The Christian Apologists were the forerunners of the Trinitarians. Yet the beginning was not here. The Babylonians worshipped one god in three persons (father, mother & child) and used the equilateral triangle as the symbol of their trinity. The Babylonian trinity was "the Eternal Father, the spirit of god incarnate in a human mother and a divine son. Ancient Egypt had a triune deity, Ra, Amon and Ptah. They also had a father, mother and son in Osiris, Isis and Hor us. Hinduism has a trinity -- Brahma the Creator, Shiva the Destroyer, and Vishnu the Preserver. Buddhism has a doctrine of a triple body or Trikaya. One is eternal, cosmic reality, a second one is a heavenly manifestation of the f irst, and the last one is an earthly manifestation of the second. (Many Buddhists worship a threeheaded statue.) An ancient religion of China, Taoism, has a trinity of gods - the Jade Emperor, Lao Tzu, and Ling Pao - the three

Purities. The philosophical trinity of Plato and Neo-platonism have already been mentioned. Paganism gave birth to trinitarianism.

The Christian Apologists sought to reconcile Christianity with Greek and Roman philosophy and the pagan world. Outwardly, they opposed gnosticism, but they adopted many of their theories. The first known Apologist was Quad- ratus of Athens (100 - 125 A.D.).

Justin Martyr was the most noted Apologist. He wrote his First Apology about 140 A.D. The Apologists believed in the baptism of the Holy Ghost and in the Gifts of the Holy Spirit, especially in healing and in casting out of demons, but they denied the oneness of God. Justin Martyr taught that the Son was a separate, divine person. Justin's influence was far-reaching. Irenaeus, Ter- tullian, Hippolytes, Cyprian, and Novatian all reflect his school of thought. Yet, in spite of his misconceptions, Justin Martyr must be respected for his steadfastness to the doctrine he believed to be the true gospel, for he died a martyr in Rome in 165 A.D.

Although the first record of the ter m "trinity" appears to have been by the Bishop of Antioch, Theophilus, in about 180 A.D., Tertullian (150 A.D. -225 A.D.) is usually credited with its origin. Justin Martyr is said to have been the first to mention a triune formula for baptism - "in the name of the Father, Son and Holy Ghost." The word "trinity" is not in the Bible and was not commonly associated with the gospel until the beginning of the third century when Tertullian of Carthage brought the term into theological use. He also made the personality of the Holy Ghost a distinct and separate person in the Godhead.

> For there are three that bear record in heaven, The Father, the Word, and the Holy Ghost,
> And these three are one.
> And there are three that bare witness in earth, The spirit, and the water, and the blood,
> All these three agree in one.
> If we receive the witness of men, The witness of God is greater; For this is the witness of God
> Which he hath testified of his Son.
>
> I JOHN 5:7 - 9

Tertullian believed the Logos doctrine of the Greek Apologists. The Trini- tarians had been quick to question the Logos (the Word) and the Son. The Greek worldly philosophy associated it with the divine Logos of their own philosophy. The church fathers related the Logos with God in much the same way that man's word is a part of an individual. It was indivisible and inseparable from the Father. The Trinitarian's concept of the Logos as a separate being was based on the philosophy of Philo.

The Modalists understood that the Son referred to the Father come in the flesh. Their distinction was in the modes or roles displayed by God at a given time. Neotus said that Jesus was the Son by reason of His birth, but He was also the Father. Jesus was the incarnation of the fullness of the Godhead.

Neotus and Praxeas emphasized Jesus' human nature and suffering. The trini- tarians did not dispute this but they considered Christ a separate person called the Son or Logos. The Modalists believed that the Father was not flesh, but was clothed or manifested in the flesh. The Son was made expressly for the salvation of mankind just as the Holy Spirit, or Holy Ghost, is not a separate being any more than the Logos (Word) but refers to God's power.

> Who, being the brightness of his glory And the express
> image of his person
> And upholding all things by the word of his power,
> When he had by himself purged our sins,
> Sat down on the right hand of the majesty on high.
>
> HEBREWS 1: 3

"The right hand of God" was yet another contention of the Trinitarians, who used it as an example of God the Father and God the Son. Yet even today the world is familiar with the terms "right hand" and "right arm" as denoting power and strength. Biblical connotations refer to God's saving power. At social affairs, pre-eminence or honor is preferred upon the one seated on the right hand of the host.

Next to be attacked was the original formula for baptizing:

> **Repent, and be baptized every one of you**
> **In the name of Jesus Christ**
> **For the remission of sins,**
> **And ye shall receive the gift of the Holy Ghost.**
>
> **ACTS 2:38**

Since idol worshippers believed in many gods and practiced dipping three times in water for cleansing, Tertullian, and others, found it convenient to advocate dipping three times, once for each person in the Godhead.

Yet, during this period the majority rejected the teachings of Tertullian. One notable example was Noetus of Smyrna. After the death of Polycarp, the church had allowed Trinitarian teaching to steal into their midst. For the rest of his life, Noetus battled the intrusion of false doctrine. He was expelled from the church at Smyrna for his strong stand on oneness. Hippolytus, a Trinitarian historian, labelled Noetus a heretic! Hippolytus was a liberal Trinitarian who also wrote on magic, astrology and philosophy. Noetus is believed to have been martyred in Ephesus about 200 A.D.

Origen, who died in 254 A.D., had the greatest effect on the East. His heretical beliefs stemmed from Greek philosophy and mystic knowledge rather than faith. His allegorical interpretations of scripture appealed to many. He believed in the pre-existence of the souls of men, denied the necessity of Christ's redemption, and believed in the ultimate salvation of all men, good or evil. His teachings were laced with Gnosticism. He had a lasting effect on the church's perception of the Holy Ghost. Origen formalized a ritual of baptismal regeneration that became widespread. The church was beginning to attach more importance to forms and ceremonies than to Christ. Even prayer for the Holy Spirit was formalized - later to be called "Confirmation." Gradually the church believed that only the bishops had the power or authority to pray for others to be f illed with the Spirit.

By the time of Jerome, about 275 A.D., a large percent of the Christian world believed the laying on of hands by the bishops and elders was a necessary means of receiving the Holy Ghost and it was received only symbolically. Al- ready, an ecclesiastical hierarchy was forming which would assume dominion over men's souls. Cyril, writing in the fourth century, describes how the church anointed the baptized with oil, symbolic of the Holy Spirit, before praying for them to receive the Holy Ghost.

In spite of the inroads on the Christian faith by persecution, Gnosticism, Neoplatonism, and Trinitarianism, there were still many oneness assemblies throughout the land. Trinitarian bishops turned to the imperial police of Rome to persecute the oneness believers, scattering their congregations, confiscating their property and executing their leaders. The true church was driven under- ground and into remote areas; decimated, but not wiped out. God will have a people called by his name and baptized in his Holy Spirit.

> Hath God cast away his people? God forbid.
> God hath not cast away his people,
> Which he foreknew.
> Wot ye not what the scripture saith of Elijah?
> How he maketh intercession to God against Israel,
> Saying, Lord they have killed thy prophets,
> And digged down thy altars,

And I am left alone and they seek my life. But what
sayeth the answer of God unto him?
I   have reserved to myself seven thousand men
Who have not bowed the knee to the image of Baal.
Even so then, at this present time also
There is a remnant according to the election of grace.

ROMANS 11:1- 5

Constantine was marching with his army, when, so his story goes, he saw a Flaming Cross superimposed upon the sun and the words "By this sign conquer." He won his battle and became co-emperor of the Roman Empire in 312 A.D. and sole emperor in 324 A.D. Constantine changed his battle standard to a cross and adopted the Christian religion. This may not have been as drastic a step as it might appear. His army was tolerant of many pagan religions - one more did not matter to them. As for Constantine, he was very f amiliar with Mithraism. There were many outward similarities. Mithraism involved an atoning sacrifice, a sacramental meal of bread and wine, resurrection, and the ultimate destruction of the world by fire. It promised immortality and redemption of sins through baptism. A ringing of bells, lighting of candles and sprinkling of holy water were common to both religions. They identified Mithra with the sun. Their baptism was literally performed by washing in the blood of a freshly killed bull.

Constantine proclaimed himself a Christian and the Christian church became the official State church, henceforth to be known as the Roman Catholic church, with himself as its head. He used the church as he used his army; to ensure his own victories. He never relinquished his faith in Mithraism; still his protec- tion rested upon the Catholic church. Sunday was declared an official day of rest, bishops could issue their own decrees, persecution and death by crucifixion were abolished; yet it did more harm to Christians than persecution ever had. Its official acceptance opened the doors to all manners of pagan rituals and doctrines.

In 314 A.D., Constantine called together a Catholic Council at Aries (France) to deal with baptism; whereby a trinitarian baptism of Father, Son and Holy Ghost was declared the only valid method and the original baptism in Jesus name was declared heretical.

> **Neither is there salvation in any other;**
> **For their is none other name under heaven given**
> **among men**
> **Whereby we must be saved.**
>
> **ACTS 4:12**

Constantine never committed himself to Christianity, but demanded de- corum in religious services. He detested disputes between his bishops and one had been brewing for some time between Arius and Athanasius as to the status of the Father and the Son. Therefore in 325 A.D., shortly after Constantine had transferred his capital from Rome to Constantinople, he called together a council of Christian bishops from all over his empire. They met at Nicea, a small town in Bithynia, and forged the Nicene Creed indicating a personal distinction between the Father and Son and a belief in the Holy Ghost. The issue was not fully resolved until 381 A.D. when the Council of Constantinople, called by Emperor Theodasius, unequivocally declared that Father, Son and Holy Ghost were three separate persons co-equal and co-eternal. This Catholic Council specifically stated that Sabellian' Jesus name baptism was invalid.

> **Thou believest that there is one God;**
> **Thou doest well:**
> **The devils also believe, and tremble.**
>
> **JAMES 2:19**

Services increased in splendor; ornate priestly robes, bells, candles, and a formalized mass leant a reflected glory to the services. Forms and ceremonies of paganism gradually were added to the worship of the Lord. Old heathen feasts became church festivals. About 405 A.D., images of saints and martyrs began to appear in the churches; first as memorials, but soon worshipped and reverenced. The adoration of the Virgin Mary was substituted for the worship of pagan gods such as Diana, Isis, Estarte and Venus. The gifts of the Spirit were no longer in the church. The Holy Ghost, speaking in tongues, miracles, and healings no longer had a part in the church, because it was led by men, not God. Those who continued to seek the truth and display signs of the Spirit, were persecuted and tortured as heretics.

It was not that the bishops and priests did not believe in God; but they had lost sight of who He is. One by one, as each fundamental truth was denied, they had traveled further away from the Lord they were seeking. There continued to be leaders who, by their eloquence and examples of holiness, still influence today's churches.

Augustine was one of these. Born in Algeria in 354 A.D. of wealthy parents, he was well educated and worldly. Converted at thirty-three years of age, he gave all his wealth to the poor, determined to live a religious life. Against his protests he was appointed Bishop of Hippo. He was a prolific writer; author of over two hundred books which f ill fifty large volumes, yet he never understood God's plan for man's salvation.

John Chrysostom, known as St John of Antioch, and Augustine were contem- poraries. John was priest of Antioch until 398 A.D. when he was made Patriarch of Constantinople, which he hated. The people loved him, but he had no patience with pomp, luxury, or the intrigues of the palace and for this was exiled to the furthermost Roman outpost. The Greek Orthodox Church has made him a saint and he is remembered as one who suffered humbly for the sins of the world and who sang angelically in his sermons.

About 450 A.D., oneness assemblies in the Antioch area came to the attention of the Catholic church at Constantinople, who hastened to declare the baptism of Sabellians invalid. Heretical baptism was discovered in northeastern Italy in 458 A.D.; people were being "rebaptized" or "repeating their baptism" allegedly through erroneous teaching. By this they meant being baptized in "Jesus name" instead of the presently accepted Catholic formula of "Father, Son and Holy Ghost."

> Now when the apostles which were at Jerusalem
> Heard that Samaria had received the word of God,
> They sent unto them Peter and John:
> Who, when they were come down,
> Prayed for them, that they might receive
> The Holy Ghost.
> (For as yet he was fallen upon none of them:
> Only they were baptized in the name of the Lord Jesus.)
> ACTS 8:14 -16

After the fall of the Western Empire in 476 A.D., Byzantium (Constantinople) became the capital of the Eastern Roman Empire. Before the fall, the Bishop at Rome had begun to acquire more influence than the others and was thought of as the "Papa" of the church. When the government lost power, this "Papa" took control of both church and state, in place of the emperor. "Papa" became known as "Pope" and gradually assumed the rule over the emperors in Europe and became the head of all the Catholic churches. The church had sunk deep into "The Dark Age", a period that lasted nearly one thousand years.

The Catholic Empire did not rule unchallenged for long. One insignificant Arab was to have a devastating impact upon the world. Muhammad was an orphan raised by a succession of relatives in the vicinity of Mecca. He was a camel-driver, trader and sheepherder until, at twenty-five years of age, a rich widow of forty found and married him. It seems to have been a happy marriage producing six children. When he was about forty, he began meditating in a nearby cave until one night an angel appeared to him in a vision and told him he would be a messenger of Allah. From that time on he had many visions. At first, only his wife, and her cousin who knew Hebrew, believed him. It was from this cousin that Muhammad received his knowledge of the Gospels and Christianity. At first his converts grew slowly. Mecca rejected him and his teachings, and he moved to Yathrib, later named Madina, where he was accepted by Jews and Arabs of that city. After his death (about 632 A.D.) his disciples gathered together his sayings which make up the Koran. To devout Muslims, this is the infallible, unchangeable word of God. Muhammad spoke often of Jesus as the Messiah with powers to heal the sick and raise the dead, and he believed that Allah, Jesus, and Mary formed a trinity. Yet the Koran denies Jesus crucifixion. Muhammad believed himself to be the last of the prophets; from Abraha m to Jesus to Muhammad.

Within ten years of his death, his Arab converts had conquered Persia, Syria, Egypt and part of Turkey. Within one hundred years, Islam covered all of North Africa and much of Spain. Damascus fell in 6 35, Jerusalem in 638. In 640 A.D. the Arab armies invaded Egypt and had captured it by 642. The Emperor at Constantinople had lost more than half of his empire. All of Europe was threatened by this Muslim religion which had so suddenly overtaken much of the Christian world.

Just as Europe was threatened by Arabs in the seventh and eighth centuries, the ninth and tenth centuries brought invasions of Norsemen down the Russian rivers to the Caspian and Black Seas and down the European coastline into England, France, Germany and Italy via their rivers. The Norse war gods, Odin and Thor, accompanied them. To the Norsemen, Odin was the father of all, creator of men, with the ability to change form at will from fish to snake to bird, etc. Odin's son, Thor, was also a god of war whose emblem was the swastika. His mother, Frigg, had more compassion for the human race than her warring husband and son.

These Scandinavian Vikings were daring marauders who had encircled Europe by 900 A.D. They came to conquer, but were instead converted by Roman and Orthodox Catholics. Grand Prince Vladimir of Russia desired to marry Princess Anne, sister of Emperors Basil II and Constantine III. They consented to the marriage if Vladimer would embrace their religion. He did; with such dedication that he ordered all the populous to be baptized while a priest read the service of baptism.

Rollo of Norway was granted the northern part of France on condition he accept Christianity and protect Normandy from further raids. Little by little, the Norsemen were assimilated into the European population, and culture, and religion.

Church buildings and art had their place and influence upon religion. By- santine mosaics dominated the churches of Turkey, Greece and Italy for a thousand years. Only fragments remain today, but enough to see the dazzling interplay of light on the brilliant fragments of glass and gold that make up the mosaics. Always Christ and the Virgin Mary were given center place; various other scenes included John the Baptist, the apostles, angels, and saints were placed round about them.

Shortly after 1,000 A.D., a great rebuilding of churches began. A new Romanesque influence was at work. Europe had faced and overcome invasions from Norsemen, Arabs, and Hungarians. As the millenium drew to a close, the people had envisioned the end of the world and of judgement day. Now they had been granted a reprieve, but with visions of God's kingdom still fresh in their minds, the Romanesque churches took on a new look. Heavy stone sculpture replaced Mosaics. These displayed a majestic Christ, strong and imposing in marble. But accompanying him were grotesque beasts and suffering martyrs.

> And behold, a throne was set in heaven,
> And one sat on the throne
> And round about the throne,
> Were four beasts full of eyes before and behind.
> And the first beast was like a lion,
> And the second beast like a calf,
> And the third beast had a face as a man
> And the fourth beast was like a flying eagle.
>   REVELATION 4:2, 6, 7

There was a strong Scythian influence to the sculpures. These ancient people who dwelt in the vicinity of the Black Sea had believed in the unity of all animals, as if they were able to change their shapes at will. This belief found a kindred spirit in the Norsemen's god, Odin, who was believed to have a like ability. From this sprang an art form that gave a strange, sinuous, unnatural life to the many carved lions and beasts adorning the churches.

Added emphasis was placed on honoring their saints and martyrs, who were regarded as sacred. Special chapels and hallways were set aside for their wor-ship. Churches were named for their saints, rather than for Christ.

The church acknowledged that the "age of miracles and speaking with tongues" was a thing of the past. The people were assured that the Spirit now worked through the Holy Church. Yet miracles were attributed to relics of the saints. The possession of relics was of utmost importance.

The most significant relic was thought to be the body of St Peter. From the second century it had been claimed that Peter was the first Bishop of Rome.

Tradition credited him as Bishop of Antioch in 34 A.D., moving to Rome in 40 and in 59 appointing Linus and Cletus his successors. No one challenged these claims. The supposed possession of both Peter's and Paul's bodies lent a powerful apostolic foundation and importance to Rome and to the Catholic Church. Basing the claim on scripture, Rome had exerted her authority over all other churches for several centuries.

> And I say also unto thee
> That thou art Peter
> And upon this rock I will build my church
> And the gates of hell shall not prevail against it.
> MATTHEW 16:18

To begin with, it was a false premise to interpret the rock as Peter instead of upon Peter's spiritual understanding that the rock is Jesus. In the second place, it seems strange that in all the time Paul and Barnabas spent at Antioch no mention was made of Peter, yet when dissension was sown among the brethren concerning circumcision, Paul and Barnabas had to go to Jerusalem to meet with him.

Neither was Peter mentioned in Paul's letter to the Romans. It does not seem likely that Paul would have failed to greet Peter had he been in Rome. Possibly the relic of Peter was no more real than some others that were highly valued such as the Lord's swaddling clothes, blood and water from his side, bread from the feeding of the five thousand, a twig from the burning bush and the rods of Moses and Aaron.

> According to the grace of God which is given unto me,
> As a wise masterbuilder, I have laid the foundation
> And another buildeth thereon.
> But let every man take heed how he buildeth thereon,
> For other foundation can no man lay
> Than that is laid, which is Jesus Christ.
> IICORINTHIANS 3:10 & 11

Abbot Suger of France was next to introduce a new architecture that would profoundly affect the churches. Gothic architecture, with its innovative arches and ribbed vaults, drastically changed their shape, allowing light and freedom to flow throughout the buildings in a manner not possible before. The first Gothic church was completed in 1130. Its introduction of ribbed vaults made large stained-glass windows possible for the first time, and with its open in- terior, gave an illusion of feminity. Previous Byzantine and Romanesque churches were essentially masculine. Not so the new Gothic churches. They belonged to the Virgin Mary and her child.

CHAPTER XVI

LINE UPON LINE

Not everyone was satisfied with the church and with the iron rule of the pope. Many were seeking for the basic faith the early apostles had known. Reformation of the church had its birth pangs in the early part of the eleventh century in remote valleys of Italy and France.

Among the first reformation groups were the Cathars (the pure) who were formed in Italy in 1028. They believed in one God, were dedicated to purity and believed that God, not the pope, was head of the church. They maintained a serenity, even as they were martyred for their faith. They rejected the mass, absolution and purgatory. They also believed the Word of Christ, who was the very God, had come into the world; but they could not conceive of the crucifixion or resurrection. (Eventually, their concept of purity took on extremes by a few, even to the food that was acceptable and to vows of chastity.) By 1200, Catharism had spread over all of northern Italy and southern France. It was not just a religion of the common people; many of the aristocracy were drawn to it. Pope Innocent III decreed the death sentence be imposed on these heretics. Catholic crusaders sought out the Cathars and whole villages were massacred. Yet Catharism flourished. Because the faith of these "heretics" was drawn from the Gospels, it became unlawful for anyone other than priests to possess any part of the Bible.

During this period, similar groups known as the Albigenses, an offshoot of the Cathars, and the Waldeneses were branded as "heretics." These people led Spirit-filled lives and were credited with "speaking in tongues." The pope sent his men to exterminate them, but like the Cathars, they could not be completely stamped out.

Pope Innocent IV in 1252 commanded the Dominicans to root out all "heretics", employing whatever torture they desired to use. Still Catharism and the Waldenses lived on.

> For precept must be upon precept,
> Precept upon precept;
> Line upon line, line upon line;
> Here a little, and there a little:
> For with stammering lips and another tongue,
> He will speak to this people.
>
> ISAIAH 28:10, 11

For every step forward there seemed to be two backward. At first, the great cathedrals had been for everyone and the only place where all the sacra- ments could be received. Increasingly, they became shrines for valuables and relics. It became more difficult to obtain a well-known saint for every cathedral, so almost any royal or princely person who came to a tragic end was considered a martyr and enshrined in the choir or santuary. This practice degenerated, until other parts of the cathedrals were filled with chantry chapels, paid for by wealthy families for daily masses for the souls of their dead, and to whom only that family was admitted. The practice of burying wealthy laymen and ecclesiastics within the confines of the cathedrals dates from the thirteenth century. Simultaneously, this practice led to the barring of the public from all but the nave. The laity had no part in the services and, from where they stood, even their vision of the service was obscured.

In the country the parish churches were primarily privately owned. In theory, everyone was expected to understand the basic elements of faith, but in practice many country priests were themselves ignorant men. The people asked only for some hope of salvation, yet over the years the church practices tended to favor only the well-to-do.

Originally, baptism and receiving of the Holy Ghost was for everyone and effectively changed the lives of those who obeyed the original plan of salvation. Gradually, as some fell back into their old sinful ways, a means of repentance was necessary. At first, it was between the sinner and God, then confession to a priest, who would intercede with God. As the form of baptism was changed and receiving of the Holy Ghost became only a formality, men were not changed. No spiritual transformation took place, and men tended more and more to drift back into their old sinful ways. Yet there remained a fear of dying and of condemnation which the church still taught.

> **Likewise, the Spirit also helpeth our infirmities,**
> **For we know not what we should pray for as we ought:**
> **But the Spirit itself maketh intercession for us**
> **With groanings which cannot be uttered.**
> **And he that searcheth the hearts**

Knoweth what is the mind of the Spirit
Because he maketh intercession for the saints.
According to the will of God.

ROMANS 8:26, 27

By the twelfth century, only private confession to a priest was valid. Absolutions came with penance and these, as meted out by the priests, tended to be extreme; such as a regimen of fasting, or fasting that went on for life, or endless pilgrimages. A man might spend his life in mortal fear of failure. Gradually a theory of purgatory was developed. Also a gradual granting of indulgences for political reasons, then for a thinly disguised monetary consideration, until indulgences were sold on almost any ecclesiastical occasion.

Early monasteries had been so influenced by the Benedictines that by 1050 they were a connecting link between the people and the church. Early in the thirteen century, they were joined by Franciscans and Dominicans. The Domin- icans were middle and upper class and literate people while the Franciscans were composed of lower classes. They took vows of poverty, lived off the land, and did a number of worthwhile services such as operate urban schools, hospitals, and serve as preachers and chaplains. Yet they were so hemmed in by man-made rules of sobriety and piety that all spirituality was lost.

As heresy continued to spread, the church developed a systematic inquisition force of Dominican friars armed with the authority to sentence and burn heretics at the stake and to torture and imprison suspects.

Some truly unorthodox movements evolved from anti-church, rebellious, superstitious, revolutionary elements. In some instances, runaway monks or priests who had fallen out with the church, provided leadership. One such radi- cal, a Hungarian monk named Jakob, taught that murdering priests was meritorious and he gathered a following of thousands who rampaged through northern France. When he was murdered, his followers quickly forsook the "cause." The organization of Dominican friars and their methods of inquisition gathered fuel from such outbreaks.

Yet a true movement for reformation had begun. John Wyclif began this movement in England. He wrote against the unscriptural practices of the Roman church. In 1380 he translated the New Testament into the English language and by 1384 had completed the Old Testament. For the first time, Englishmen had the opportunity to gain first-hand knowledge of God's word. For many years it had been church policy to keep the Bible out of the hands of the laity. John Wyclif was called into court and sentenced to be burned to death. When the Pope died first, his orders were not carried out. John Wyclif died a natural death years later, but he had dealt such a blow to the church that forty years after his death, the church commanded his body be dug up and burned!

All scripture is given by inspiration of God.
And is profitable for doctrine,
For reproof, for correction,

> **For instruction in righteousness:**
> **That the man of God may be perfect,**
> **Thoroughly furnished unto all good works.**
> **II TIMOTHY 3:16, 17**

At the fall of Constantinople in 1453 to the Mohammedans, and their sub- sequent capture and control of the whole Eastern Empire, Catholicism was dealt a blow they never fully recovered from. The Eastern Greek Catholic church had been separate since 1054 from the Western Roman Catholic church. The Eastern church was made up of a peace-loving people who had resisted the eff orts of the Roman Pope to seize power over them. Both churches had fallen far from God's plan of salvation, but the loss of Constantinople and the Eastern church to the Turks brought about a spiritual awakening among the people and the beginning of the end of the Dark Age.

Martin Luther is credited with the biggest impact in effecting Reforma- tion of the church system. When Pope Leo X required huge sums of money to build St. Peter's church at Rome, he turned to the church practice of granting indulgences; carrying it to new extremes by selling certificates, signed by him- self , granting pardons for all manner of sins, without repentance. Anyone could buy "forgiveness" for friends, living or dead. He promised souls would rise out of purgatory to heaven upon purchase of his certificates.

This act was too much for Martin Luther who had only recently been impressed with the Biblical phrase "the just shall live by faith," and an understanding that salvation came not through good works.

> **For I am not ashamed of the gospel of Christ;**
> **For it is the power of God unto salvation**
> **To everyone that believeth;**
> **To the Jew first, and also to the Greek.**
> **For therein is the righteousness of God**
> **Revealed from faith to faith:**
> **As it is written, The just shall live by faith.**
> **ROMANS 1:16, 17**

Luther believed he had been given the truth and a responsibility to relay it to the people. His first action, in October of 1517, was to nail a list of ninety- five declarations against the church to its cathedral door. Martin Luther's greatest asset was a spiritual force derived from hours of personal prayer. He was a prolific writer and laid out the Lutheran doctrine of justification by faith in simple terms that appealed to laymen.

When social and economic unrest mingled with the religious reform move- ment, it took the form of a peasant's revolt in 1524. Luther allied himself with a conservative, established order; disassociating himself from the revolutionaries, and thereby gained the support of the princely German rulers. By 1539, Luther and his church were securely established. One step had been taken away from the mother church.

The time had come for new growth. Just as springtime triggers a new awakening of dormant trees and the sap begins to flow and the limbs to put forth new buds, so it was within the hearts and minds of men. Christian Univer- sities had begun to re-examine the fundamental beliefs of the church; to study scripture and re-evaluate the writings of the early fathers. The spread of the new intellectual movement was facilitated by the development of printing. In 1500, there were hundreds of presses in Europe. The church had claimed exclusive right to the Bible since the Ninth Century, but by the end of the Four- teenth Century the Bible was available to much of the public. With the introduc- tion of printing, the New Testament became available in several languages. There were fourteen different versions in the German language alone.

Erasmus was a reformer and scholar who believed there should be no inter- mediaries between the individual and the Scriptures, and that the Bible must be studied. He believed in private devotion and prayers, and that man's salva- tion came through knowledge of God. He rejected indulgences, masses for the dead, and believed the Catholic church was corrupt. But neither was he in agree- ment with Lutheran or Calvinist theology. Considerably older than either of these reformers, he was nevertheless highly respected and his opinions were valued by many in influential positions. Erasmus was a pacifist; Luther believed in violent measures for those who did not conform to his doctrine.

John Calvin was a Frenchman, and contemporary of Martin Luther, who brought the reformation to Switzerland. He taught that men were not only predestined to be saved, but also some to be lost.

> **And we know that all things**
> **Work together for good**
> **For them that love God,**
> **For them who are the called**
> **According to his purpose.**
> **For whom he did foreknow,**
> **He also did predestinate**
> **To be conformed to the image of his Son,**
> **That he might be the first born**
> **Among many brethren.**
>
> **ROMANS 8:28, 29**

Calvin taught salvation was possible for everyone who elected to become a member of his church for "whoever finds himself in Jesus Christ, and is a member of his body by faith, is assured of salvation." His church employed elders and councils to enforce a strict moral code by excommunication of those who did not conform.

By the mid-Sixteenth Century, there were three accepted state religions: the Catholic church in Italy, Lutheranism in Germany, and Calvinists in Switzerland and Scotland. This did not mean acceptance of each other's religions; on the contrary, they opposed and hated each other.

There was another reformer, Michael Servetus, who stood apart from all the others, for he stressed the "oneness" of God and did not understand why anyone who claimed separation from the Catholic church would cling to the trinity doctrine, which he called a "three-headed monster." Servetus was burned at the stake for his convictions. Although John Calvin was primarily responsible for the martyrdom of Servetus, both Catholics and Protestants were in favor of it. They had found a united cause.

The Protestant movement spread to the British Isles. The great majority of the people became Anglican, members of the Church of England, with a small dissenting group of Presbyterians, Congregationalists, Baptists and Quakers. It was automatically assumed everyone was a member of a church - a state church - just as they were a citizen of a country. Very little diversity or freedom of worship was allowed until the settlement of the American colonies.

The English government took a tolerant religious attitude toward the new colonists, primarily because of the economic need to attract settlers to this wild, uncivilized country. Jails were emptied, the impoverished and adventurers were recruited, but it soon became apparent that those seeking religious freedom were highly dependable settlers worth cultivating. For example, when Peter Stuyvesant tried to suppress religious freedom in New Amsterdam, Dutch author- ities quickly ordered hi m to stop, lest he discourage other settlers from coming to the New World. English policy was the same; grants were made to Lord Balti- more and William Penn specifically allowing freedom of worship.

For many, this new beginning, coupled with separation from their homeland, was looked upon as the Lord's doing. America was a land of opportunity, a land where an "open door" was awaiting them. It was the promised land where all things would be made new. Many believed that colonizing America was no acci- dent; that God had kept America hidden for a divine purpose and that His pre- determined time had come to fulfill America's destiny and that it was related to God's f inal act of redemption.

> **And when they were come,**
> **And had gathered the church together,**
> **They rehearsed all that God had done with them,**
> **And how he had opened the door of faith**
> **Unto the Gentiles.**
>
> **ACTS 14:27**

Virginia, the first colony to be settled (in 1607) was also the only one to have religious restrictions imposed upon it. The Church of England, and its Anglican established religion, had sent Chaplains along with the first settlers to enforce conformity to the church. By this time the Church of England had severed all ties with the Roman Catholic church, and the English monarch was the "supreme governor" of the church. Prayers for the dead had been abolished, worship was conducted in English and a strong Puritan movement had begun.

North Carolina, South Carolina and Georgia were nominally Anglican, but religious toleration was practiced from the first. Maryland was founded in 1634 by Lord Baltimore, who was Catholic, but the Roman Catholics were a minority, even on his first ship that set sail for America.

In 1629 a group of Non-separatist Congregationalists obtained a royal charter for the Massachusetts Bay Company and, by a questionable oversight, immediate control by the English monarch was not included, signifying independence. The stockholders were called "freemen." New Hampshire and Connecticut were extensions of Massachusetts. Rhode Island became the refuge for those who opposed the predominant Congregational religion. This sect had broken away from the Church of England because they believed church members should determine church affairs as well as retaining the authority of ordination within their own congregation. Their places of worship were called "meeting houses" so that people would not mistakenly think that the church was a building.

> And has put all things under his (Christ's) feet,
> And gave him to be the head
> Over all things in the church,
> Which is his body (congregation);
> The fullness of him that filleth all in all.
>   EPHESIANS 1:22, 23

Because the Duke of York owed a huge debt to his deceased father, William Penn accepted a vast territory in the New World in payment. William Penn was well pleased for he desired to establish a society based upon Quaker faith and idealism. This land was named Pennsylvania and was founded in 1681. A year later, William Penn purchased Delaware.

George Fox had initiated the Quaker Friends' Societies in an effort to bring new lif e into dead, formal English churches by a real spiritual worship of God. George Fox, a poor uneducated cobbler, began his preaching without followers, without a church, without training.

> For ye see your calling, brethren,
> How that not many wise men after the flesh,
> Not many mighty, not many noble, are called.
> But God hath chosen the foolish things
> Of the world to confound the wise;
> And God hath chosen the weak things of the world
> To confound the things which are mighty.
> I CORINTHIANS 1:26, 27

He rivalled Paul in persecution; he was beaten, stoned and imprisoned fre- quently, as were his followers. George Fox and the early Quakers were repeatedly jailed for their convictions, for not conforming to the state church, for refusing to serve in the army or navy. From the beginning of the movement, the Friends opposed war and slavery of every kind. They were the leaders in many reforms such as freeing women from bondage, abolition of capital punishment for minor offenses, and imprisonment for debt and religious persecution. In spite of their radical ideals, George Fox and the early Quakers gained favor with God and the respect of men. People found they could be trusted; consequently their businesses prospered.

George Fox was born in 1624 in England. From an early age, it was evident a Godly influence rested upon him. Step by step, he was drawn to a deeper Christian experience. Soon after he began to preach, word spread his ministry was different, and people came from far off to hear him. Fox became mightily used of God as those who heard him preach were convicted of their sinful natures and the Lord's Spirit began to shake them.

Fox called the state churches "steeplehouses", pointing out that the people who truly believed in Christ were the real church of God.

> **What?   Know ye not that your body**
> **Is the temple of the Holy Ghost**
> **Which is in you, which ye have of God, And ye are**
> **not your own.**
> **I CORINTHIANS 6:19**

A remarkable spiritual power was characteristic of his preaching. He went everywhere afoot, often meeting opposition and ridicule, yet converting the greatest disbelievers. Fox often preached of the Lord's power poured out to direct the people through His Spirit to better understand the scriptures.

> **Now we have received,**
> **Not the spirit of the world,**
> **But the Spirit which is of God; That we might know**
> **the things That are freely given to us of God.**
> **I CORINTHIANS 2:12**

Fox went all over Britain and overseas to Germany, Holland, the West Indies, and America preaching with great Spiritual power. On numerous occasions, the power of the Lord was so great that as the people trembled and shook, so did the steeplehouse! He profoundly desired to turn people from outward forms and ceremonies and to direct them to the need of real holiness of heart and lifestyle. Fox taught as Jesus taught in His Sermon on the Mount, emphasizing a need to be pure in heart, meek in spirit, and to love God and neighbors.

The Quakers were quiet of speech, plainly dressed, honest and restrained in behavior. They gathered in silence for worship until one of them was led by the Spirit to speak. Surprisingly, they were great missionaries and nowhere were they more successful than America. By the close of the colonial period, the Quakers ranked fif th numerically of all the denominations.

Presbyterian churches were established on Long Island, in New Jersey, Pennsylvania, Maryland, and South Carolina. Although there were scattered groups of Scotch-Irish in the colonies by 1680, most did not come to America until after 1720. John Knox, impressed by John Calvin, had introduced this church to Scotland. It did not differ greatly from other continental reformed churches.

The Baptists were another variation of the Puritan movement. They were Congregationists who believed baptism should be restricted to those accountable for their faith; they were Calvinistic in nature and similar to the Presbyterians. Initially they rejected infant baptism. Churches were first formed in New Jersey, Pennsylvania, and Delaware, but soon spread to all thirteen colonies and by the American revolution had become one of the major religious groups in America.

Religions in America were primarily protestant. Roman Catholics were few, primarily located in Maryland, New York, and Pennsylvania. German and Dutch settlers introduced the Mennonites, Dunkers, and Moravians. Because of William Penn's liberal policies, many settled in Pennsylvania. Primarily, they were plain people who sought to abide by New Testament principles. The Dunkers differed in that they baptized by a three-fold immersion rather than by pouring. German Lutherans and German Reformed also migrated, although on a more individual basis.

Jews were also represented in colonial America, but they were few in num- ber. The earliest known Jewish synagogue was built in 1730 in New Amsterdam.

The liberty of freedom to worship and proliferation of religions in America was misleading because initially the majority of people belonged to no church. The first Puritans had come with great expectations, but by the second and third generations, a moral apathy and sense of duty pervaded the churches.

Primarily in Europe, and to some extent in America, the eighteenth century brought an increase in scientific knowledge and a corresponding doubt in eternal hell-fire. Hell remained, but educated, sophisticated people were inclined to reject references to it from the pulpit. They preferred to believe that a loving God would not subject sinners to everlasting fire. Consequently, as ministers catered to their congregations and no longer preached of hell, crime and sin flourished. To counter this, governments were compelled to impose stiffer and stiffer penalties.

> **Knowing this, that the law is not made for a righteous man, But for the lawless and disobedient, For the ungodly and for sinners, For unholy and profane, for murderers....**
> **I TIMOTHY 1:9**

A counter-measure, or great awakening, occurred on both sides of the Atlantic, spontaneously, from several sources. One of the first began with Theodore Frelinghuysen, believed to be a German Pietist, who began an evangelistic movement in the Dutch Reformed church. William Tennent and his sons were responsible for revival among the Presbyterians as they fought against smugness and complacency by preaching against sin.

Jonathan Edwards sparked a revival at Northampton, Massachusetts in 1734 that continued until 1737. He published an account of this revival that greatly influenced George Whitefield and John Wesley. By 1740, revivals had spread through every colony, touching every class of people. George Whitehead, the first successful open-air preacher, was born in England and a scholar at Oxford, ordained by the Church of England, and touched by the Holy Spirit. He was a minister of great faith and power, endowed with an extraordinary voice. From the beginning he attracted huge crowds. Soon he was barred from the state churches because of his Spirit-filled preaching. Rather than hindering him, this proved to be a blessing as he gathered crowds too large for any church wherever he chose to preach. Before he began his open air ministry, he had preached in one church where a thousand people had to be turned away. This prompted his outdoor ministry which he conducted in such diverse places as churchyards, coalmines, the roughest parts of London, and Kennington Common, where he drew a more refined audience. He was close friends with the Wesleys, but they did not always agree on points of theology. During his lifetime, he was mightily used of God. He made seven visits to America; literally preaching until the day he died on his last visit in 1770. As a direct result of his preaching, many people separated from their original churches and ultimately found their way to Baptist churches.

John Wesley, and his brother Charles, were born of a long line of Church of England ministers. John himself was an ordained minister of the Church of England. While at Oxford, he started the Methodist Societies; small groups who gathered to study scripture and books on holy living and to visit the poor, sick and imprisoned; becoming actively involved in Christian service.

In 1735, John and Charles sailed for America, intending to become missionaries to the Indians. During this voyage, John met, and was strongly influenced by Moravian missionaries. This visit to America met with little success.

Returning to England, he sought to learn more from the Moravians and was surprised to learn that almost all conversions to Christ came instantaneously, through faith. Wesley had a great longing for a deep experience of God. At last God's power f ell mightily upon him, filling him with joy and praise for the Lord. This powerful anointing of the Spirit remained and from that time his preaching took on a new dimension.

> Now unto him that is able to keep you from falling.
> And to present you faultless
> Before the presence of his glory
> With exceeding joy.
>
> JUDE 24

Whitefield now requested Wesley take over his open-air ministry. After witnessing Whitefield's success, he too became a famous open-air minister, preaching to even larger crowds. Conviction of sin rested upon the people as they cried out or swooned until obtaining forgiveness and peace. Powerful moves of the Holy Ghost accompanied Wesley's preaching. Scoffers and disbelievers were in turn "slain in the Spirit" and usually found peace in Christ when prayed for. It was not uncommon to hear cries of "What must we do to be saved?"

John Wesley insisted on modesty of dress, abstinence from worldly amusements, stressed daily holy living and advocated:

> Follow peace with all men, and holiness,
> Without which no man shall see the Lord.
>
> HEBREWS 12:14

In 1765 Wesley sent lay preachers to America. Notable among them was Devereaux Jarrett, who knew both Whitefield and Wesley. Through his zealous preaching, several churches were established. Reactions to his preaching also produced revival as whole congregations would be bathed in tears of repentance, some seized with trembling and others dropping unconscious to the floor, while some were lost in a spirit of love and praise. Not until after the death of Wesley, did the Methodist Societies break away from the Anglican Church. Two centuries later they were numbered among the largest of the Protestant denominations.

The "Great Awakening" had brought a new, spiritual awareness and emphasis upon religion. The swelling ranks of church goers necessitated additional churches and ministers, which, in turn, produced a number of new colleges and universities to prepare the ministry. Washington & Lee, Brown University, Rutgers and Dartmouth, to name a few, were established at this time.

A profound effect of this religious awakening was to bind the colonists together. Christianity became a voluntary movement, a unifying force and generated a common interest and common cause which reinforced the conviction that God had a special destiny for America. Without this new cohesiveness which bound the colonists together as never before, it is doubtful if the American Revolution would have occurred. Hand in glove with religious freedom went political liberty. Religious evangelism was a national force which transcended colonial differences. The diversity of American religions was no barrier to unity since most rested on a protestant base and religious toleration had reached a new height. By definition, a "sect" is exclusive but "denomination" is neutral and implies a diversity "within a whole." On this basis the churches worked together as never before.

The victory and independence achieved by the American Revolution reinforced a general conviction that America was God's new Israel and was expressed in Hebraic terms such as chosen people, covenanted nation, Egyptian bondage, promised land, etc. The people were fully aware that the eyes of the world were upon them.

Quakers, Mennonites and Moravians suffered most during the war years. The peace churches, in opposition to war, lost many members who defected to fight for independence. Never again would the Quakers be a major denomina tion. The Anglican church, with its close ties to the mother church in England, and to the king, suffered the most until a new generation brought recovery through the Episcopal church.

The alliance between Congregationalists and Presbyterians brought about new growth for their churches as they pushed westward. By 1800, Baptists had become the largest of the denominations, with their greatest gains in the East. Methodists had a phenominal growth record, primarily due to their travelling preachers and "circuit system." Yet all of these denominations differed only slightly in their doctrinal beliefs. Of greater import was the rapid expansion westward and the efforts of all denominations to establish churches and provide a ministry throughout this vast new territory.

God has always been available to those who earnestly seek him. This period was no exception.

But the natural man receiveth not
The things of the Spirit of God.
For they are foolishness unto him:
Neither can he know them
Because they are spiritually discerned.
I CORINTHIANS 2:14

Lorenzo Dow was one who sought God at an early age. Born in Connecticut in 1777, he had been taught the old Calvinistic doctrine that God would save His own elect in His own way. When the Methodists came into his town, his family and friends were set against them, yet Lorenzo Dow went to their meetings. He had decided if he was one of God's elect, they could not harm him, or if he was eternally reprobated, they could do him no additional harm. At the Methodist's prayer meeting, conviction overcame him. Feeling the Saviour's forgiveness, his soul was at peace and filled with joy. He was called to preach and licensed by the Methodists. Uneducated, inexperienced, he did not have an auspicious beginning. Many criticized his ignorance, and his preaching was so uncompromising as to rouse anger wherever he went. Many times he was so discouraged he felt he could never preach again. Yet God compelled him to continue. At last, the power of the Holy Ghost overcame him, and from that day a sweet peace was continually with him, undergirding him at all times. His meetings and preaching began to kindle revival; people by the thousands flocked to hear him. Strange manifestations occurred during his services, principally "the jerks. " It was interesting to note that those op posed to his preaching (persecutors, scoffers, and half -hearted Christians) were the ones affected. Ultimately, many of these were saved.

Peter Cartwright was another famous Methodist minister with little pre vious education. About 1800, in the upper part of Kentucky, a meeting of Pres byterian ministers was unexpectedly and inexplicably moved upon by God's Spirit. This began a revival that drew ministers of all denominations. As word of this miracle spread, thousands of people came and hundreds fell prostrate under the powerful surge of God's power. This might well have been the first authentic camp meeting ever held. Cartwright was converted to Christ and attended several camp meetings among the Methodists and Presbyterians, taking an active part in the meetings. He was given an exhorters license and then permission to form a circuit in another region of Kentucky. Cartwright received the baptism of the Spirit while preaching his first sermon. His meetings continued to be Spirit-f illed, and thousands of souls were won to Christ. Always caref ul not to quench any honest move of the Holy Spirit, he was quick to recognize and stop any unruly outbursts not of God. He described his own meetings as revivals where the awesome power of God frequently felled many of the congregation as they cried aloud for mercy and salvation. At times, the Holy Spirit would move upon unbelievers in his congregation, producing the same "jerks" as Lorenzo Dow witnessed. The more they resisted, the more they jerked. Cartwright believed this was judgement sent from God to bring sinners to repentance, and to prove God's power was real and greater than men's.

As might be expected in a climate of tolerance and religious freedom, some groups moved into gnosticism, claiming to discover secret texts or know ledge. One such sect was founded by Joseph Smith who grew up in an atmosphere of hysteria which pervaded the area. Visions, strange apparitions and manifest- ations were so common in the region it was called the "burned-over district" of New York. Money-digging madness, abetted by treasure hunting with "seer-stones" was accepted practice. Joseph Smith was the proud owner of a seer-stone from which he claimed great powers of divination. (Old court-house records confirm he was arrested for defrauding one greedy treasure hunter.) An active imagination, plus inspiration from Masonic lore which had been printed in 1802, and with remarkable similarities in the Book of Mormon, brought forth the nucleus of a new religion. The parallels of the Masonic legend of Enoch and Joseph Smith's subsequent finding and translating of the golden plates, as related by himself, were more than coincidental. Mormonism, fabricated in a climate of occultism, perpetrated as a hoax, may well have provided egress to Satanic forces beyond the control of Joseph Smith and his companions, because the original Book of Mormon contained some true gospel. It has since undergone many changes. The fraudulent character of the Book of Mormon necessitated further revelations. The Church of Jesus Christ of Latter-Day Saints is based first of all on the testimony that Joseph Smith was a true prophet inspired by visiting god-men.

> **Beware of false prophets,**
> **Which come to you in sheep's clothing.**
> **But inwardly they are ravening wolves.**
> **Ye shall know them by their fruits.**
> **MATIHEW 7:7, 15, 16**

By 1830, Joseph's book had been published, and a new church formed. Soon Joseph Smith and his followers moved to Kirtland, Ohio. The church growth was astounding, but failure of Smith's "Anti-Banking Company" forced them to relocate. At Nauvoo, Illinois, Joseph Smith received many "revelations" and the church was transformed, as its roots sank deeply into ancient mysteries of pagan occultism. Smith revealed that men may become gods through a compli- cated system of uncreated "gods-in-embryo" and that Jesus Christ and Lucifer are brothers. A plurality of gods, as well as wives, and baptism for the dead were accepted. After Joseph Smith was initiated into the Nauvoo Masonic Lodge, he had other revelations; secret, pagan, temple rituals, which accepted Lucifer as the Light-bearer and their god.

> **For such are false apostles,**
> **Deceitful workers,**
> **Transforming themselves into the apostles of Christ.**
> **And no marvel, for Satan himself**
> **transformed into an angel of light.**
> **IICORINTHIANS 11:13, 14**

Secret mystery rituals in the temple paralleled those of the Masons as they re-enacted the drama of Adam and Eve with a Luciferic twist while gnostic "knowledge" was imparted by the serpent. This, of course, was hidden from all but the very elect.

Smith was eventually murdered by a mob in Nauvoo in 1844. Mormonism lived on through a new leader, Brigham Young, who led the sect on an exodus to a new far-west settlement, destined to become Salt Lake City and home of the Mormon Temple.

The 1830s saw several movements away from Christianity. Transcendentalism, the Oneida Community who believed conversion brought complete release from sin, the Millerites, Mesmerism, and Spiritualism were all briefly popular. Thereafter, there was a steady slipping away, especially by mid-century, under the impact of Darwin. The intellectual advances of the nineteenth century thrust some Protestants into agnosticism and other "isms."

The greatest fear was of Catholicism. An influx of Catholic emigrants was seen as a Catholic political ploy to gain control of America. After the Civil War, this migration was readily apparent as Catholics from Ireland and Europe migrated by the millions. Also, Catholicism gained new power through its historic appeal. After all, it had stood unchanged and unchangeable over the centuries. At a time when history and science were undermining faith in the infallibility of God's Word, this stability was of utmost importance to many people.

Following the Civil War, the African-American churches became the fastest growing of any in the country. The largest group was Baptist, with Methodists second. Church popularity among the African-Americans may have been because this was the first social outlet they could claim as their own. It provided for community assistance and, of utmost importance, a personal relationship with God. Before the war, most had been allowed to attend the church of their masters, but with little or no personal participation.

As discoveries of gold, silver and copper drew multitudes to the West, further discoveries that cattle could survive the winters and that wheat flourished, encouraged many more. Railroads were built, and at every community churches literally sprang into existence. Methodists, Presbyterians, Congregationalists, and Baptists, in that order, brought religion to the new settlements. Episcopalians were hampered by a lack of ministers. Lutherans brought churches to German communities. Roman Catholics were especially welcomed in Spanish-speaking communities of the southwest. Also, many of the Irish Catholics located in the northern states and established their own churches.

In 1870 there were four million Catholics in America, in 1880 there were six million, in 1890 there were nine million, and by the twentieth century there were twelve million. By 1920, every sixth person and one third of all church members were Catholic. The immigrant flood into America had continued, and they remained loyal to the Roman Catholic religion. Now that their numbers had swelled so prodigiously, many Catholics did not hesitate in proclaiming Protestants were infidels.

Increasingly, both Protestants and Catholics, in a lesser measure, were effected by the stress placed upon evolution and science, and as fallacious accusa tions were raised against the Bible, they were put on the defensive in defending God's Word.

Catholics had long supplemented a Biblical foundation with "tradition" and affirmed papal infallibility in the interpretation of scriptures. In addition, the church had never encouraged individual study of the Bible, so many Catholics were not too concerned with worldly, scientific refutation of God's Word.

On the other hand, it was of vital importance to Protestants and threatened the whole basis of their theology. New scientific theories were unquestioningly accepted by some, seriously undermining their faith in God's Word. Others, not so easily daunted, sought to emphasize the essential doctrines of Christianity with a "back to Christ" movement.

> But if our gospel be hid,
> It is hid to them that are lost
> In whom the God of this world {Satan)
> Hath blinded the minds of them which believe not.
> Lest the light of the glorious gospel of Christ,
> Who is the image of God,
> Should shine unto them.
>
> II CORINTHIANS 4:3, 4

A religion begun in 1875 by Helen Petrovna Blavatsky was in opposition to Christianity and to science. Her Theosophical Society taught that all world religions had common truths, yet she had an abiding hatred of Christianity.

Ms Blavatsky had travelled widely and become heavily influenced by Oriental occultism. While in Tibet, she was instructed by "masters", or seers, adept in Spiritualism. She adapted her knowledge of Buddhism and reincarnation to evolution. For many years she was a spiritistic medium under the control of a "master." Achieving "illumination" was a Theosophist goal, and their inspiration was derived from "spirits." Following promptings from the spirits, the Theosophic leadership, now including Colonel Olcott, moved to India in 1875 and added Hindu elements to their religion. Further revelations bid them keep certain of their teachings secret. At the death of Ms Blavatsky, Annie Besant assumed leadership. One of her books, The Lesser Mysteries, stated "The greater will never be published through the printing press; they can only be given by Teacher to pupil, from mouth to ear." As a religion, Theosophy is gnostic ancient wisdom which taught "dig deep into yourself to find God" - this is yet another "Man is a god" concept.

Anne Besant was replaced by Alice Ann Bailey, aptly qualified for leader- ship because of her hatred of orthodox Christianity and loyalty to occultism and Eastern mysticism. Although she called herself a Christian, her many pub- lications belie that fact. She taught the divinity of man and reincarnation. The Lucifer Publishing Company was formed in 1922 primarily to disseminate her books. Too blatant, the name was soon changed to Lucis. Theosophy was to remain low profile until its 1975 revelation of a New Age and plans for a mandatory world religion.

Jehovah's Witnesses evolved through desire for a doctrine which would deny eternal punishment. It survived many changes in doctrine and leadership. In 1879, Charles Russell published his Zion's Watchtower and Herald of Christ's Presence, followed by Studies in the Scriptures. At his death, Judge Rutherford continued to publish the Watchtower and the Golden Age, later changed to A wake, plus the Yearbook of Jehovah's Witnesses. An unending flow of books and pamphlets continued to guide Jehovah's Witnesses through successive revelations as their interpretation of the Bible grew increasingly estranged from that of other churches and of scripture.

> And many of them that sleep
> In the dust of the earth,
> Shall awake, some to everlasting life,
> And some to shame and everlasting contempt.
> DANIEL 12:2

Franz Mesmer, A German physician and student of psychotherapy, discovered the power of one man over another. This power, known as hypnotism, or mesmerism, became a mixed blessing, depending on how and by whom it was used. It also became the foundation of a deeply mystic religion. Charles Poyen, a French hypnotist, introduced mesmerism to New England and to Phineas Quimby, who experimented with the sick, and in so doing discovered the power of mind over matter. He wrote his philosophy in long hand and shared it with his patients.

Unity drew from his studies. Both Charles and Myrtle Fillmore suffered from debilitating diseases. Mrs Fillmore was healed after hearing a lecture on metaphysical healing, based on the findings of Phineas Quimby. She, in turn, brought about her husband's healing and then abetted healings in her neigh borhood, primarily by the principle of "I am a child of God and therefore I do not inherit sickness." Gradually, this became a religious movement, culminating in the Unity School of Christianity, which continues to publish weekly and monthly magazines and pamphlets, operates a broadcasting station, and a training school that believes in healing through the mind; that God is all in all. Originally, Unity's teaching concentrated solely on healing; later, on health, prosperity and happiness; all of which are inspirational and common desires of everyone, but harmful by themselves, for they overlook the obedience necessary for salvation.

The Fillmores believed that God is Principle, Law, Being, Mind, Spirit and All-Good. Their teachings bore a marked resemblance to Christian Science, and small wonder, for Mrs Patterson came to Phineas Quimby for healing in 1862. Mrs Patterson had suffered from a spinal weakness all her life and obtained relief after being treated by Mr Quimby. She later remarried and became famous as Mary Baker

Eddy who founded Christian Science and taught God is All, God is Life, and therefore Sickness and Death are non-existent. Needless to say, many cures have been effected through faith. Medical science later recognized psychosomatic illness and the interaction between the physical and spiritual man. Since man tends to regard the Bible as a book of both truth and error, it was not hard for Christian Scientists to rely heavily on Mrs Eddy's book "Science and Health" and confirm her word with scripture.

Knowing this first,
That no prophecy of the scripture
Is of any private interpretation.

II PETER 1:20

Man's search for comfort and reassurance in this life have led him down many avenues. Even when that narrow way, which leads to life is discovered, not all men are willing to follow it but prefer their own way. Nevertheless, there is a spiritual need in everyone that can only be satisfied by God.

CHAPTER XVII

IN DUE SEASON

To everything there is a season
And a time for every purpose under the heaven.
I know that whatsoever God doeth,
It shall be forever:
Nothing can be put to it,
Nor anything taken from it.

And God doeth it that man should fear before him.
That which hath been is now;
And that which is to be hath already been,
And God requireth that which is past.

ECCLESIASTES 3:1

In 1900 Mr Parham started the Bethel Bible School at Topeka, Kansas in an old rock mansion called "Stone's Folly.11 Patterned after an English castle, it was a magnificent three-story structure containing many cupolas and turrets. One of these became the prayer tower of the forty students who took three hour prayer shifts, praying around the clock. Brother Parham felt the churches of his day were missing something that God had for them; that the Bible held out promises which were not being received. Consequently, his school dedicated itself to an in-depth study of the scriptures. He was particularly interested in the baptism of the Holy Ghost, and in December of 1900 requested they all independently search the scriptures for a true Biblical sign of this baptism. The answer was unanimously "speaking in other tongues as the Spirit gave utter- ance." With renewed prayer and fasting and great desire, the people sought God for this experience.

At the turn of the century, on January 1, 1901, Agnes Ozman was heard to speak another language, and a halo of light appeared around her head. On January 3, twelve ordained ministers from different denominations were filled with God's Spirit, speaking in tongues as the Spirit gave the utterance.

> But this is that which was spoken by the prophet Joel
> It shall come to pass in the last days, saith God,
> I will pour out my Spirit upon all flesh
> And it shall come to pass, that whosoever
> Shall call on the name of the Lord
> Shall be saved.
>
> ACTS 2:16, 17, 21

When this was made public, crowds gathered and marvelled to hear men and women speaking unknown languages fluently, just as on the day of Pentecost. Brother Parham received the Holy Ghost, and nearly every hungry soul he laid hands on and prayed for received this holy baptism of the Spirit. St Louis news-papers carried accounts of the phenomenon of speaking in tongues, others came bringing language experts and interpreters who attested to the legitimacy of the languages the Holy Ghost filled believers were speaking. This Holy Ghost fire quickly spread to Kansas City, Galena, Baxter Springs and a number of neighboring towns, where the first churches were established. From here workers spread further abroad, carrying the message that

Pentecost was as real in 1901 as in the year 33 A.D. Not only was the Holy Spirit and speaking in tongues in evidence, but miracles of healing and prophecy blessed their revivals. By 1905 it had spread to Houston, Texas which later became the headquarters of the Apostolic Faith Movement, as it was then known. From Houston the fire spread to Chicago and even to New York.

Brother Seymour, an African-American Baptist preacher from Houston, had received an understanding of the Pentecostal message, and even though he had not yet received an infilling of the Holy Spirit, was called to Los Angeles to help in a work there. In 1906 God's Spirit was showered upon that city and Brother Seymour became a prominent leader in Azusa Street. Hundreds of ministers, Christian workers, and missionaries came to hear and receive; black and white intermingled with no thought of race as they united in a search for truth and God's Spirit.

Many of these ministers were disappointed, and replaced, when they returned to their own congregations to find them full of unbelief, preferring traditional worship, even after witnessing the power and glory of God manifest through His Spirit.

> In the law it is written,
> With men of other tongues and other lips
> Will I speak unto this people,
> And yet for all that
> They will not hear me, saith the Lord.
>
> I CORINTHIANS 14:21

God's work was not to be stopped. Many dedicated men and women carried His Word to the highways and by-ways, sacrificing homes and jobs, literally trusting in God for their daily bread. Through unbelievable hardships, many early church leaders faithfully labored to bring the Apostolic doctrine to those who had not heard it. In many cases, the hungry hearted were also the hungry. Seldom did the prosperous citizens accept this new, humbling experience. After the initial outpouring of God's Spirit, it became harder to find honest hearted souls who were ready to openly declare themselves on the side of this new doctrine and risk the censure of their peers. Other churches raised opposition to this upstart religion that placed so much emphasis on receiving the Holy Ghost and its claim to similarity to the church first founded by Jesus' apostles. Also, it was a threat, for this Apostolic movement drew its membership from the denominational churches. Still, the faithful leaders persevered, slowly establishing churches throughout America, particularly in the South. This movement became organized in 1914 under the General Council of the Assemblies of God.

In 1913, the first world-wide camp meeting was held in Los Angeles. Hun- dreds of preachers from all over A merica and Canada were present. There was an air of expectancy about this meeting, a feeling God was going to reveal a new thing, yet when it came they were not ready for it. Evangelist McAlister preached on baptism, mentioning the various methods that had been used during the past nineteen centuries.

He touched on the triune baptism of dipping separately for the Father, Son, and Holy Ghost and then remarked that the apostles baptized only once in the name of Jesus Christ. The other ministers quickly rejected this, falling back on Matthew 28:19. Gradually conviction gripped the hearts of some.

> **And whatsoever ye do in word or deed**
> **Do all in the name of the Lord Jesus**
> **Giving thanks to God and the Father by him.**
> **COLOSSIANS 3:17**

The apostolic commandment had always been to be baptized in the name of Jesus Christ, which was the only name given for the Father, for the Son, and for the Holy Ghost. A number of ministers saw this truth and were rebaptized in the name of the Lord Jesus Christ and established this procedure in their churches.

After many strategies to block this "Oneness" movement, a General Camp Meeting convened at Little Rock, Arkansas in August 1915. Pastor Hall of Illinois was speaker and took the following scripture for his text throughout the meeting.

> **For in him dwelleth**
> **All the fullness of the Godhead bodily...**
> **Buried with him in baptism,**
> **Wherein also ye are risen with him**
> **Through the faith of the operation of God.**
> **COLOSSIANS 2:9, 12**

By this time illumination of Scripture had revealed the fullness of God in Christ to many who were present as they understood the reason for baptism in Jesus' name and saw that the long standing trinity baptism was a denial of His Oneness. Simultaneously God's Holy Spirit was revealing this truth through personal revelation to certain ones at the Camp Meeting.

A large number of those present refused to accept this new step to salva- tion and fought by every means within their power to overturn this "Oneness" doctrine. For a year the battle raged as each side sought to convince the other. When this new baptism could not be stopped, the General Council of the As- semblies of God saw the issue must be resolved between the Trinitarian theory and the Oneness theory. As they met in June 1916 to attempt to iron out their differences, it became apparent reconciliation was not possible. Over one hundred and fifty ministers were expelled that day. It was not because the Oneness men disagreed with baptism of the Holy Ghost, healings, miracles and holiness, but because of their stand for the name of Jesus Christ.

> **And daily in the temple,**
> **And in every house,**
> **They ceased not to teach**
> **And preach Jesus Christ.**

ACTS 5:42

The displaced Oneness ministers felt the need for organization and joined another group of Oneness people called Pentecostal Assemblies of the World in 1917. This was a unique fellowship of

African-American and white, united in spirit and truth. Gradually problems arose, primarily because Northern African-American ministers resented the segregation still practiced in the South. In a meeting at St Louis in 1924, it was decided to let the African-American ministers retain the Pentecostal Assemblies of the World and the white ministers would form a new organization, The Pentecostal Ministerial Alliance. In 1945 The Pentecostal Assemblies of the World, The Pentecostal Ministerial Alliance, The Pentecostal Assemblies of Jesus Christ and the Pentecostal Church, Inc. united to form just that - the United Pentecostal Church. This merger brought together about 1,800 ministers and 900 churches with their general headquarters at St Louis, Missouri. God's primary purpose was, and continues to be, to restore the original faith and power of the apostles to his church and to prepare a people "called by His name" for His soon coming.

After World War II, Pentecostals were elevated to middle class status but the stigmas attached to them were not necessarily removed. Charges had been made that they were fanatical, mentally unstable, ignorant, lower class, holy rollers, even that speaking in tongues (glossolalia) was of the devil and only slowly were these misconceptions eradicated as the Pentecostals prospered.

While growth rates of the major mainline churches declined, Pentecostal growth accelerated. Even so, the Pentecostal fire was only a small flame in a dark world.

Protestant denominations tended to hold to the belief that all men and women are saved through God's mercy. Evangelicals opposed this and taught that God requires repentance and acceptance of His plan for salvation, that He is a God of mercy and justice, and some will be sentenced to eternal hell. Therefore, evangelism is a necessary part of Christianity.

In 1949, Southern Baptist Billy Graham launched his international evangel- istic career in a revival tent at Los Angeles. In 1950 he began his Hour of Deci- sion radio broadcasts and a monthly magazine which reached millions. He preached repentance and belief in the Gospel (notwithstanding the fact he rejected Pentecost). His public endorsement of Nixon for United States president in 1972 began a trend of alliances between the presidency and religious aff iliations that continued. Thousands of sinners responded to his calls for repentance and made new commitments to the Lord. But as sincere as Billy Graham has been in his evangelistic commitment to saving souls, his message to the world has not gone far enough.

> He said unto them
> Have ye received the Holy Ghost since ye believed?
> And they said unto him,
> We have not so much as heard
> Whether there be any Holy Ghost.
> And he said unto them
> Unto what were ye baptized?
> And they said, Unto John's baptism.
> Then said Paul, John verily baptized with a baptism of
> repentance.

Saying unto the people, that they should believe on him
Which should come after him, that is, on Christ Jesus.
When they heard this, they were baptized
In the name of the Lord Jesus.
And when Paul had laid his hands upon them
The Holy Ghost came on them, and they spoke with tongues
And prophesied.

ACTS 19:2 - 6

Ye are the temple of the living God;
As God hath said,
I will dwell in them and walk in them
And I will be their God.
And they shall be my people.
Wherefore come out from among them,
And be ye separate, saith the Lord.

II CORINTHIANS 6:16, 17

Occurring in 1967, the most unbelievable penetration of the Holy Spirit was into the Catholic Church which had shown little interest in the Pentecostal movement. During the first part of the Twentieth Century, immigration aided the growth of the Catholic churches in America. They were not concerned with the dwindling membership that plagued protestants. Yet, by 1960 growth had stopped. Parochial schools were closing, priests and nuns were forsaking the church. Early in 1960, Pope John XXIII convened Vatican II, a council that met from 1962 until 1965. This council was referred to by the pope as a "new Pentecost" and he ordered daily prayer by all Catholics for the three-year period. At the end of Vatican II, revolutionary changes were effected which made dialogue bet ween protestants and catholics possible. For the first time, pastors and priests participated in each other's services.

Vatican II emphasized the Holy Spirit and charisms (special spiritual gifts or power) which belonged to the church. The council stated a belief in present day manifestations of all the gifts of the Spirit. The ground work had been laid and preparation made for a Pentecostal movement which began at Duquesne University, Pittsbugh, Pennsylvania, a school run, believe it or not, by the Holy Ghost Fathers. Two professors in a search for the Spirit arranged the first known Pentecostal prayer meeting. After study of the book of Acts and prayer, many of the young seekers received the in-filling of the Holy Spirit and acted just like Spirit-filled Pentecostals. Soon Notre Dame University in Indiana, received the same experience. Professors and University students led this fast growing Catholic Pentecostal movement through prayer groups. There was never any question of separation from the mother church; after all the church had always claimed the charisms. To establish their own identity, they called this move of God's Spirit "charismatic." There was little outward change in those who received the Holy Ghost. It only intensified their devotion to Mary and the church.

> **Know ye not, that so many of us**
> **As were baptized into Jesus Christ**
> **Were baptized into his death?**
> **Therefore we are buried with him**
> **By baptism into death.**
> **That like as Christ was raised from the dead**

By the glory of the Father
Even so, we also should walk in newness of
life...Knowing this, that our old man is crucified with
him, That the body of sin might be destroyed.
ROMANS 6:3, 4, 6

Putting off the "old man" and assuming the "new" through baptism in the name of Jesus Christ is a cleansing process necessary for continued habitation of his Holy Spirit. Through understanding of His Word, a few did separate them- selves from Catholicism and became "Oneness" Pentecostals.

Further acceptance of the Pentecostal experience by the Catholic church was through Cardinal Suenens of Belguim who, after joining the movement, was appointed by the Pope as Charismatic advisor to the Vatican. The Catholic church had decided to allow this spiritual movement to develop under the church's guidance. In 1975, the Feast of Pentecost was celebrated at St Peter's and 10,000 charismatics gathered to hear Pope Paul VI and to attend a charismatic mass conducted by Cardinal Suenens.

Despite the Vatican's acceptance of God's Holy Spirit, basically the church remains unchanged. In 1939, Pope Pius XII extended plenary indulgence (freedom from punishment in purgatory for sins) to radio and, at a later date, to TV audiences. Christmas week, 1985, Pope John Paul II extended this power to his Bishops who can now dispense this plenary indulgence via radio and TV to all listening Catholics.

And the scribes and the Pharisees began to reason
Saying, Who is this which speaketh blasphemies? Who
can forgive sins, but God alone?

LUKE 5:21

Pope John Paul II is unique in many ways. His election in 1978 was the first time in over 400 years a non-Italian had been selected. Born in Poland, Karol Wojytla was an extremely skilled linguist who obtained instant rapport with the tremendous crowds who flocked to obtain his blessings. His extensive travels took him to more countries than any other pope, and he was invariably met by millions as whole populations turned out to greet him. His charismatic personality allowed him to impart doctrine and discipline contrary to those of the countries visited and yet retain their devotion to himself. He was idolized by millions. He was unwavering in his desire to restore the old, rigid disciplines to the church and to the ecclesiastical body. He strongly opposed artificial birth control, abortion, divorce, extramarital sex and homosexual relationships. He exalted the Virgin Mary and had the highest regard for the Black Madonna in Poland.

Yet in meetings with leaders of Protestant churches, he upheld the confessional statement of Catholic evangelists which deplores the isolation and separation of Christians from one another, and believed Christ desires unity among his people. Pope John Paul expressed his desire to remove the real divisions that existed and to restore the full unity in the faith; at the same time insisting the Catholic doctrine must not be compromised or deviated from.

Many American priests and much of the laity opposed this rigid and inflexible stand, yet thousands fell at his feet during his visit to A merica as if mesmerized.

The neo-pentecostal or charismatic movement could no longer be denied by Protestant denominations. Presbyterian, Episcopalian, Lutheran, and Methodist denominations accepted this inevitable invasion of the Spirit. The least receptive were Baptists and Nazarenes. A growing malaise within the churches had prompted some members to drop out, or join earlier defections such as the Southern Methodist Church or independent Christian churches and Churches of Christ. It was only surprising that so many had remained with their original churches. A new infusion of the Spirit was necessary if the churches were to live.

Assemblies of God minister, Dave Wilkerson, began an outreach to young drug addicts in New York City. He claimed baptism in the Holy Spirit surpassed any other cure for drug addiction. In a similar move, California "hippies" sought release from drugs by turning to Reverend Smith and his Calvary Chapel Foursquare Church in Costa Mesa for help. In a matter of months, thousands of converts had been baptized in the Pacific Ocean. Soon similar Pentecostal ministries had sprung up across America as word was spread by the "Jesus People" that the only force powerful enough to break the drug habit was the Holy Ghost.

Soon known as a "born again" movement, it included a conversion experience, reliance on and belief in the reliability of the Bible and acceptance of the birth, miracles, and resurrection of Christ. Requirements for "born-again" varied with each church; many no longer considered evidence of receiving the Holy Ghost necessary, and a large number of "born again Christians" felt an awareness of the Holy Spirit, but never actually received it and never understood the importance of Jesus' name baptism.

> Having the understanding darkened,
> Being alienated from the life of God
> Through the ignorance that is in them,
> Because of the blindness in their heart..
>
> EPHESIANS 4:18

Jimmy Carter, elected President of the United States in 1976, did much to foster acceptance of the "born again" evangelical movement with his unabashed claim to being a "born again" Christian. Alt hough a Baptist himself , Jimmie Carter was quick to laud his sister, Ruth Carter Stapleton, a charis-matic faith-healing evangelist.

The infusion of the neo-pentecostal charismatic movements into Catholic and Protestant churches had brought Trinity Pentecost to the attention of the religious world. A 1979 Gallop Poll reported twenty nine million Americans called themselves either pentecostal or charismatic. Only six million said they had spoken in tongues.

Today these neo-pentecostal/charismatic converts do not consider a holy standard of living necessary. Drinking, smoking, drugs, immodest apparel, language, or personal habits are little changed although most report these practices are more moderate than before.

> I beseech you therefore, brethren,
> By the mercies of God
> That ye present your bodies a living sacrifice,
> Holy, acceptable to God
> Which is your reasonable service.
> And be not conformed to this world:
> But be ye transformed by the renewing of your mind,
> That ye may prove what is that good,
> And acceptable, and perfect will of God.
>
> ROMANS 12:1, 2

During the 1980's, an unprecedented divorce rate, liberal abortion laws, homosexuality, sexual promiscuity, child molestation, pornography, drugs, and crime have all had their devastating effect on homes and families. Many evangelicals linked conversion and christianity with politics in efforts to stem the tide of evil in society. Recently religious leaders have become involved in campaigns for, or against, gay rights, legalized abortion, public prayer in schools, harrassment of Christian private schools by government institutions, equal rights for women, and other issues. In their desire for moral reforms, these issues have drawn support from Protestant, Catholic, Pentecost, and Jews alike, uniting them as nothing else could.

The Reverend Jerry Falwell and his successful Moral Majority is a classic example. For med in 1979, it has become an important political force.

In 1986 Jerry Falwell began expansion of Moral Majority by forming a new "Liberty Federation" which will also involve balancing the budget, fighting communism, and backing conservative Christian candidates for political offices. His critics accuse him of wrapping the Bible in politics, yet he continues to appeal to a large number of religious factions.

An International Missionary Council, formed in Edinburgh in 1910, and A merican organized "Fair and Order Movement" found it strategic to unite with the World's Christian Student Federation in missionary endeavors. From this it was easy to envision the World Council of Churches which led to its establishment in 1948. Originally founded by Protestant denominations, within two years it drew unofficial observers from the Roman Catholic church. The success of the World Council of Churches has been due to a growing desire for unity and peace through a vision of a one-world government and one-world religion that has been the desire of mankind for millenium.

The World Council of Churches predicts by the year 2000 A.D. over fifty percent of all Christians, world-wide, will be non-white, Pentecostal, or charismatic and in the Southern Hemisphere. This is not surprising, f or Africa, Mexico, Central and South America, and the Philippines, as well as other Third World countries, have seen a phenomenal pentecostal conversion recently. Throughout these countries a latter-day revival is reality as desperate, starving, hopeless people receive the Holy Ghost, are willingly baptized in the name of Jesus, and daily lay down their lives for the Truth that America and much of the world rejects.

Woe unto America! A land and a people blessed by God. A nation with a devine destiny.

> Behold, I stand at the door, and knock:
> If any man hear my voice, and open the door,
> I will come in to him,
> And will sup with him, and he with me.
> To him that overcometh will I grant
> To sit with me in my throne,
> Even as I also overcame
> And am set down with my Father in his throne,
> He that hath an ear, let him hear
> What the Spirit saith unto the churches.
>   REVELATION 3: 20 - 22

God's Spirit reached out time and again, knocking at the heart and soul of man; through George Fox and the Quakers, through revivals led by Whitefield and Wesley, Dow, Cartwright, Moody, Parham, and Seymour. Line upon line, here a little and there a little, each time revealing a little more of the Truth.

Yet each time man again turned to his own way, preferring to "do his own thing" rather than fully open the door to the Lord.

For the time will come
When they will not endure sound doctrine
But after their own lusts
Shall they heap to themselves teachers,
Having itching ears
And they shall turn away their ears from the truth
And shall be turned unto fables.

IITIMOTHY 4:2 - 4

Man continually fails to recognize the Almighty God in the role he chose (that of the Son and of the sacrificial lamb) to save mankind, which is also the mode of Himself He expressly desires to be recognized and worshipped as Savior and Redeemer and Jesus Christ. This is Truth! Only those who worship in Spirit and in Truth while on this earth can expect to share eternity with Him. Lukewarm, half-way measures are not acceptable to God.

Countdown is almost complete as the Lord's dispensation of grace draws to an end. And as for America,_ you must listen closely to detect any pulse, because this nation is dying!

CHAPTER XVIII

THE DAY OF THE LORD

The great day of the Lord is near, it is near and hasteth
greatly,
Even the voice of the day of the Lord:
The mighty men shall cry there bitterly.
That day is a day of wrath, a day of trouble and distress.
A day of wasteness and desolation, a day of darkness and
gloominess,
A day of clouds and thick darkness.
A day of the trumpet and alarm
Against the fenced cities, and against the high towers
And I will bring distress upon men
That they shall walk like blind men
Because they have sinned against the Lord:
And their blood shall be poured out as dust and their
flesh as the
dung.
Neither their silver nor their gold shall be able to deliver
them
In the day of the Lord's wrath:
But the whole land shall be devoured by the fire of his
jealousy:
For he shall make even a speedy riddance
Of all them that dwell in the land.

ZEPHANIAH 1 : 14 - 18

The first two thousand years from Adam and Eve to Abraham covered a period of time in which Jehovah dealt on an individual basis with Adam and Eve; with Enoch who walked with God and died not for God took him; and with Noah through whom He saved mankind from complete eradication. Yet man continually sought evil.

For the next two millenium, Almighty God concentrated on a people whom He made a nation. Separating Abraham from his pagan background, Jehovah made an everlasting covenant with Abraham and his descendents who became the Jewish race. His promises of a Messiah and an everlasting kingdom still stand. The fact they did not recognize their Messiah when he came the first time did not negate that promise - it only postponed it for another two thousand years.

The past two millenium Jehovah/Jesus dispensed salvation to all Gentiles who would come to Him in Spirit and in Trut h. To them He holds out a promise that is referred to as "the Rapture."

> For the Lord himself shall descend from heaven
> With a shout, with the voice of the archangel,
> And with the trump of God:
> And the dead in Christ shall rise first,
> Then we which are alive and remain
> Shall be caught up together with them in the clouds.
> To meet the Lord in the air:
> And so shall we ever be with the Lord.
> I THESSALONIANS 4:16, 17

For the past two thousand years, man has held to the hope he would experience this miracle in his lifetime. Paul wrote the above scripture to the church when the first Christians died and doubt was sown among them. It was a reassurance that not all would live to see the Rapture, but if they belonged to God, he would call them from the grave when the time came. After all, Jesus had called Lazarus forth after four days. Not hing can prevent his calling as many as He wills.

As the year 1,000 A.D. approached, men grew anxious and awaited the Rapture, and the end of the world, with trepidation and alarm. They had witnessed "signs of the end times" with the invasion of Norsemen into all Europe and despite the fact the world did not end at that time, their church architecture took on the foreboding aspect of the Book of Revelation.

> And as he sat upon the mount of Olives,
> The disciples came unto him privately, saying,
> Tell us, when shall these things be?
> And what shall be the sign of thy coming,
> And of the end of the world?
> And Jesus answered and said unto them:
> Take heed that no man deceive you.
> For many shall come in my name,
> Saying, I am Christ, and shall deceive
> many. And ye shall hear of wars and rumors of
> wars; See that ye be not troubled
> For all these things must come to pass,
> But the end is not yet.
> For nation shall rise against nation,
> And kingdom against kingdom.
> And there shall be famines and pestilences,
> And earthquakes in divers places.
> All these are the beginning of sorrows.
>
> MATTHEW 24:3-8

During t he past thousand years, nine hundred and eighty-five to be exact, cults have sprung up based upon the coming of the Lord. Seventh Day Adventist's beginning stems from William Miller's prophecy that the Lord would return to earth in 1843, and when Jesus Christ failed to appear, Miller revised the date to October 1844. Undaunted, but with a different prophecy, and a mission to honor the "true Sabbath" on Saturday, Seventh Day Adventists still await the Lord's coming and his earthly kingdom; ignoring scriptures concerning the rapture and the great tribulation during which time the Anti- Christ will be allowed free reign over the world. The late Herbert W. Ar m-strong's World-wide Church of God, his "The World Tomorrow" broadcasts and his "Plain Truth" magazines are also predicated upon his philosophy which bypasses or ridicules unpleasant scriptures pertaining to judgement day, hell, tribulation, and rule and reign of the Anti-Christ. He too encourages his followers to look for the "earthly" coming of the Lord.

> **For we must all appear before the judgement seat of Christ;**
> **That everyone may receive the things done in his body, According**
> **to that he hath done, Whether it be good or bad.**
> **IICORINTHIANS 5:10**

But the Lord has mercifully made provision for those who seek Him while they yet live. His pardon is available only because:

> **God was in Christ,**
> **Reconciling the world unto himself,**
> **Not imputing their trespasses unto them;**
> **And hath committed unto us,**
> **The words of reconciliation.**
> **II CORINTHIANS 5:19**

385

Paul did have the words of reconciliation and he faithfully led the church in the way God desired: to wit, repentance, baptism in Jesus' name, and infilling of the Holy Ghost with evidence of speaking in other tongues. Never did he teach any other doctrine. It is still man's only hope of salvation. Today the world truly stands on the brink of eternity as this millenium draws to a close, and as the door will be shut to the Gentiles and again opened to his Hebrew children.

> And he shall set up an ensign for the nations
> And shall assemble the outcasts of Israel,
> And gather together the dispersed of Judah
> From the four corners of the earth.
>
> ISAIAH 1 : 12

Ejected from Jerusalem by the Roman Empire in 70 A.D., sporadic uprisings culminated in their complete ouster from Palestine in 135 A.D. The Jews became a homeless nation, rejected, hated, mistrusted, and persecuted as no other people before or since. Though they were scattered throughout the world, to the four corners of the earth, they retained their identity and religion. Nothing could shake an ingrained, deeply imbedded instinct that they were still God's chosen people, and Jerusalem was their holy city.

> And they shall fall by the edge of the sword
> And shall be led away captive into all nations;
> And Jerusalem shall be trodden down of the Gentiles
> Until the time of the Gentiles be fulfilled.
>
> LUKE 21:24

Jerusalem was captured by the Muslims in 638. In 691, t he Mosque of the Dome of the Rock was erected on the platform that had once contained Israel's Temple of God. Still standing, it is sacred to Muslims who believe Mohammed was carried from this spot up through Islam's seven heavens into God's presence. In 1099, Crusaders captured Jerusalem and, for the century they retained it, put the stamp of Christianity upon it as they built churches to honor the death, burial, and resurrection of Jesus Christ and for Mary, mother of Jesus. Again Arabs gained control of the holy city. The sixteenth century brought the Turks and Sultan Suleiman the Magnificent who rebuilt the city walls of the old city. Little by little, Jews had been allowed to return and in the 1850's the Jewish settlement, Yemin Moshe began to take shape outside the city walls, the nucleus of a new city.

In 1917, after 400 years of Turkish control, Jerusalem passed to the British. As the British Army entered the holy city, led by Commanding General Sir Edmund Allenby, he was moved to humbly walk through the old Jaffa Gate in respect for the sanctity of this city which was chosen by God above all others.

On November 2, 1917, British Foreign Secretary, Arthur J. Balfour, issued a declaration on behalf of his government which established a national homeland for Jewish people in Palestine. Gradually the people returned to their land. It has been estimated there were 25,000 Jews in Palestine in 1917; by 1945, over half a million had settled primarily in agricultural lands purchased with Zionist Federation funds. To a large extent, dedicated Jewish youth established farming communes (kibbutzim) on land considered worthless. With unparalleled zeal and dedication, these young men and women literally grubbed garden spots from the wilderness, simultaneously fighting Arabs and malaria. God's blessing was poured out in an amazing increase in rainfall and in an abundance of fruit and vegetables of astounding size.

> He shall cause them
> That come out of Jacob to take root,
> Israel shall blossom and bud,
> And fill the face of the world with fruit.
>
> ISAIAH 27:6

Although a British mandate authorized this Jewish homeland, they did little to support it. In fact, as Arab and Jewish conflicts and guerrilla warfare increased, Britain issued a White Paper favoring Arab control of the area. In 1947, the United Nations planned to partition Palestine into Jewish and Arab states with Jerusalem under United Nations control, but circumstances prevented it. No sooner had the last British Army contingent departed than Jews and Arabs opened fire on each other, contending for possession of Jerusalem. In May 1948, Israel declared the establishment of the State of Israel. The United States was the first country to recognize their Statehood. The end of the War of Independence in June 1949 left Jerusalem a divided city.

A small, ill-equipped Jewish militia had become a seasoned fighting force that astounded the world as it defeated seven Arab nations and increased their territory by six hundred miles.

David Ben-Gurion became Israel's first prime minister. There were no longer restrictions on immigration, and Jews returned to their homeland from every direction: east from Babylon, north from Russia and Hitler's prison camps, and from southern Arab nations. Notable among these were Yemenite Jews who heard a new "David" was in power. Yearning for their homeland, and considering themselves exiles, they began their journey afoot, leaving everything they could not carry behind. Israel organized an airlift, using converted bombers. The crew was apprehensive as they loaded Yemenites who had never seen airplanes before, having no idea how they would react when the planes took off. They need not have worried. The Yemenites just smiled and explained God had promised:

.......They shall mount up with wings as eagles....
ISAIAH 40:31

When the United Nations accepted Israel as a nation, their flag was displayed at Lake Success, New York. Although Israel was not aware of it, divine guidance had much to do with its design. Its white flag bears two horizontal blue stripes and between them, also in blue, is a religous emblem, two interlaced triangles forming the Shield of David, commonly called the Star of David. It is the one emblem which stands for Israel's God. Ancient Hebrew used no vowels and God's name as revealed to Moses was written YHVH, translated Jehovah or Yahweh. At one time men held God's name to be so holy that only the High Priest could pronounce it once a year on the Day of Atonement. The Hebrews devised methods to refer to His name. One way was to print a fraction of the letters within the Shield of David. Today Israel's flag tells the world that God is One God, and that His name is holy. Jesus declared Himself to be the star:

> I, Jesus, have sent my angel
> To testify unto you these things in the churches.
> I am the root and the offspring of David,
> And the bright and morning star.
> REVELATION 22:16

The Jews do not yet understand, but Jesus is the central figure of their flag. From the beginning there have been only three ways that God has mani- fested Himself: in creation (Father), redemption (Son) and revelation (Holy Ghost). Man, made in the image and likeness of God, is likewise symbolized by a triangle composed of spirit, body and soul. God was manifest in the flesh and represents both triangles as Son of god and Son of man - Jesus Christ. Soon Israel will know who their flag represents for God has truly set up an ensign for the nations!

For nineteen years Jerusalem remained divided, until June 1967. During the third day of the Six Day War, Israel gained control of all of Jerusalem and gained access to the Western or Wailing Wall which is the only visible portion remaining of Herod's Temple and the most precious remnant of the most sacred site to all Israelites. They also gained access to the old walled city of Jerusalem, precious in its own right. For the first time in 1900 years, the Holy City was controlled by Jews.

Against astronomical odds, Jerusalem had defeated the armies of Egypt, Jordan, Syria, and Lebanon, who were supported by the rest of the Arab world. God was again protecting his ancient people. Firmly entrenched, Israel was back in the promised land to stay. All end-time Bible prophecy hinges on this event.

Following the War of 1967, Israelites extended the boundaries of Jerusalem to contain territory conquered from Jordan. Neither the United States nor the United Nations has acknowledged the annexation or the capital status that Israel claims for Jerusalem. Further expansion, which is opposed by all nations, entails Jewish settlements, sponsored by the government, which subtly take possession of the land regained through war.

Again, Israel was forced to fight the War of 1973 as Egypt attacked the Sinai Peninsula, and Syria attacked Golan Heights while devout Jews were in their synagogue on Yom Kippur. Even supported by eleven Arab nations, Egypt and Syria were unable to conquer the tiny nation of Israel. Russia demanded peace, and the major powers brought pressure upon Arabs and Jews to cease fighting. Israel survives!

Today an uneasy peace exists as Israel must be constantly on alert, for her borders are threatened by hostile neighbors and terrorists attacks. As never before, the Middle East is a volatile brew of hate; a powder keg with a sputtering fuse which is growing dangerously short.

"A homeland for displaced Palestinians" is the professed goal of diverse Arab nations and organizations. It is the justification claimed for indiscriminate terrorist tactics committed or abetted by Libyan leader Moammar Khadafy, who in reality is a megalomaniac with grandiose visions of becoming leader of all the Arab world. Utilizing his country's oil wealth, he has obtained sophisticated weapons and missiles from Russia (and also Russian advisors) with which he threatens neighboring Arab nations of Chad, Sudan, and Egypt, Israel, and A merica whom he hates and sees as a threat to himself.

Khadafy supports the Abu Nidal Group, the most dangerous of all the Middle East terrorist organizations. Abu Nidal was a former PLO representa tive who split from Yasser Arafat in 1973, because he had become too moderate. Hatred of Israel and of A merica and of Arafat motivate and sustain a blood lust that is satiated by indicriminate terrorist attacks. Abu Nidal and his "Fatah Revolutionary Council" has demonstrated its ability to operate in any country it chooses. Western Europe has been hard hit by air hijackings; and airport, restaurant, and hotel bombings in which innocent bystanders from many nations, including America, have been killed. This terrorist group is committed to violence to destroy all attempts to reconcile Israel and Arab nations. They also desire the destruction of Jordan, Egypt, and Arafat, whom they see as too moderate.

At different times, Iraq and Syria have supported Nidal and sponsored his group in moves against their own enemies. Syria's peacekeeping bid in Lebanon may very well result in a complete military takeover of that country. Syria is backed by Russia who supplies armament to them. The Soviets support Syria's President Hafez Assad as a part of their own long-range strategy.

Another dangerous fanatic is Iranian leader Ayatollah Ruhollah Khomeini and his Islamic Jihad who seeks to unseat all Arab rulers and replace them with Muslim fanatics in a vision of a new Islamic empire.

Russia supplied instigation, money, and weapons to Arab nations enabling them to attack Israel in the past. Her hatred of Israel has not diminished, and control of the Mediterranean and the Arab oil lands is of utmost importance in her overall plans for world dominion.

The USSR's willingness to threaten and use military force under certain conditions has been demonstrated by their control and domination of Hungary in 1956 as Soviet tanks crushed a bid for freedom, and of Czechoslovakia in 1968 when they sought to establish a more liberal socialist regime. In 1979, their brutal invasion of Afghanistan shocked the world but brought only verbal protests and a minimum of covert aid for the beleagued Afghan nation. Again, a quiescent world watched as Russia squelched the Solidarity Labor Movement in Poland in 1980 - 81.

Cuba and North Korea are supported by Russia and, in turn, are used by Russia as important bases to further their Communistic expansion. Through Cuba and Nicaragua, the Soviets foster guerrilla warfare in El Salvador and Guatamala and Honduras, threatening the Western Hemisphere. But Russia has gained the most ground in the Mideast and North Africa as she supplies weapons and advisors to allies such as Syria, Libya, Algeria, North and South Yemen, Iran, Iraq, Angola, and Ethiopia.

> Thus saith the Lord God;
> Behold I am against thee, 0 Gog,
> The chief prince of Meshech and Tubal
> And I will bring thee forth, and all thine army
> Persia, Ethiopia, and Libya with them,
> All of them with shield and helmet:
> Gomer, and all his bands; the house of Togarmah
> Of the north quarters, and all his bands,
> And many people with thee
> In the latter years thou shalt come into the land
> That is brought back from the sword
> And is gathered out of many people.
> Against the mountains of Israel
> Thou shalt ascend and come like a storm
> Thou shalt be like a cloud to cover the land,
> Thou and all thy bands,
> And many people with thee.
>
> EZEKIEL 38:3 - 9

Gog, Meshech, Tubal, Gomer, and Togarmah are the ancient tribal names of Japeth's sons whom the Lord scattered from the Tower of Babel. Magog fathered the Scythians who became modern Russia: h e. is their ruler, or chief prince. Tubal, also Russian, founded Tobolsk, in northeast Siberia; Moscow was named for Meshech, or Moschi. Togarmah originally in southwest Armenia, migrated north and west, possibly into Poland. Gomer settled in eastern Europe, probably today's East Germany.

Thus Russia and its European Communist allies, will band together with Libya, Iran, and Ethiopia in a move against Israel. Today the stage is set and only God knows how soon or what incident will trigger this attack. Maybe not this week, this month or this year, but soon, for it was foretold 2,500 years ago by the prophet Ezekiel, and all conditions have been f ulfilled.

> And thou shalt come up against my people Israel,
> As a cloud to cover the land;
> It shall be in the latter days.
> And I will bring thee against my land
> That the heathen may know me,
> When I shall be sanctified in thee
> O Gog, before their eyes.
>
> EZEKIEL 38:16

The defeat of Russia and all her allies will be so decisive and miraculous that the children of Israel, and all the world, cannot but give credit and honor to the Lord. Ezekiel mentions a great earthquake that will destroy mountains and level everything within its path. There will be dissention amongst Russia's allies as, in their distrust of everyone, they turn their weapons against each other. Pestilence, and overflowing rain, great hailstones, fire and brimstone will all take their toll until five sixths of this great army has been destroyed and their bodies left unburied upon the mountains of Israel.

> And I will send a fire on Magog
> And among them that dwell carelessly in the isles:
> And they shall know that I am the Lord.
> EZEKIEL 39:6

America cannot afford to stand idly by as Russia attacks Israel, for it is apparent this is a decisive step in her bid to take over all of the oil-rich Arab world. A Russian victory would undoubtedly cut off America's oil supply. This, coupled with loss of respect by the rest of the world, and a communist threat from Cuba and Central and South America could render her virtually impotent. To prevent this, America must take drastic action to stop Russia and her hordes. Millions of Jews living in America will also put pressure upon the American government to act in defense of Israel. In this case, money, supplies, and weapons would be inadequate. Whatever method America chooses to stop Russia, it could easily escalate to a point of no return as these super powers confront each other, and one or the other launches the first nuclear warheads.

> Blow ye the trumpet in Zion,
> And sound an alarm in my holy mountain.
> Let all the inhabitants of the land tremble
> For the day of the Lord cometh,
> For it is nigh at hand.
> A day of darkness and of gloominess,
> A day of clouds and of thick darkness.

As the morning spread upon the mountains,
A great people and a strong;
There hath not ever been the like,
Neither shall be any more after it,
Even to the years of many generations.
A fire devoureth before them.
And behind them a flame burneth,
The land is as the garden of Eden before them,
And behind them a desolate wilderness,
Yea, and nothing shall escape them.
Before their face the people shall be much pained
All faces shall gather blackness

JOEL 2:1- 6

Paralysis and disbelief grip the world in the wake of devastation of such magnitude that mere words cannot begin to describe it. Once a mighty nation, within hours America will be reduced to a land so crippled and scarred that it will indeed take generations to recover.

But of the times and seasons, brethren,
Ye have no need that I write unto you
For yourselves know perfectly
That the day of the Lord
So cometh as a thief in the night.

I THESSALONIANS 5:2

Millions killed or missing, whole cities destroyed, communications severed, nuclear fallout contaminating everything in its path; panic, riots, chaos. Who would notice or understand that God had "raptured" his church during this holocaust; that the people called by His Name were on their way to a wedding supper?   Paul told his Jesus' name church:

Behold, I show you a mystery. We shall not all sleep (die).
But we shall all be changed, in a moment
In the twinkling of an eye, at the last trump.
For the trumpet shall sound
And the dead shall be raised incorruptible
And we shall be changed.

I CORINTHIANS 15:51, 52

With the rapture of the Lord's church, the door of salvation is forevermore closed to Gentiles. Until the "rapture", Jesus is still calling for the lost; ever ready to forgive the repentant, and share His Name and Holy Spirit with those who seek him. But as in the days of Noah, the disbelieving will be doomed. Because this age has not witnessed a "rapture" does not mean it will not happen. In Noah's day, the world had not witnessed rain, but on the Lord's appointed day, the only door into the ark was closed by God Himself, and the rains came. Salvation was no longer possible.

With Russia and America powerless, the European Community (Common Market nations) will emerge as the most stable, reliable source of government in the world. After witnessing the unutterable impact and devastation on the world through atomic warfare, a strong central government and peaceful coexistence will be of prime importance to all nations, great or small.

Let no man deceive you by any means;
For that day shall not come, except their come a falling
away first.
And that man of sin be revealed, the son of perdition;
Who opposeth and exalteth himself

Above all that is called God, or that is worshipped;
So that he as God sitteth in the temple of God,
Showing himself that he is God (Antichrist).
And now ye know what withholdeth
That he might be revealed in his time.
For the mystery of iniquity doth already work.
Only he who now letteth will let until he be taken out
of the way.
And then shall that wicked be revealed,
Whom the Lord shall consume with the spirit of his mouth,
And shall destroy with the brightness of his coming.
Even him, whose coming is after the working of Satan.
With all power and signs and lying wonders.
With all deceivableness of unrighteousness in them that
perish.

II THESSALONIANS 2:3 - 10

Within the European Community one will emerge to rule the world. He will be a strong, dynamic leader with solutions to all the world's greatest problems of economics, famine, strife. Not aware that God's church is no longer on earth, people will willingly accept a world religion as an extension of their traditional churches, a universal monetary system, and a world leader.

He will win their support through promises of peace. One of his first acts will be a covenant guaranteeing Israel's security. Aided and abetted by the False Prophet (religious leader) and given power by Satan, it will appear to many that he is their long awaited Christ come to establish his earthly kingdom.

In actuality, the antichrist will rule on earth for seven years only because it is God's will that he do so. During this period, God's wrath will be poured out upon the world through the judgements of the seven seals, the seven trum- pets, and the seven vials.

The first angel sounded
And there followed hail and fire mingled with blood
And they were cast upon the earth;
And the third part of trees were burnt up,
And all green grass was burnt up.

REVELATION 8:7

This was followed by a great mountain, burning with fire, cast into the sea and killing a third of all marine life and destroying a third of all ships upon the seas. A third of all river water was poisoned, a third of the sun and moon and stars were darkened, and daylight hours shortened. Considering that John, who visualized and wrote the book of Revelation, could have had no knowledge of thermonuclear weapons and atomic power, this is a graphic description of the war that opened the way for the antichrist.

Although the door of salvation is closed to all Gentiles, God's grace is poured out to his Israelite children during this tribulation period. The seal of the living God is placed upon the forehead of 144,000 Israelites, 12,000 from each of twelve tribes; at last opening their understanding. These will go out proclaiming Jesus Christ is the true Messiah.

The Lord will also provide two powerful prophets, able to work miracles, who will witness for three and one half years. Some evidence indicates these prophets may be Moses and Elijah. When their testimony is finished, the antichrist will be allowed to kill them. Their testimony will be resented by the world which desires no part of the truth. Consequently, as these prophets lie dead on the streets of Jerusalem and are shown to the world via satellite, everyone will rejoice.

> **And they that dwell upon the earth**
> **Shall rejoice over them, and make merry,**
> **And shall send gifts one to another;**
> **Because these two prophets**
> **Tormented them that dwell on the earth.**
> **REVELATION 11:10**

But after three and one half days, God's Spirit of Life enters the bodies of the slain prophets and as they stand upon their feet, all the people hear a great voice from heaven calling them and watch their ascension. Within the hour a great earthquake destroys a tenth of Jerusalem and 7,000 residents are killed. God's wrath is no small thing!

Although the antichrist promises peace, he cannot contend with the Lord who causes the bottomless pit to be opened. From it emerge locusts with the power of scorpions, sent to seek out all men who do not have the seal of God in their foreheads. Their mission is to torment, not kill, but those afflicted will suffer such extreme torment that death would be preferable to living.

> **And the shapes of the locusts were like unto horses**
> **Prepared unto battle,**
> **And they had breastplates, as it were breastplates**
> **of iron;**

And the sound of their wings was as the sound of chariots
Of many horses running to battle.

REVELATION 9:7 - 9

Pentegon Defense Advanced Research Projects Agency plans and develops prototypes of exotic computerized land and air systems. On their drawing board are plans for a ten-foot tall Hexapod, a six-legged vehicle that looks like a cross between a grasshopper and a horse. God's Word will be fulfilled. What sounded outrageous and unbelievable a few short years ago, has become reality!

At the end of three and one half years, the world worshipped the devil and his agents, the antichrist and the false prophet, because they had not a love of the truth ---

And all that dwell upon the earth shall worship him,
Whose names are not written in the book of life of the Lamb
Slain from the foundation of the world.
And he causeth all, both small and great,
Rich and poor, free and bond.
To receive a mark in their right hand, or in their foreheads.
And that no man might buy or sell,
Save he that had the mark,
Or the name of the beast, or the number of his name.
For it is the number of a man;
And his number is six hundred three score and six.

REVELATION 13: 8, 16-18

Inexorably, this system is being refined. With the advent of computeriza- tion, world-wide implementation of a numbering system is at hand: 666 - a number frequently associated with computer systems; and electronic funds transfer system and electronic deposit of salaries, laser beam identification, and microchips that can easily be imbedded beneath the skin and read by laser beams; increasing use of social security numbers for identification, replacing other I.D. and account numbers for all transactions. With the full implementation of a cashless society, and only one means of identification, man can no longer exist without this mandatory mark for truly he will be unable to buy or sell. Computer tatoos or chips are imminent. There will be no resistance to the final implementation of this mark because:

They have received not a love for the
truth, That they might be saved.
And for this cause God shall send them strong delusion,
That they should believe a lie.
That they all might be damned
Who believed not the truth
But had pleasure in unrighteousness.
II THESSALONIANS 2:10-12

Only Jews have a hope of salvation at this time. The 144,000 from the twelve tribes of Israel are redeemed from the earth and those who were victor- ious over the beast and his image and over his mark and his number sing the song of Moses and the song of the Lamb from heaven.

Woe unto those who did receive the mark of the beast, for they shall be tormented with fire and brimstone forever.

As the antichrist demands worship of his image, and as he persecutes Jews, he breaks his covenant with Israel and even defiles their temple.

> And from the time that the daily sacrifice
> Shall be taken away,
> And the abomination that maketh desolate set up,
> There shall be a thousand two hundred ninety days.
>   DANIEL 12:11

Until this time, even some of the Jews had looked upon the antichrist as their Messiah. Now they flee Jerusale m as they see their holy place within the temple defiled. Until Christ's return, many will seek refuge in a wilderness hiding place where God's protection will cover them. Possibly this place will be Petra, the ancient city of altars south of the Dead Sea, easily guarded and inaccessible except by foot or on mules.

God's wrath will be increasingly severe as putrid sores and boils inflict those who carry the mark of the beast. The Lord has all the forces of nature at his command and natural catastrophes such as earthquakes, volcanoes, and floods, can be as devastating as nuclear war. Even now the earth groans with the severity of catastrophic weather and eruptions on this planet. In October, 1985, Brazil experienced an unusual hailstorm lasting fifteen minutes that damaged over 2,000 homes and froze, drowned or crushed over 2 0 people by hailstones weighing about two pounds each. When the storm was over, one street alone was covered wit h a slab of ice five f eet deep and one hundred feet long.

In September 1985, without warning, an earthquake shook Mexico City and the surrounding area, leveling thousands of buildings and killing an estimated 20,000. A volcanic eruption and resulting mudslides in Columbia buried as many as 25,000 people.

Only recently it became evident that radon is seeping up through the soil from natural uranium deposits which are part of a geologic formation called Reading Prong located in eastern Pennsylvania and extending across northern New Jersey and into New York state. It is estimated 100,000 people live in this area and over a period of time it poses a threat of lung cancer, particularly as it accummulates in air tight buildings. Radon seepage may exist in many other locations of the world that have not been identified as yet.

The 1980's brought awareness of a new disease known as acquired im mune deficiency syndrome (AIDS) and although its origin is unknown, scientists and doctors believe that the lif e-style and practices of homosexuals are a major f actor. It has spread to other segments of society through blood transfusions and contaminated needles used by drug addicts.

> Because that when they knew God,
> They glorified him not as God, neither were thankful;
> But

became vain in their own imaginations,
And their foolish hearts were darkened.
Wherefore God also gave them up to uncleanness
Through the lusts of their own hearts.
To dishonor their own bodies between themselves.
Who changed the truth of God into a lie,
And worshipped and served the creature
More than the Creator, who is blessed forever.
For this cause God gave them up unto vile affections;
For even their women did change the natural use
Into that which is against nature.
And likewise also the men, leaving the natural use of
the woman,
Burned in their lust one toward another; men with men.
Working that which is unseemly, and receiving in
themselves
That recompense of their error which was meet.

ROMANS 1 : 21 - 27

It is evident the world is reaping what men have sown. When homosexuality "came out of the closet" it brought AIDS to mankind. The first recorded cases were in America in 1978. By 1987, heterosexual transmission was also a reality. It has been estimated that as many as 2,500,000 Americans may have been infected with the virus by the end of 1984. In 1987, the U.S. Public Health Service reported over 33,000 cases of AIDS in America and over 19,000 deaths from the disease.

**And the fourth angel poured out his vial upon the sun;
And power was given unto him to scorch men with fire.
And men were scorched with great heat,
And blasphemed the name of God**

Which had power over these plagues:
And they repented not to give him glory.
REVELATIONS 16:8, 9

It is believed that the fiery core of our sun attains 27,000,000 degrees Fahrenheit, converting hydrogen to helium and releasing electrons, photons and neutrinos. A wealth of information on the sun has been gathered by a manned Skylab spacecraft and later by an unmanned observation satellite, the Solar Maximum Mission (SMM). Scientists have found that the solar corona, the sun's outer atmosphere, displays huge loops of magnetic force where solar flares occur. Solar flares are powerful explosions on the sun that propel matter into space and bombard the earth with high-energy radiation and atomic particles. Magnetic storms, auroral displays, and radio interference are direct results of sun flares during which X-ray and ultraviolet emissions are thought to erupt simultaneously. If it is God's will, these solar flares could increase in intensity, scorching the earth with great heat .

Since 1979, scientists have observed a hole over the South Pole that is relatively ozone-free. Life on earth depends upon an ozone layer in the upper atmosphere (12 to 30 miles above sea level) for protection from the sun's ultraviolet radiation. This protective layer has become thinner each year and the area is expanding.

And the sixth angel poured out his vial
Upon the great river Euphrates
And the waters thereof were dried up,

> That the way of the kings of the east
> Might be prepared.
>
> REVELATION 16:12

A thousand Russians and 12,000 Syrians spent ten years building a great earthen dam across the Euphrates River, forming Lake Assad which stretches for fifty miles and, when full, stores 420 billion cubic feet of water. Man is assisting in fulfilling this prophecy:

> And I saw three unclean spirits
> Like frogs come out of the mouth of the dragon.
> And out of the mouth of the false prophet
> For they are the spirits of devils, working miracles,
> Which go forth unto the kings of the earth
> And of the whole world to gather them to the battle
> Of that great day of God Almighty.
>
> REVELATION 16:13, 14

All the promises of peace and prosperity promised by the antichrist had come to naught. It would not take much to awaken hostility, anger, and suspicion among the nations of the world. Malicious rumors and accusations would be sufficient to arouse people and nations who were at a breaking point from all the onslaughts of God's wrath; people who continue to blaspheme the Lord because of their pains and sores and have no thought or desire to repent of their sins.

Mighty armies will assemble and converge in the Valley of Esdraelon - the plain of Megiddo - Ar mageddon, a site that had experienced many wars.

Gideon and his men fought the Midianites here, the Philistines defeated Saul on nearby Mount Gilboa, Barak and Deborah defeated Sisera, to name a few. But this war cannot be compared with any other, in magnitude, nor in scope. For these great armies from every nation from the east, from the south and from the north are assembled with the forces of Satan and the antichrist to do battle with Almighty God (and his heavenly army - those who were raptured seven years before). As the almighty forces of God converge on planet earth.

> **There were voices, and thunders, and lightnings;**
> **And there was a great earthquake.**
> **Such as was not since men were upon the earth,**
> **So mighty an earthquake, and so great.**
> **REVELATION 16:18**

And Jerusalem was divided into three parts, and the cities of the nations, fell and great Babylon, and every island fled, and mountains were not found. Simultaneously, upheavals so mighty that the whole world rocks and splits asunder as forces deep within the earth give vent to the tremendous heat and pressure trapped in the center of our planet; as tectonic plates shift and grind against each other; as fault lines such as the Afar Triangle located at the junction of the Red Sea, the Gulf of Aden, and the African Rift Valley are wrenched apart; the earth is shaken as never before during the history of mankind. Great Babylon, that city of seven hills, that wicked city that had led so many astray, a city of much wealth and power, who had stolen the souls of men is Rome and is destroyed in one hour.

And in her was found the blood
Of prophets, and of saints,
And of all that were slain on earth.

REVELAITON 18:24

Babylon is Rome as it was in Paul's day; home of emperors who ruled a mighty empire and demanded the worship of men and who persecuted and took the lives of Christians who worhsipped the Lord Jesus Christ. Babylon is Rome, the Vatican and the Popes who have guided and misled Catholics by a trinitarian doctrine that denies one God and Jesus Christ who is that God. Babylon is all denominations who cling to a trinitarian system, and who are destined to become a part of the one world religion which will give allegiance to the antichrist and the false prophet. Babylon is that ancient pagan religion that took root in Babylon during the days of Nimrod, a religion fostered by Satan whose tendrils have reached into every religion known to man. The only way to withstand it is through repentance, baptism in Jesus name and infilling of the Holy Ghost as the apostles found out on the day of Pentecost. Half measures will fail for they deny that God Himself came to earth, clad in a fleshly garment, shed his precious blood, and died on a cross that those who believe might receive remission from sin and power to overcome by His name, Jesus, and His Spirit, the Holy Ghost.

Is it any wonder that everyone in heaven rejoices to see Babylon destroyed? That ungodly, worldly system no longer will reign over

planet earth, but the Lord God omnipotent, the Lamb, who has become
as a roaring lion, the King of Kings and Lord of Lords, will vanquish,
by the power of His Word, all the mighty armies assembled at Ar
mageddon to do battle against Him.

> **And I saw the beast, and the kings of the earth,**
> **And their armies, gathered together**
> **To make war against him that sat on the horse,**
> **And against his army.**
> **And the beast was taken.**
> **And with him the false prophet.**
> **These both were cast alive**
> **In a lake of fire burning with brimstone.**
> **And the remnant were slain**
> **With the sword of him that sat upon the horse,**
> **Which sword proceeded out of his mouth;**
> **And all the fowls were filled with flesh.**
>
> **REVELATION 19:19 - 21**

The antichrist and the false prophet can never again rule mankind.
But what of Satan, that driving force of evil that motivated them? He
will be bound and imprisoned in a bottomless pit for a thousand years;
then released for a short time to again work his guile and deception upon
the world.

CHAPTER XIX

OMEGA

And I saw thrones, and they sat upon them,
And judgment was given unto them.
And I saw the souls of them that were beheaded
For the witness of Jesus, and for the word of God,
And which had not worshipped the beast,
Neither his image, neither had received his mark
Upon their foreheads, or in their hands;
And they lived and reigned with Christ a thousand years
But the rest of the dead lived not again
Until the thousand years were finished.
This is the first resurrection.

REVELATION 20:4, 5

John visualized the millennial kingdom of Christ that the Jews had anticipated and longed for since the last king of Jerusalem, Zedekiah, was taken prisoner by Nebuchadnezzer, king of Babylon, and their nation taken captive. The apostles expected Jesus to return and set up his kingdom in their lifetime. Just before Jesus ascended to heaven, they asked him if he would restore the kingdom to Israel. Little did they realize it would not happen for almost two thousand years. Yet God's promises will be fulfilled at the appropriate time. The faithful Jews who suffer the persecution of the antichrist and the great tribulation will be resurrected to rule with the Lord for a thousand years. Gentiles have no part in this resurrection. If they are not included in the catching away of Christ's church at the beginning of the tribulation, they will be forever doomed.

> Behold, the days come, saith the Lord,
> That I will perform that good thing
> Which I have promised unto the house of Israel
> And to the house of Judah.
> In those days, and at that time
> Will I cause the Branch of righteousness
> To grow up unto David
> And he shall execute judgment and righteousness in
> the land.
> In those days shall Judah be saved,
> And Jerusalem shall dwell safely.
>
> JEREMIAH 33:14 - 16

The reign of Jesus Christ will be diametrically opposite the rule of the antichrist, for out of Zion shall go forth righteousness and the word of the Lord, who is a just judge. He will heal the nations and bring peace for a thousand years. Never in the history of mankind has there been an extended period of peace. The Bible mentions war as early as the days of Abraham. Certainly, the world today is filled with strife. Imagine, if you can, the wealth of the world diverted to peaceful means instead of defense and armament.

> And they shall beat their swords into plow shares,
> And their spears into pruning hooks:
> Nation shall not lift up sword against nation,
> Neither shall they learn war anymore.
>
> ISAIAH 2:4

The world will suffer untold ravages during the tribulation period. Coupled with today's pollution of land, sea, and air, great climatic changes can be expected. The Environmental Protection Agency (EPA) estimates that 1.5 trillion gallons of pollutants leak into the ground each year from sprayed and fertilized fields, septic tanks, holding ponds, landfills, and accidental chemical and oil spills. Aquifers, underground water sources, and streams are poisoned by seepage of these contaminated waste products. The tribulation period will bring atomic warfare as well as the wrath of God upon the earth.

> Now when I had returned, behold
> At the bank of the river were very many trees
> On the one side and on the other.
> Then he said unto me
> These waters issue out toward the east country
> And go down to the desert, and go into the sea.
> The waters shall be healed.
> And it shall come to pass, that everything that liveth,
> Which moveth, wither soever the rivers shall come,
> shall live;
> And there shall be a great multitude of fish
> Because these waters shall come thither
> For they shall be healed.
> And everything shall live whither the river cometh.
>   EZEKIEL: 47: 7 - 9

This water flows from the temple of God in Jerusalem, but the Lord's healing will be for all people who believe in Him. He will require a yearly visit from everyone which will be of greater benefit to mankind than anyone can imagine. Spiritual and physical healing will be direct results.

Today many scientists have become increasingly concerned about climatic changes as numerous studies and reports indicate a warming trend resulting

from a greenhouse effect. Carbon dioxide levels have increased considerably due to burning of coal, oil, synthetic fuels, and natural gas. CO_2 lets visible light pass through, but absorbs energy at infra-red wavelengths; blocking

heat from escaping in the same manner that glass traps the sun's heat in a greenhouse.

There is cause for alarm. The Environmental Protection Agency (EPA) believes significant changes will be noticed by 1990. Unknown factors include the part other gases may have on the greenhouse effect. These include nitrous oxide, ozone, chloroflourocarbons, and methane. These are better infra-red absorbers than carbon dioxide and could raise the heat level substantially.

Methane gas is suddenly increasing in the atmosphere six percent a year, posing a significant threat.

Another factor could be the effect of clouds. It is not known if they might block sunlight from reaching earth or, because they are good inf ra-red insulators, accelerate the warming trend.

One result of the greenhouse effect is that carbon dioxide makes photosynthesis more efficient, increasing crop yields. Longer growing seasons and warmer climates could again bring the earth to a lush, tropical environment similar to the earth in the beginning before the flood wiped out all of mankind except for Noah and his family. Once again, all flesh will become vegetarians.

> And they shall build houses and inhabit them,
> And they shall plant vineyards
> And eat the fruit of them
> They shall not build and another inhabit
> They shall not plant, and another eat,
> For as the days of a tree are the days of my people.
> The wolf and the lamb shall feed together,
> And the lion shall eat straw like the bullock:
> And dust shall be the serpent's meat.
> They shall not hurt nor destroy in all my holy mountain,
> Saith the Lord.
>
> ISAIAH 65:21-25

The presence of the Lord among men will provide many blessings. Again, man's life span will become many hundreds of years and some may live for the entire thousand years of the Lord's earthly kingdom. Absence of sin and disease, of stress and of worry will all play a part in man's well being. Primarily, the Lord's love and concern for his people is responsible. There will still be some who are rebellious and have no love for Jesus Christ and His righteousness. These shall be cut of f .

> There shall be no more thence an infant of days,
> Nor an old man that hath filled his days;
> For the child shall die a hundred years old,
> But the sinner being a hundred years old
> Shall be accursed.
>
> ISAIAH 65:20

Mortal man will be given this period of time free from the temptations and deceptions of Satan. He will experience all the benefits of love, peace, and prosperity yet at the end of the thousand year reign of Jesus Christ when the devil is let loose, many will turn to that sinful, evil deceiver. Satan will again be able to muster an army of innumerable volunteers who will gather around Jerusalem to make war against Jesus and his saints; to no avail, for fire will come from God out of heaven and consume them.

> And the devil that deceived them
> Was cast into the lake of fire and brimstone,
> Where the beast and the false prophet are,
> And shall be tormented day and night
> Forever and ever.
>
> REVELATION 20:10

Hell, Hades, Sheol, the grave, the pit, the abyss, and Gehenna all refer to the same destination. Jesus used the word "Gehenna" to refer to hell. Outside of Jerusalem was a gorge known as Ge-Hinnom or Valley of Hinnom, which for centuries was considered an evil place. Eventually it became the garbage dump, the repository of all the city's refuse. The continual burning and numerous maggots and crawling things feasting on rotten matter was used by Jesus as a comparison to hell where sinners, unbelievers, and lost souls will spend eternity.

> Where their worm dieth not,
> And the fire is not quenched.
>
> MARK 9:48

Today many churches, if they preach on hell, teach that hell is not real. Beware, for God's Word says it is, and that all must face judgment. The Lord does not wish that anyone should have to be sentenced to eternal torment. Hades was originally intended for Satan and the rebellious angels who followed him. But the rebellious and sinful nature of unrepentant man will bar him from God's presence in heaven, and there must be a place for him.

> For if God spared not the angels that sinned,
> But cast them down to hell,
> And delivered them into chains of darkness,
> To be reserved unto judgment.
> And spared not the old world,
> But saved Noah the eighth person,
> A preacher of righteousness,
> Bringing in the flood upon the world of the ungodly.
> And turned the cities of Sodom and Gomorrah into ashes,
> II PETER 2:4 - 6

How can ungodly men today expect to escape a like judgment? At the end of the millenial reign and after Satan has been cast into the lake of fire and brimstone, it becomes man's turn. Until now, all the dead sinners, and ungodly unbelievers have awaited their call to judgment. The sea will give up its dead, and death and hell will deliver their dead to f ace God at the great white throne. No one can escape; everyone from the famous, powerful and rich to the lowliest beggar, will face the same examination, as the books are opened. At birth everyone's name is recorded in the Book of Life; life on earth determines whether it remains or is blotted out. Other books record every deed - good or bad.

> And I saw a great white throne,
> And him that sat on it,
> From whose face the earth and the heaven fled away;
> And there was found no place for them.
> And death and hell were cast into the lake of fire.
> This is the second death.
> And whosoever was not found
> Written in the book of life
> Was cast into the lake of fire.
>
> REVELATION 20:11, 14, 15

A greenhouse effect will result in a tropical temperature upon earth during the millenial reign, but even now scientists are worried earth may follow the example of Venus where a runaway greenhouse effect is thought to account for surface temperatures approaching 900 degrees Fahrenheit. Venus's cloud-shrouded atmosphere is about 97 percent carbon dioxide.

Astonomers have always believed it takes at least 100,000 years for stars to undergo any significant change. Sirius, the brightest star in the night sky has astronomers completely baffled. Ancient manuscripts, including ones from Biblical Babylon, describe the star as bright red. Today it is clearly bluish-white. A star's color indicates its temperature. Red stars are rela- tively cool, bluish white ones are very hot and both ordinarily take eons to change. Historical records indicate Sirius has undergone a drastic change in only two or three thousand years. Scientists cannot say with any certainty that our earth will not undergo extreme changes within the next thousand years, to wit:

> But the heavens and earth, which are now,
> By the same word are kept in store,
> Reserved unto fire against the day of judgment,
> And perdition of ungodly men.
> The Lord is not slack concerning his promise,
> As some men count slackness:
> But is long suffering to us-ward,
> Not willing that any should perish,
> But that all should come to repentance,
> But the day of the Lord will come
> As a thief in the night;
> In the which the heavens shall pass away
> With a great noise, and the elements
> Shall melt with fervent heat,
> The earth also and the works
> That are therein shall be burned up.
>
> II·PETER 3: 7, 9 and 10

As for those who were called in the first resurrection and rapture of the Lord's Jesus name church, they will ever be with the Lord. For them he has prepared a new Jerusalem, having the glory of God. It will have twelve gates of pearl, bearing the names of the twelve tribes of the children of Israel, and twelve foundations named for the twelve apostles of Jesus Christ.

> And the building of the wall of it was of jasper,
> And the city was pure gold, like unto clear glass.
> And the foundations of the wall of the city

Were garnished with all manner of precious stones.
REVELATION 21: 18, 19

Gold has always symbolized purity and His bride will be without spot, wrinkle, or blemish, changed to immortal, incorruptible beings who can look upon God face-to-face.

> And they that feared the Lord spoke often one to another,
> And the Lord hearkened, and heard it,
> And a book of remembrance was written before him
> For them that feared the Lord,
> And that thought upon his name.
> And they shall be mine, saith the Lord of hosts
> In that day when I make up my jewels;
> And I will spare them,
> As a man spareth his own son that serveth him.
>
> MALACHI 3 : 16,17

New Jerusalem will have no need of sun or moon, for the Lord Himself is the light thereof. Only those whose names are found in the Lamb's book of life can enter the city. No sin or abomination or lies will be found within its walls. A pure river of water of life will flow from the throne of Almighty God, the Lord Jesus Christ. On either side of this river will be the tree of life which will bare twelve kinds of fruits and the leaves will heal the nations (possibly people from every nation). This tree is the same as the tree of life that grew in the Garden of Eden. God had always intended for man to partake of this tree and receive the benefits of eternal life; but because of disobedience and self-will and the resulting sin that was introduced into the world, it had to be withheld as Adam and Eve were cast from the garden. Only those redeemed by the blood of the Lamb and who have His name will walk the golden streets of the New Jerusalem and partake of this precious fruit.

> And there shall be no more curse,
> But the throne of God and of the Lamb shall be in it.
> And His servants shall serve Him.
> And they shall see His face
> And His name shall be in their foreheads.
>
> REVELATION 22: 3 &: 4

For Jesus Christ is the face of God and there is but ONE GOD. Only those who understand and believe this and who accept the Lord's plan of salvation in its entirety will ever see Him face to face.

When God poured out the baptism of the Holy Ghost upon the students of Bethel Bible College and upon C. F. Parham, its founder and teacher, they sought God's will concerning water baptism. Finally, the Spirit of God spoke, "We are buried by baptism unto His death - God the Father, and God the Holy Ghost never died." They then understood that baptism in the name of the Father and the Holy Ghost was meaningless and that a triple immersion was unnecessary. Therefore, through faith in the divinity of Jesus Christ, they baptized by single immersion, in the name of Jesus, signifying the death, burial and resurrection whereby they were saved. Reverend Parham baptized in the name of Jesus, understanding that Jesus is the only door to salvation. But, through lack of organization in this new movement, many ministers who received the baptism of the Holy Ghost failed to grasp the significance of Jesus name water baptism and continued to use the old formula they were accustomed to. Later it was decided, to keep unity within the new movement, they should use the old formula, Father, Son and Holy Ghost.

What would today's churches be like and how many would have been reached with the true gospel if those early ministers had only grasped the importance of Jesus name baptism? Today it is not too late for you, but tomorrow may be.

> And behold, I come quickly;
> And my reward is with me.
> To give every man according as his work shall be.
> I am Alpha and Omega,
> The beginning and the end,
> The first and the last,
> Blessed are they that do his commandments,
> That they may have right to the tree of life,
> And may enter in through the gates into the city.
>
> REVELATION 22:12 - 14

> He which testifieth these things saith,
> Surely, I come quickly. Amen. Even so, come, Lord Jesus.
>
> REVELATION 22:20

BIBLIOGRAPHY

Alexander, David and Pat. Eerd man's Hand book to the Bible. Grand Rapids, Mich: Eerd man's Publishing Co. 1973

Bernard, David K. The Oneness of God. Hazelwood, Mo: Word Afla me Press 1983 Bicklein, Roy Prophetic Time Periods. Orlando, Florida: Bookworld Publishing Co. Inc. 1985

Blaiklock, E. M. Com mentary on the New Testament. Old Tappan, N.J.: Fle ming H. Revell Co. 1977

Bouquet, A. C. Everyday Lif e in New Testament Times. New York: Charles Scribner's Sons 1953

Calk, Daniel Prophecy Digest 1982-1983. Houston, TX: Believe Publications 1982 Chalfant, W m. B. Ancient Champions of Oneness. Hazelwood, Mo.: World Afla m e Press 1979

Cornfield, Gaalyah, The Historical Jesu . New York: M cMillan Publishing Co. 1983

Daniel - Rops Jesus & His Ti mes. New York: E. P. Dutton & Co., Inc. 1954

Dayan, Moshe, Living With the Bible. New York & Great Britain: W m Morrow & Co., Inc. 1978

Decker, Ed and Hunt, Dave. The God Makers. Eugene, Oregon: Har
vest Hoqse Publishers 1984

DeCoulanges, Fustel. The Ancient City. Balti more: The John Hopkins
University Press 1980

Ewart, Frank J. The Phenom enon of Pentecost. Hazelwood, Mo.:
Word Afla me Press 1975

Forbush, W. Bryon Fox's Book of Martyrs. Grand Rapids, Mich:
Zondervan Publishing House 1978

Foster, Fred J. Their Story: 2 0th Century Pentecostals. Hazelwood,
Mo: Word Aflame Press 1981

Goss, Ethel E. The Winds of God. Hazelwood, Mo: Word Afla
me Press 1977 Harkness, Georgia Mysticism, Its Meaning and
Message. Nashville: Abingdon Press 1973

Heller, Dr John H. Report on the Shroud of Turin. Boston: Houghton
Mifflin Co. 1983

Hudson, Winthrop S. Religion in America. New York: Chas Scribner's
Sons 1981

Hunt, Dave Peace, Prosperity and the Coming Holocaust. Eugene,
Oregon: Harvest House Publishers 1960

Johnson, Paul A History of Christianity. New York: Athenium 1976

K eller, Werner The Bible as History. New York: William Morrow & Co. 1981 Lahaye, Tim Revelation. Grand Rapids, Mich: The Zondervan Publishing House 1973, 1975

Lawson, James Gilchrist. Deeper Experiences of Famous Christians. Anderson, Indiana: The Warner Press 1911

Magnusson, Magnus Archaeology of the Bible. New York: Simon & Schuster 1977

Meilsheim, D. The World of Ancient Israel. New York: Tudor Publishing Co. 1973 Miller, Madeline S. and Lane, J. Harper's Bible Dictionary. New York: Harper and Row Publishers 1973

Pagels, Elaine The Gnostic Gospels. New York: Random House 1979

Payne, Robert The Christian Centuries. New York: W. W. Norton & Co., Inc. 1966 Quebedeaux, Richard The Worldly Evangelicals. Harper & Row, Publishers 1973 Sagan, Carl Cosmos. New York: Rando m House 1980

Shephard, J. W. The Christ of the Gospels. Grand Rapids, Mich: W m. B. Eerd man's Publishing Co. 1939

Stevenson, K enneth E. and Haber mas, Gary R. <u>Verdict on the S</u>hroud. Ann Arbor, Michigan: Servant Books 1981

Swihart, Stephen D. Ar mageddon 198?. Plainfield, N.J.: Haven Books 1980 Synan, Vinson In <u>the Latter D</u>ays. Ann Arbor, Mich: Servant Books 1984

Van Baalen, Jan Karel <u>The Chaos of Cults.</u> Grand Rapids, Mich: W m. B. Eerd man's Publishing Co. 1938 - 1981

Van Impe, Jack with Campbell, Roger F. <u>Israel's Final Holocaust</u>. Nashville: Thomas Nelson Publishers 1979

Vos, Howard F. <u>An Introduction to Bible Archeology,</u> Chicago: Mood y Press 1983 Walvoord, John F. The Nations in Prophecy. Grand Rapids, Mich: Zondervan 1967 Walzer, Michael The <u>Revolution of the S</u>aints. London: Weidenf eld & Nicolson 1966

Printed in the United States
By Bookmasters